MY PAST AND THOUGHTS

MY PAST AND THOUGHTS

The Memoirs of Alexander Herzen

VOLUME III

*Translated from the Russian
by Constance Garnett*

faber and faber

This edition first published in 2008
by Faber and Faber Ltd
3 Queen Square, London WC1N 3AU

Printed by Books on Demand GmbH, Norderstedt

All rights reserved
Translation © Constance Garnett, 1924

The right of Constance Garnett to be identified as translator of this work
has been asserted in accordance with Section 77 of the
Copyright, Designs and Patents Act 1988

This book is sold subject to the condition that it shall not, by way of
trade or otherwise, be lent, resold, hired out or otherwise circulated
without the publisher's prior consent in any form of binding or cover other than
that in which it is published and without a similar condition including this
condition being imposed on the subsequent purchaser

A CIP record for this book is available from the British Library

ISBN 978-0-571-24543-7

Our authorised representative in the EU for product safety is
Easy Access System Europe, Mustamäe tee 50, 10621 Tallinn, Estonia
gpsr.requests@easproject.com

CONTENTS

PART V

PARIS—ITALY—PARIS

(1847–1852)

SECTION ONE

BEFORE THE REVOLUTION AND AFTER IT

CHAPTER XXXIV:—THE JOURNEY—The Lost Passport—Königsberg—The Hand-made Nose—We Arrive!—
And Depart *page* 1

CHAPTER XXXV:—THE HONEYMOON OF THE REPUBLIC—The Englishman in the Fur-Jacket—The Duc de Noailles—Freedom and her Bust in Marseilles—The Abbé Sibour and the Universal Republic in Avignon *page* 10

APPENDIX I:—1. The Dream—11. In the Storm
page 18

CHAPTER XXXVI:—La Tribune des Peuples—Mickiewicz and Ramon de la Sagra—The Chorus of the Revolution of June 13, 1848—Cholera in Paris—Departure
page 31

CHAPTER XXXVII:—A Babel of Tongues—The German Umwalzungsmänner—The French Red Montagnards—The Italian Fuorusciti in Geneva—Mazzini, Garibaldi, and Orsini—The Roman and the German Traditions—A Trip on 'The Prince Radetsky' *page* 58

CHAPTER XXXVIII:—Switzerland—James Fazy and the Refugees—Monte Rosa *page* 102

APPENDIX II:—1. Il Pianto—II. Post Scriptum
page 130

CHAPTER XXXIX-.—Money and Police—The Emperor James Rothschild and the Banker Nicholas Romanov—Police and Money *page* 150

CHAPTER XL:—The European Committee—The Russian Consul at Nice—Letter to A. F. Orlov—Persecution of a Child—The Vogts—Transference from the Grade of Upper Court Councillor to that of Simple Peasant—Reception at Châtel *page* 171

CHAPTER XLI:—P. J. Proudhon—Publication of the 'Voix du Peuple'—Correspondence—The Significance of Proudhon *page* 210

CHAPTER XLII:—The *Coup d'État*—The Procureur of the late Republic—The Voice of the Cow in the Wilderness—Banishment of the Procureur—Order and Civilisation Triumphant *page* 246

SECTION TWO
RUSSIAN SHADOWS

I. N. I. SAZONOV *page* 255

II. THE ENGELSONS *page* 277

PART V

PARIS—ITALY—PARIS

(1847–1852)

AS I begin to publish yet another part of *My Past and Thoughts*, I pause in hesitation at the fragmentariness of my narratives, my pictures, and the running commentary of my reflections. There is less external unity about them than about those of the earlier parts. I cannot weld them into one. In filling in the gaps, it is very easy to give the whole thing a different background and a different lighting—the truth of the period would be lost. *My Past and Thoughts* is not an historical monograph, but the reflection of historical events on a man who has accidentally been thrown into contact with them. That is why I have decided to leave my disconnected chapters as they were, stringing them together like the mosaic pictures in Italian bracelets—all of which refer to one subject but are only held together by the setting.

My *Letters from France and Italy* are essential for completing this part, especially in regard to the year 1848; I had meant to make extracts from them, but that would have involved so much reprinting that I did not attempt it.

Many things that have not appeared in *The Polar Star* have been put into this edition, but I cannot give everything to my readers yet, for reasons both personal and public. The time is not far off when not only the pages and chapters here omitted, but the whole volume, which is most precious to me, will be published.

GENEVA, 29*th July* 1866.

SECTION ONE

BEFORE THE REVOLUTION AND AFTER IT

Chapter 34

THE JOURNEY

THE LOST PASSPORT—KÖNIGSBERG—THE HAND-MADE
NOSE—WE ARRIVE!—AND DEPART

IN Lautzagen the Prussian gendarmes invited me into their office. The old sergeant took the passports, put on his spectacles, and with extreme distinctness began reading aloud all that was unnecessary:

Auf Befehl S.K. M. Nikolai des Ersten . . . alien und jeden, denen daran gelegen, etc. etc. . . . Unterxeichner Peroffski, Minister des Innern, Kammerherr, Senator und Ritter des Ordens St. Wladimir . . . Inhaber eines goldenen Degens mit der Inschrift fur Tapferkeit . . .

This sergeant who was so fond of reading reminded me of another one. Between Terracino and Naples a Neapolitan carbineer came to the diligence four times, asking every time for our visas. I showed him the Neapolitan visa: this and the half *carlino* were not enough for him; he carried off the passports to the office, and returned twenty minutes later insisting that my companion and I should go before the brigadier. The latter, a drunken old officer, asked me rather rudely, 'What is your surname and where do you come from?' 'Why, that is all in the passport.' 'I can't read it.' We conjectured that reading was not the brigadier's strong point. 'By what law,' asked my companion, 'are we bound to read aloud our passports? We are bound to have them and to show them, but not to dictate them; I might dictate anything.' '*Accidenti*,' muttered the old man, '*va ben, va ben!*' and he gave back our passports without writing anything.

The learned gendarme at Lautzagen was of a different type; after reading three times in the three passports all the decorations of General Perovsky, including his buckle for an unblemished record, he asked me: 'But who are you, *Euer Hochwohlgeboren*?' I stared, not understanding what he wanted of me. '*Fräulein Maria E., Fräulein Maria K., Frau H.*—they are all women, there is not one man's passport here.' I looked: there really were only the passes of my mother and two of our friends who were travelling with us; a cold shudder ran down my back.

'They would not have let me through at Taurogen without a passport.'

'*Bereits so*, but you can't go on further.'

'What am I to do?'

'Perhaps you have forgotten it at the office. I'll tell them to harness a sledge for you; you can go yourself, and your family can keep warm here meanwhile. *Heh! Kerl! Lass er mal den Braunen anspannen.*'

I cannot remember that stupid incident without laughing, just because I was so utterly disconcerted by it. The loss of that passport of which I had been dreaming for years, which I had been trying to obtain for two years, the minute after crossing the frontier, overwhelmed me. I was certain I had put it in my pocket, so I must have dropped it—where could I look for it? It would be covered by snow. . . . I should have to ask for a new one, to write to Riga, perhaps to go myself: and then they would send in a report, would notice that I was going to the mineral waters in January. In short, I felt as though I were in Petersburg again; visions of Kokoshkin and Sartynsky, Dubbelt and Nicholas, passed through my mind. Good-bye to my journey, good bye

to Paris, to freedom of the press, to concerts and theatres
. . . once more I should see the clerks in the ministry,
police—and every other sort of—officers, town constables
with on their back the two bright buttons with which
they look behind them . . . and first of all I should
see again the little wrinkled soldier in a heavy casque
with Number 4 mysteriously inscribed on it, the frozen
Cossack horse . . . I might even see the nurse again
at 'Tavroga,' as she had called it.

Meanwhile they put a big, melancholy, angular horse
into a little sledge. I got in beside a driver in a military
overcoat and high boots, he gave the traditional lash with
the traditional whip—when suddenly the learned sergeant
ran out into the porch, in his shirt-sleeves, and shouted:
'*Halt! Halt! Da ist der vermaledeite Pass,*' and he
held it unfolded in his hands.

I was overtaken by hysterical laughter.

'What are you doing with me? Where did you
find it?'

'Look,' he said, 'your Russian sergeant folded them
one inside the other: who could tell it was there? I
never thought of unfolding them.'

And yet he had three times over read: *Es ergehet
deshalb an alle hohen Mächte und an alle und jede, welchen
Standes und welcher Würde sie auch sein mögen*. . . .

I reached Königsberg tired out by the journey, by
anxiety, by many things. After a good sleep in an
abyss of feathers, I went out next day to look at the
town. It was a warm winter's day: the hotel-keeper
suggested that we should take a sledge. There were
bells on the horses and ostrich feathers on their heads
. . . and we were gay; a load was lifted from our
hearts, the unpleasant sensation of fear, the gnawing feeling of suspicion, had vanished. Caricatures of Nicholas
were exposed in the window of a bookshop; I rushed
in at once to buy a stock of them. In the evening I

went to a small, dirty, and inferior theatre, and came back from it excited, not by the actors but by the audience, which consisted mostly of workmen and young people; in the intervals between the acts every one talked freely and loudly, all put on their hats (a very important thing, as important as the right to wear a beard, etc.). This ease and freedom, this element of greater serenity and liveliness impresses the Russian abroad. The Petersburg government is still so coarse and crude, so absolutely nothing but despotism, that it positively likes to inspire fear; it wants everything to tremble before it—in fact, it desires not only power but the theatrical display of it. To the Petersburg Tsars the ideal of public order is the discipline of the waiting-room and the barracks.

. . . When we were setting off for Berlin I got into the carriage, and a gentleman muffled up in wraps took the seat beside me; it was evening, I could not see him distinctly. Learning that I was a Russian, he began to question me about the strictness of the police and about passports; I, of course, told him all I knew. Then we passed to Prussia; he spoke highly of the disinterestedness of the Prussian officials, the excellence of the administration, praised the king, and finally made a violent attack on the Poles of Posen on the ground that they were not good Germans. This surprised me; I argued with him, I told him bluntly that I did not share his views, and then said no more.

Meanwhile it was getting light; only then I noticed that my neighbour, the conservative, spoke through his nose, not because he had a cold in it, but because he had not one at all, or at least had not the most conspicuous part. He probably noticed that this discovery did not afford me any special satisfaction, and so thought fit to tell me, by way of apology, the story of how he had lost his nose and how it had been restored. The first part was somewhat confused, but the second was very circumstantial: Diffenbach himself had carved him a new nose out of his hand; his hand had been bound to his face for six weeks; *Majestät* had come to the hospital to look at it, and was graciously pleased to wonder and approve.

> 'A dit: c'est vraiment étonnant,
> Le roi de Prusse en le voyant.'

Apparently Diffenbach had been preoccupied with something else and had carved him a very ugly nose. But I soon discovered that his hand-made nose was the least of his defects.

Getting from Königsberg to Berlin was the most difficult part of our journey. The belief has somehow gained ground among us that the Prussian posting service is well organised: that is all nonsense. Travelling by post-chaise is only pleasant in France, Switzerland, and England. In England the post-chaises are so well built, the horses so elegant, and the drivers so skilful that one may travel for pleasure. The carriage moves at full speed over the very longest stages, whether the road runs uphill or downhill. Now, thanks to the railway, this question is becoming one of historical interest, but in those days we learned by experience what German posting chaises and horses could be. They were worse than anything in the world except perhaps the German post-drivers.

The way from Königsberg to Berlin is very long; we took seven places in the diligence and set off. At the first station the conductor told us to take our luggage and get into another diligence, sagaciously warning us that he would not be responsible for our things being safe. I observed that I had inquired at Königsberg and was told that we should keep the same seats: the conductor spoke about snow, and said that we had to get into a diligence provided with runners; there was nothing to be said to that. We had to transfer ourselves with our goods and our children in the middle of the night in the wet snow. At the next station there was the same business again, and the conductor did not even trouble himself to explain the change of carriages. We did half the journey in this way; then he informed us quite simply that we 'should be given only five seats.'

'Five? Here are my tickets.'

'There are no more seats.'

I began to argue; a window in the posting station was thrown open with a bang and a grey-headed man with moustaches asked rudely what the wrangling was about. The conductor said that I demanded seven seats, and that he had only five; I added that I had tickets and a receipt for the fares for seven seats. Paying no attention to me, he said to the conductor in an insolent, husky, Russo-German military voice: 'Well, if this gentleman does not want the five seats, throw his things out; let him wait till there are seven seats free.' Whereupon the worthy stationmaster, whom the conductor addressed as *Herr Major*, and whose name was Schwerin, shut the window with a slam. On considering the matter, we, as Russians, decided to go on. Benvenuto Cellini in like circumstances would, as an Italian, have brought out his pistol and shot the stationmaster.

Our friend who had been repaired by Diffenbach was at the time in the restaurant; when he clambered on to his seat and we set off, I told him what had happened. He was in a very genial mood, having had a drop too much; he showed the greatest sympathy with us, and asked me to give him a note on the subject when we got to Berlin. 'Are you an official in the posting service?' I asked. 'No,' he answered, still more through his nose; 'but that doesn't matter . . . you . . . see . . . I am in what is called here the central police service.'

This revelation was even more distasteful to me than the hand-made nose.

The first person to whom I expressed my liberal opinions in Europe was a spy—but he was not the last

Berlin, Cologne, Belgium—all passed rapidly before our eyes; we looked at everything half absent-mindedly, in passing; we were in haste to arrive, and at last we did arrive.

. . . I opened the heavy, old-fashioned window in the Hotel du Rhin; before me stood a column:

> '. . . with a cast-iron doll,
> With scowling face and hat on head,
> And arms crossed tightly on his breast.'

And so I was really in Paris, not in a dream but in reality: this was the Vendôme column and the Rue de la Paix.

In Paris—the word meant scarcely less to me than the word 'Moscow'! Of that minute I had been dreaming from childhood. If I might only see the Hôtel de Ville, the Café Foy in the Palais Royal, where Camille Desmoulins picked a green leaf and, fixing it on his hat for a cockade, shouted '*A la Bastille!*'

I could not stay indoors; I dressed and went out to stroll about the streets . . . to look up Bakunin, Sazonov: here was Rue St.-Honoré, the Champs-Élysées —all those names which had been familiar for long years . . . and here was Bakunin himself. . . .

I met him at a street corner; he was walking with three friends and, just as in Moscow, discoursing to them, continually stopping and waving his cigarette. On this occasion the discourse remained unfinished; I interrupted it and took him with me to find Sazonov and surprise him with my presence.

I was beside myself with happiness!

And at that happiness I will stop here.

I am not going to describe Paris once more. My first

acquaintance with European life, the glorious tour in Italy just awakened from sleep, the revolution at the foot of Vesuvius, the revolution before St. Peter's, and finally the news—like a flash of lightning—of the 24th of February—all that I have described in my *Letters from France and Italy*. I could not with the same vividness reproduce now impressions half effaced by time and overlaid by others. They make an essential part of my *Records*—what is a letter but a record of a brief period?

Chapter 35
THE HONEYMOON OF THE REPUBLIC
The Englishman in the Fur-Jacket — The Due de Noailles — Freedom and her Bust in Marseilles — The Abbé Sibour and the Universal Republic in Avignon

'*T*O-MORROW we are going to Paris; I am leaving Rome full of life and excitement. What will come of it all? Can it last? The sky is not free from clouds; at times there is a chilly blast from the sepulchral vaults bringing the smell of death; the odour of the past; the historical tramontano is strong, but whatever happens I am grateful to Rome for the five months I have spent there. The feelings I have passed through remain in the soul, and the reaction will not extinguish quite everything.'

This is what I wrote at the end of April 1848, sitting at my window in the Via del Corso and looking out into the 'People's square,' in which I had seen and felt so much.

I left Italy in love with her and sorry to leave her: there I had met not only great events but also the very nicest people — but still I went. It would have seemed like being faithless to all my convictions not to be in Paris when there was a republic there. Doubts are apparent in the lines I have quoted, but faith got the upper hand, and with inward pleasure I looked in Città at the consul's seal on my visa on which was engraved the imposing words, 'République Française' — I did not reflect that the very fact that a visa was needed showed that France was not a republic.

We went by a mail steamer. There were a great many passengers on board, and as usual they were of all sorts: there were passengers from Alexandria, Smyrna, and Malta. One of the terrible winds common in spring blew up just after we passed Leghorn: it drove the ship along with incredible swiftness and with insufferable rolling; within two or three hours the deck was covered with sea-sick ladies; by degrees the men too succumbed, except a grey-headed old Frenchman, an Englishman from Canada in a fur-jacket and a fur-cap, and myself. The cabins, too, were full of sufferers, and the stuffiness and heat in them were enough alone to make one ill. We three sat at night on our portmanteaus, covered with our overcoats and railway rugs, in the howling of the wind and the splashing of the waves, which at times broke over the fore-deck. I knew the Englishman; the year before I had travelled in the same steamer with him from Genoa to Città Vecchia. It happened we were the only two at dinner; he did not say a word all through the meal, but over the dessert, softened by the marsala and seeing that I on my side had no intention of entering upon a conversation, he gave me a cigar and said that he had brought his cigars himself from Havana. Then we talked: he had been in South America and California, and told me that he had long been intending to visit Petersburg and Moscow, but should not go until there were *proper* means of communication and a direct route between London and Petersburg.[1]

'Are you going to Rome?' I asked, as we approached Città.

'I don't know,' he answered.

I said no more, supposing that he considered my question impertinent, but he immediately added:

'That depends on whether I like the climate in Città.'

'Then you are stopping here?'

'Yes; the steamer leaves to-morrow.'

At that time I knew very few Englishmen, and so I could hardly conceal my laughter, and was quite unable

[1] There is this now.—(*Author's Note*.)

to do so when I met him next day, walking by the hotel in the same fur-coat, carrying a portfolio, a field-glass, and a little dressing-case, followed by a servant laden with his portmanteau and various belongings.

'I am off to Naples,' he said as he came up to me.

'Why, don't you like the climate?'

'It's horrid.'

I forgot to mention that on our first journey together he occupied the berth which was directly over mine. On three occasions during the night he almost killed me, first from fright, and then with his feet; it was fearfully hot in the cabin, he went several times to have a drink of brandy and water, and each time, climbing down and climbing up, he trod on me and shouted loudly, in alarm: 'Oh—beg pardon—*J'ai avals soif.*' '*Pas de mal!*'

Consequently we met this time like old friends; he spoke with the greatest approbation of my immunity from sea-sickness, and offered me his Havana cigars. As was perfectly natural, the conversation soon turned on the revolution of February. The Englishman, of course, looked upon the revolution in Europe as an interesting spectacle, as a source of new and curious observations and experiences, and he described the revolution in New Colombia.

The Frenchman took a different interest in these matters . . . within five minutes an argument had sprung up between him and me: he answered evasively, cleverly, and with the utmost courtesy, yielding nothing, however. I defended the republic and revolution. Without directly attacking it, the old gentleman championed the traditional forms of government as the only ones durable, popular, and capable of satisfying the just claims of progress and the necessity of settled security.

'You cannot imagine,' I said to him in joke, 'what a peculiar satisfaction you give me by your implied criticisms. I have been for fifteen years speaking about the monarchy just as you speak about the republic. The parts are changed; in defending the republic, I am the conservative, while you, defending the legitimist monarchy, are a *perturbateur de l'ordre politique*.'

The old gentleman and the Englishman laughed. A tall, gaunt gentleman, whose nose has been immortalised by *Charivari*[1] and Philipon, the Comte d'Argout,[2] came up to us. (*Charivari* used to declare that his daughter did not marry because she did not want to sign herself 'So-and-so, *née d'Argout'*.) He joined in the conversation, addressed the old gentleman with deference, but looked at me with a surprise not far removed from repulsion; I noticed this, and began to be at least four times as *red* in my remarks.

'It is a very remarkable thing,' the grey-headed old Frenchman said to me: 'you are not the first Russian I have met of the same manner of thinking. You Russians are either the most absolute slaves of your Tsar, or—*passez-moi le mot*—anarchists. And it follows from that, that it will be a long time before you are free.' Our political conversation continued in that strain.[3]

When we were approaching Marseilles and all the passengers were busy looking after their luggage, I went up to the old gentleman and, giving him my card, said that I should like to think that our discussion on the swaying boat had left no unpleasant impression. The old gentleman said good-bye to me very charmingly, delivered himself of another epigram at the expense of the republicans whom I should see at last at closer

[1] *Le Charivari* was the French *Punch* (earlier in date, however, *Punch* being called 'The London Charivari' as a sub-title), founded in 1831 by Charles Philipon, a caricaturist of great talent.

[2] The Comte d'Argout had much to do in bringing about the fall of Charles x., and held several important ministerial appointments under Louis-Philippe.—(*Translator's Notes.*)

[3] I have heard this criticism a dozen times since.—(*Author's Note.*)

quarters, and gave me his card. It was the Due de Noailles, the kinsman of the Bourbons, and one of the leading counsellors of Henry the Fifth.[1]

Though this incident is quite unimportant, I describe it for the benefit and education of our 'dukes' of the three highest ranks. If some senator or privy councillor had been in Noailles' place he would simply have taken what I said for insolence and breach of discipline and would have sent for the captain of the boat.

A Russian minister of the year 1850[2] sat with his family in his carriage on the steamer to avoid all contact with passengers who were common mortals. Can one imagine anything more ridiculous than sitting in an unharnessed carriage . . . and on the sea, too, and for a man double the ordinary size into the bargain!

The arrogance of our great dignitaries is not due to aristocratic feeling—the grand gentleman is dying out; it is the feeling of liveried and powdered flunkeys in great houses, extremely abject on one side and extremely insolent on the other. The aristocrat is a personality, while our faithful servants of the throne are entirely without personality; they are like Paul's medals, which bear the inscription: 'Not to us, not to us, but to thy name.' Their whole training leads up to this: the soldier imagines that the only reason why he must not be beaten with sticks is that he wears the Anna ribbon; the station superintendent considers his position as an officer the barrier that protects his cheek from the traveller's hand; an insulted clerk points to his Stanislav or Vladimir ribbon—'not for ourselves, not for ourselves . . . but for our rank!'

On leaving the steamer at Marseilles, I met a great procession of the National Guard, which was carrying to

[1] The Comte de Chambord, grandson of Charles x., was by the oyalists called Henri Cinq.—(*Translator's Note*.)

[2] The celebrated Victor Panin.—(*Author's Note*.)

the Hôtel de Ville the figure of Liberty, *i.e.* of a woman with immense curls and a Phrygian cap. With shouts of *'Vive la République!'* thousands of armed citizens were marching in it, and among them workmen in blouses who had been enrolled in the National Guard. I need hardly say that I followed them. When the procession reached the Hôtel de Ville, the general, the mayor, and the commissaire of the Provisional Government, Démosthéne Ollivier, came out into the portico. Démosthène, as might be expected from his name, prepared to deliver an oration. An immense circle formed about him: the crowd, of course, moved forward, the National Guards pressed it back, the crowd would not yield; this offended the armed workmen, they lowered their guns and, turning round, began with the butt-ends hitting the toes of the people who stood in front; the citizens of the 'one and indivisible republic' stepped back....

This proceeding surprised me the more because I was still completely under the influence of the manners of Italy, and especially of Rome, where the proud sense of personal dignity and the inviolability of the person is fully developed in every man—not merely in the *facchino* and the postman, but even in the beggar who holds out his hand for alms. In Romagna such insolence would have been greeted with twenty *coltellate*.[1] The French drew back—perhaps they had corns?

This incident made an unpleasant impression on me. Moreover, when I reached the hotel I read in the newspapers what had happened at Rouen.[2] What could be

[1] *I.e.* stabs with a dagger.
[2] At the Rouen elections for the Constituent Assembly in April, the Socialist candidates were heavily defeated; the workmen, suspecting some fraud, assembled, unarmed, before the Hôtel de Ville, to protest. They were attacked by soldiers and National Guards; eleven were killed and many wounded.—(*Translator's Notes.*)

the meaning of it? Surely the Duc de NOAILLES was not right?

But when a man wants to believe, his belief is not easily uprooted, and before I reached Avignon I had forgotten the butt-ends at Marseilles and the bayonets at Rouen.

In the diligence with us there was a thick-set, middle-aged abbé of dignified deportment and attractive exterior. For appearance' sake he took up his breviary, but to avoid dropping asleep put it back soon afterwards in his pocket and began talking charmingly and intelligently, with the classical correctness of the language of Port-Royal and the Sorbonne, and with many quotations and chaste witticisms.

Indeed, it is only the French who know how to talk. The Germans can make declarations of love, confide their secrets, give lectures, and scold. In England routs are so much liked just because they make conversation impossible . . . there is a crowd, no room to move, every one is pushing and being pushed, no one knows anybody; while if people come together in a small party they immediately have wretchedly poor music, singing out of tune, or boring little games, or with extraordinary heaviness the hosts and guests try to keep the ball of conversation rolling, with sighs and pauses reminding one of the luckless horses who almost at their last gasp under the whip drag a heavy-laden barge against the stream.

I wanted to taunt the abbé with the republic, but I did not succeed. He was very glad that liberty had come without excesses, above all without bloodshed and fighting, and looked upon Lamartine as a great man, something in the style of Pericles.

'And of Sappho,' I added, without, however, entering upon an argument. I was grateful to him for not saying a word about religion. So talking, we arrived at Avignon at eleven o'clock at night.

THE ABBE SIBOUR

'Allow me,' I said to the abbé as I filled his glass at supper, 'to propose a rather unusual toast: "To the republic, *et pour les hommes d'église qui sont républicains.*" The abbé got up, and concluded some Ciceronian sentences with the words: 'À la République future en Russie.'

'À la République universelle!' shouted the conductor of the diligence and three men who were sitting at the table. We clinked glasses.

A Catholic priest, two or three shopmen, the diligence conductor, and Russians—we might well drink to the universal republic!

But it really was very jolly.

'Where are you bound for?' I inquired of the abbe, as we took our seats in the diligence again, and I asked his pastoral blessing on a cigar.

'For Paris,' he answered; 'I have been elected to the National Assembly. I shall be delighted to see you if you will call; this is my address.' He was the Abbe Sibour, *doyen* of something or other and brother of the Archbishop of Paris.[1]

A fortnight later there came the fifteenth of May, that sinister *ritournelle* which was followed by the terrible days of June. That all belongs not to my biography but to the biography of mankind. . . .

I have written a great deal about those days. I might end here like the old captain in the old song:—

> 'Ici finit tout noble souvenir,
> Ici finit tout noble souvenir.'

But with those accursed days the last part of my life begins.

---

1 Sibour, Marie Dominique Auguste (1792-1857), was appointed on 10th of July 1848, by General Cavaignac, to the archi-episcopal see of Paris to replace Affre, who died of wounds received in the June days. He was himself assassinated in church by the Abbé Vergur, whom he had interdicted.—(*Translator's Note.*)

Appendix I

(*From 'West European Sketches—Notebook I.'*)

I

The Dream

DO you remember, friends, how lovely was that winter day, bright and sunny, when six or seven sledges accompanied us to Tchornaya Gryaz, when for the last time we clinked glasses and parted, sobbing?

. . . Evening was coming on, the sledge crunched through the snow, you looked mournfully after us and did not divine that it was a funeral and a parting for ever. All were there but one, the dearest of all; he alone was far away, and by his absence seemed to wash his hands of my departure.

That was the 21st of January 1847.

Seven years[1] have passed since then, and what years! Among them were 1848 and 1852.

All sorts of things happened in those years, and everything was shattered—public and personal: the European revolution and my home, the freedom of the world and my individual happiness.

Of the old life not one stone remained standing. At that time my powers had reached their fullest development; the previous years had given me pledges for the future. I left you full of daring and reckless self-reliance, with haughty confidence in life. I was in haste to tear myself away from the little group of people who had been so closely knit together and had come so close to each other, bound by a deep love and a common grief. I was lured by distance, space, open conflict, and free speech. I was seeking an independent arena, I longed to try my powers in freedom. . . .

[1] Written at the end of 1853.

THE DREAM

Now I expect nothing: after what I have seen and experienced, nothing will move me to much wonder or to deep joy; joy and wonder are curbed by memories of the past and fear of the future. Almost everything has become a matter of indifference to me, and I desire as little to die to-morrow as to live long years; let the end come as accidentally and senselessly as the beginning.

And yet I have found all that I sought, even recognition from this old self-complacent world—and at the same time I have lost all my faith, all that was precious to me, have met with betrayal, treacherous blows from behind, and indeed a moral corruption of which you in Russia have no conception.

It is hard for me, very hard, to begin this part of my story; avoiding it, I have written the preceding parts, but at last I am brought face to face with it. But away with weakness: what one could live through, one must have the strength to remember.

From the middle of the year 1848 I have nothing to tell of but agonising experiences, unavenged insults, undeserved blows. My memory holds nothing but melancholy images, my own mistakes and other people's: mistakes of individuals, mistakes of nations. When there was hope of salvation, death crossed the path. . . .

. . . The last days of our life in Rome conclude the happy part of my memories, that begin with the awakening of thought in childhood and youthful vows on the Sparrow Hills.

Alarmed by the Paris of 1847, I had opened my eyes to the truth for a moment, but was carried away again by the current of events seething about me. All Italy was 'awakening' before my eyes! I saw the King of Naples tamed and the Pope humbly asking the alms of the people's love—the whirlwind which set everything in movement carried me, too, off my feet; all Europe took up its bed and walked—in a fit of somnambulism which we took for awakening. When I came to myself, all was over; la Sonnambula, terrified by the police, had fallen from the roof; friends were scattered or were furiously slaughtering one another. . . . And I found myself alone, utterly alone, among the graves and the cradles—their guardian, defender, avenger, and I could do nothing just because I tried to do more than the common.

And now I sit in London where chance has flung me—and I stay here because I do not know what to do. An alien race swarms about me and hurries hither and thither, wrapped in the heavy breath of ocean; a world dissolved into chaos, lost in a fog in which all outlines are blurred, in which light becomes a murky glimmer.

. . . And that other land—washed by the deep blue sea under the canopy of deep blue sky . . . it is the one bright spot left on this side of the grave.

O Rome, how I love to return to your deceptions, how gladly I recall day by day the time when I was intoxicated with you!

. . . A dark night. The Corso is filled with people, here and there are torches. It is a month since a republic has been proclaimed in Paris. News has come from Milan—there they are fighting, the people demand war, there is a rumour that Charles Albert is on the way with troops. The talk of the angry crowd is like the intermittent roar of waves which alternately break with a splash and pause for a breathing space. The crowds form into ranks. They go to the Piedmont Ambassador to find out whether war has been declared.

'Fall in, fall in with us,' shout dozens of voices.

'We are foreigners.'

'All the better; Santo Dio, you are our guests.'

We joined the ranks.

'The front place for the guests, the front place for the ladies, *le donne forestiere*!'

And with passionate shouts of approval the crowd parted to make way. Ciceruacchio and with him a young Roman poet, the author of the people's songs, pushed their way forward with a flag, the tribune shook hands with the ladies and with them stood at the head of ten or twelve thousand people—and all moved forward in that majestic and harmonious order which is peculiar to the Roman people.

The leaders went into the Palazzo, and a few minutes later the drawing-room doors opened on the balcony. The ambassador came out to appease the people and to confirm the news of war; his words were received with frantic joy. Ciceruacchio was on the balcony in the glaring light of torches and candelabra, and beside him under the Italian flag stood four young women, all four Russians—was it not strange? I can see them now on that stone platform, and below them the swaying multitude, mingling with shouts for war and curses for the Jesuits, '*Evviva le donne forestiere*!'

In England, they and we should have been greeted with hisses, abuse, and perhaps stones. In France, we should have been taken for *agents provocateurs*. But here the aristocratic proletariat, the descendants of Marius and the ancient tribunes, gave us a warm and genuine welcome. We were received by them into the European struggle . . . and with Italy alone the bond of love, or at least of warm memory, is still unbroken.

And was all that . . . intoxication, delirium? Perhaps—but I do not envy those who were not carried away by that beautiful dream. The sleep could not last long in any case: the ruthless Macbeth of real life had already raised his hand to murder sleep and . . .

My dream was past—it has no further changed.[1]

---

[1] English in the original.—(*Translator's Note.*)

II

IN THE STORM

On the evening of the 24th of June, coming back from the Place Maubert, I went into the Quai d'Orsay. A few minutes later L heard a discordant shouting, and the sound came nearer and nearer. I went to the window: a grotesque comic *banlieu* marched in from the suburbs to the support of order; clumsy, rascally Fellows, half peasants, half shopkeepers, a little bit drunk, in wretched uniforms and old-fashioned casques, they moved rapidly but in disorder, with shouts of '*Vive Louis-Napoléon!*'

It was the first time I heard that ill-omened shout. I could not restrain myself, and when they reached the café I shouted at the top of my voice: '*Vive la République!*' Those standing near the windows shook their fists at me, an officer muttered some word of abuse, brandishing his sword; and for a long time afterwards I could hear the shouts of welcome to the man who had come to strangle half the revolution, to destroy half the republic, to inflict himself upon France, as a punishment for forgetting in her hysteria both other nations and her own proletariat.

At eight o'clock in the morning of the 26th of June, Annenkov and I went out to the Champs-Élysées. The cannonade we had heard in the night had ceased; only from time to time there was an interchange of shots and the beating of drums. The streets were empty, but the National Guards stood on each side of them. On the Place de la Concorde there was a detachment of the *Garde mobile*; near them some poor women with brooms, some ragpickers and *concierges* from the houses near, were standing. The faces of all were gloomy and horror-stricken. A lad of seventeen leaning on his gun was telling them something; we joined them.

IN THE STORM 23

He and all his comrades, boys like himself, were half drunk, their faces blackened with gunpowder and their eyes bloodshot from sleepless nights and drink; many were dozing with their chins resting on the muzzle of their gun. . . . 'And what happened then there's no need to describe.' After a pause he went on: 'Yes, and they fought well, too, but we paid them out for our comrades! What lots of them fell! I stuck my bayonet up to the hilt in five or six of them; they'll remember us,' he added, trying to assume the air of a hardened criminal. The women were pale and silent; a man who looked like a *concierge* observed: 'Serve them right, the blackguards!'. . . but this savage comment evoked not the slightest response. They were all of too ignorant a class to be moved to pity by the massacre and by the wretched boy whom others had turned into a murderer.

Silent and mournful, we went on to the Madeleine. Here we were stopped by the National Guards. At first, after searching our pockets, they asked where we were going, and let us through; but the next cordon beyond the Madeleine refused to let us through and sent us back; when we went back to the first cordon, we were stopped again. 'But you saw us pass here just now!' 'Don't let them pass,' shouted an officer.' 'Are you laughing at us, or what?' I asked. 'It's no use your talking to me,' answered the shopman in uniform rudely.' 'Take them to the police: I know one of them' (he pointed to me); 'I have seen him more than once at meetings. I dare say the other is the same sort too; they are neither of them Frenchmen, I'll answer for it—march.' Two soldiers in front, two behind, and one on each side escorted us. The first man we met was a *représentant du peuple* with the silly badge in his button-hole; it was De Tocqueville, the writer on America. I appealed to him and told him what had happened: it was not a joking matter;

they kept people in prison without any sort of trial, threw them into the cellars of the Tuileries, and shot them. De Tocqueville did not even ask who we were; he very politely bowed himself off, delivering himself of the following banality: 'The legislative authority has no right to interfere with the executive.' He might well be a minister under Napoleon III.!

The 'executive authority' led us down the boulevard to the Chaussée d'Antin to the *commissaire de police*. By the way, it may not be out of place to observe that neither when we were arrested, nor when we were searched, nor when we were on our way, did I see a single policeman; all was done by the bourgeois soldiers. The boulevard was completely empty, all the shops were closed; the inmates rushed to their doors and windows when they heard our footsteps, and kept asking who we were: *'Des émeutiers étrangers,'* answered our escort, and the worthy bourgeois looked at us and gnashed their teeth.

From the police-station we were sent to the Hôtel des Capucines; the Ministry of Foreign Affairs has its quarters there now, but at that time there was some temporary police committee there. We went with our escort into a large study. A bald old gentleman in spectacles, dressed entirely in black, was sitting alone at a table; he asked us over again all the questions that the commissaire had asked us. 'Where are your passports?' 'We never carry them with us when we go for a walk.' He took up some manuscript book and spent a long time looking in it, apparently found nothing, and asked one of our convoy: 'Why did you arrest them?' 'The officer gave the order; he says that they are very suspicious characters.' 'Very well,' said the old man; 'I will inquire into the case; you can go.'

When the escort had gone, the old man asked us to

explain the cause of our arrest. I put the facts before him, adding that the officer might perhaps have seen me on the fifteenth of May near the Assembly; and then described the incident of the previous day. I had been sitting in the Café Comartine when suddenly there was a false alarm, a squadron of dragoons rushed by at full speed, the National Guard began to form ranks. Together with some five people who happened to be in the café, I went up to the window; a National Guard standing below shouted rudely, 'Did you hear that the windows were to be shut?' His tone justified me in supposing that he was not addressing me, and I did not take the slightest notice of his words; besides, I was not alone, though I happened to be standing in front. Then the defender of order raised his gun, and, as all this took place in the *rez-de-chaussée*, tried to thrust at me with his bayonet, but, seeing his movement, I stepped back and said to the others: 'Gentlemen, you are witnesses that I have done nothing—is it the habit of the National Guard to stick foreigners!' '*Mais c'est indigne, mais cela n'a pas de nom!*' my neighbours chimed in. The panic-stricken café-keeper rushed to shut the windows; a vile-looking sergeant commanded him to turn every one out of the café—I fancied he was the same man who had ordered us to be detained. Moreover, the Café Comartine was but a few steps from the Madeleine.

'So that's how it is, gentlemen: you see what imprudence leads to. Why walk out at such a time?—minds are exasperated, blood is flowing. . . .'

At that moment a National Guard brought in a maid-servant, saying that an officer had caught her in the very act of trying to post a letter addressed to Berlin. The old man took the envelope and told the soldier he could go.

'You can go home,' he said to us; 'only, please do not go by the same streets as before, and especially not by the cordon which arrested you. But stay, I will send some one to escort you; he'll take you to the Champs-Élysées—you can get through that way.'

'And you,' he said, addressing the servant, giving her back the letter, which he had not touched, 'post it in some letter-box further away.'

And so the police protected us from the armed bourgeois!

On the night between the 26th and the 27th of June, so Pierre Leroux relates, he went to Sénart to beg him to do something for the prisoners who were being suffocated in the cellars of the Tuileries. Sénart, a man well known as a desperate conservative, said to Pierre Leroux: 'And *who* will answer for their lives on the way? The National Guard will kill them. If you had come an hour earlier you would have found two colonels here: I had the greatest difficulty in bringing them to reason, and ended by telling them that if these horrors went on I should give up the president's chair in the Assembly and take my place in the barricades.'

Two hours later, on returning home, the *concierge* made his appearance accompanied by a stranger in a dress coat and four men disguised as workmen, though they had the moustaches of *municipales* and the deportment of gendarmes. The stranger unbuttoned his coat and waistcoat and, pointing with dignity to the tricoloured scarf, said that he was the commissaire of police, Barlet (the man who on the 2nd of December, in the National Assembly, took by the collar the man who had himself taken Rome—General Oudinot), and that he had orders to search me. I gave him my key, and he set to work exactly as Police-master Miller did in 1834.

My wife came in: the commissaire, like the officer of gendarmes who once came to us from Dubbelt, began apologising. My wife looked calmly and directly at him, and when at the end of his speech he begged her indulgence, said: 'It would be cruelty on my part not to enter into your position; you are sufficiently punished by being forced to do what you are doing.'

The commissaire blushed, but did not say a word. Rummaging among the papers and laying aside a whole heap of them, he suddenly went up to the fireplace, sniffed, touched the ashes, and, turning to me with an important air, asked: 'What was your object in burning your papers?'

'I haven't been burning papers.'

'Upon my word, the ash is still warm.'

'No, it is not warm.'

'*Monsieur, vous parlez à un magistrat!*'

'The ash is cold, all the same, though,' I said, flaring up and raising my voice.

'Why, am I lying?'

'What right have you to doubt my word? . . . here are some honest workmen with you, let them try it. Besides, even if I had burnt papers: in the first place, I have a right to burn them; and in the second, what are you going to do?'

'Have you no other papers?'

'No.'

'I have a few letters besides, and very interesting ones; come into my room,' said my wife.

'Oh, your letters . . .'

'Please don't stand on ceremony . . . why, you are only doing your duty; come along.' The commissaire went in, glanced very slightly at the letters, which were for the most part from Italy, and was about to go. . . .

'But you haven't seen what is below—a letter from the Conciergerie, from a convict, you see; don't you want to take it with you?'

'Really, Madame,' answered the policeman of the republic, 'you are so prejudiced; I don't want that letter at all.'

'What do you intend to do with the Russian papers?' I asked.

'They will be translated.'

'The point is, where you will take your translator from. If he is from the Russian Embassy, it will be as good as betraying people to the Russian Government; you will ruin five or six people. You will greatly oblige me if you will mention at the *procès-verbal* that I beg most urgently that a Polish *émigré* should be chosen as a translator.'

'I believe that can be done.'

'I thank you; and I have another favour to ask of you: do you know Italian at all?'

'A little.'

'I will show you two letters; in them the word France is not mentioned. The man who wrote them is in the hands of the Sardinian police; you will see by the letters that it will go badly with him if they get into the hands of the police.'

'*Mais, ah ça!*' observed the commissaire, his dignity as a man beginning to be aroused; 'you seem to imagine that we are connected with the police of all the despotic powers. We have nothing to do with other countries. We are unwillingly compelled to take measures at home when blood is flowing in the streets and when foreigners interfere in our affairs.'

'Very well, then, you can have that letter.'

The commissaire had not lied; he certainly did know *very little* Italian, and so, after turning the letters over, he put them in his pocket, promising to return them.

With that his visit ended. The Italian letters he gave back next day, but my papers vanished completely.

A month passed; I wrote a letter to Cavaignac,[1] inquiring why the police did not return my papers nor say what they had found in them—a matter of very little consequence to them, perhaps, but of the greatest importance for my honour.

What gave rise to this last phrase was as follows. Several persons of my acquaintance had intervened on my behalf, considering the visit of the commissaire and the retention of my papers outrageous. 'We wanted to make certain,' Lamoricière[2] told them, 'that he was not *an agent of the Russian Government.*' This was the first time I heard of this abominable suspicion; it was something quite new for me. My life had been as open, as public, as though it were lived in a glass hive, and now all at once this terrible accusation, and from whom? —from a republican government!

A week later I was summoned to the prefecture. Barlet was with me. We were received in Ducou's room by a young official very like some Petersburg head-clerk of the free-and-easy type. 'General Cavaignac,' he told me, 'has charged me to return your papers without examination. The information collected concerning you renders it quite superfluous; no suspicion rests upon you; here is your portfolio. Will you please first sign this?'

It was a receipt stating that all the papers had been returned to me complete.

I stopped and asked whether it would not be more in order for me to look through the papers first.

---

[1] Cavaignac, Louis-Eugène (1802-1857), the youngest of the three distinguished Frenchmen of that name, was commander-in-chief in 1848, and an unsuccessful candidate for the presidency of the Republic when Louis-Napoleon (afterwards Napoleon III.) was elected on 10th December 1848.

[2] Lamoricière, Louis de (1806-1865), a prominent politician and general, was exiled in December 1848, and afterwards took command of the Papal troops.—(*Translator's Notes.*)

'They have not been touched. Here is the seal, indeed.'

'The seal has not been broken,' observed Barlet soothingly.

'My seal is not here. Indeed, it was not put on them.'

'It is my seal, but you know you had the key.'

Not wishing to reply with rudeness, I smiled. This enraged them both: the head-clerk became the head of a department; he snatched up a penknife and, cutting the seal, said in a rather rude tone: 'Pray look, if you don't believe, but I have no time to waste,' and walked out with a dignified bow. Their resentment convinced me that they really had not looked at the papers, and so, after a cursory glance at them, I signed the receipt and went home.

Chapter 36

LA TRIBUNE DES PEUPLES—MICKIEWICZ AND RAMON DE LA
SAGRA—THE CHORUS OF THE REVOLUTION OF JUNE 13,
1848—CHOLERA IN PARIS—DEPARTURE

I LEFT Paris in the autumn of 1847, without having formed any ties there; I remained completely outside the literary and political circles. There were many reasons for that. No direct occasion of contact with them occurred, and I did not care to seek it. To visit them simply in order to stare at celebrities, I thought unseemly. Moreover, I particularly disliked the tone of condescending superiority which Frenchmen assume with Russians: they approve of us, encourage us, commend our pronunciation and our wealth; we put up with it all, and behave as though we were asking them a favour, or even apologising for ourselves, delighted when, from politeness, they affect to take us for Frenchmen. The French overwhelm us with a flood of words, we cannot keep pace with them; we think of an answer, but they do not care to hear it; we are ashamed to show that we notice their blunders and their ignorance—they take advantage of all that with hopeless self-complacency.

To get on to a different footing with them, one would have to impress them with one's consequence; to do so, one must possess all sorts of privileges, which I had not at that time, and of which I took advantage at once when they were at my disposal.

Moreover, it must be remembered that there are no people in the world with whom it is easier to strike up a nodding acquaintance than the French—and no people with whom it is more difficult to get on to really intimate terms. A Frenchman likes to live in company, so as to display himself, to have an audience, and in that respect he is as much a contrast to the Englishman as in everything else. An Englishman is always looking at people because he is bored; he looks at men as though from a stall in a theatre; he makes use of people as an entertainment, or as a means of obtaining information. The Englishman is always asking questions, the Frenchman is always giving answers. The Englishman is always wondering, always thinking things over; the Frenchman knows everything for certain, he is finished and complete, he will go no further: he is fond of preaching, talking, holding forth—about what, to whom, he does not care. He feels no need for personal intimacy, the café satisfies him completely. Like Repetilov in *Woe from Wit*, he does not notice that Tchatsky is gone and Skalozub is in his place, that Skalozub is gone and Zagoretsky is in his place—and goes on holding forth about the Chamber, about the jury, about Byron (this he pronounces as though it were a French name), and other important matters.

Coming from Italy, with the enthusiasm of the February revolution still fresh in my heart, I stumbled on the 15th of May, then passed through the agony of the June days and the state of siege. It was then that I obtained a deeper insight into the *tigre-singe* of Voltaire —and I lost even the desire to become acquainted with the mighty ones of this republic.

On one occasion a possibility arose of common work which would have brought me into contact with many persons, but that did not come off. Count Xaveri Branicki gave seven million francs for a magazine to deal with foreign politics and other nations, and especially with the Polish question. The usefulness and appropriateness of such a magazine were obvious. French papers show little interest or knowledge in dealing with what is happening outside France; during the republic, they thought it sufficient to encourage from time to time all the nations of the world with the phrase *solidarité des peuples*, and the promise that as soon as they had time to turn round at home they would found a worldwide republic resting upon universal brotherhood. With the means at the disposal of the new magazine, which was to be called *La Tribune des Peuples*, it might have been made the Moniteur of the international movement and progress. Its success was the more certain as there was no other international periodical; there are sometimes excellent articles in *The Times* and the *Journal des Débats* on special subjects, but they are occasional and disconnected. The *Augsburg Gazette* would be the most international organ if its *black-and-yellow* proclivities were not so glaringly conspicuous.

But it seems that all the excellent projects of the year 1848 were doomed to be prematurely born and to perish before cutting their first tooth. The magazine turned out poor and feeble—and died at the slaughter of the innocents after the 14th of June 1849.

When everything was ready and on the point of beginning, a house was taken and fitted up with big tables covered with cloth and little sloping desks; a lean French *littérateur* was engaged to watch over the international mistakes in spelling; to edit it, a committee was nominated from former Polish nuncios and senators, and at the head of this Mickiewicz was appointed, with Hoetsky as his assistant;—all that was left to arrange was a triumphal opening ceremony, and what date could be more suitable for that than the anniversary of February the 24th, and what form could it more suitably take than that of a supper?

The supper was to take place at Hoetsky's. When I arrived I found many of the guests already there, and among them scarcely a single Frenchman; on the other hand, other nationalities, from the Sicilians to the Croats, were fully represented. I was really interested in one person only—Adam Mickiewicz; I had never seen him before. He was standing by the fireplace with his elbow on the mantelpiece. Any one who had seen his portrait in the French edition of his works, taken, I believe, from the medallion executed by David d'Angers,[1] could recognise him at once in spite of the great change wrought by the years. Many thoughts and sufferings had left their trace on his face, which was rather Lithuanian than Polish. The whole impression made by his figure, his head, his luxuriant grey hair and weary eyes, was suggestive of past suffering, of acquaintance with spiritual pain, and of the exaltation of sorrow— he was the plastic embodiment of the destiny of Poland. The same impression was made on me later by the face of Worcell, though the features of the latter, in spite of being even more expressive of suffering, were more animated and gracious than those of Mickiewicz. It seemed as though Mickiewicz were held back, preoccupied, distracted by something: that something was the strange mysticism into which he retreated further and further away.

I went up to him. He began questioning me about Russia: his information was fragmentary; he knew little of the literary movement after Pushkin, having stopped short at the time when he left Russia. In spite of his leading idea of a fraternal league of all the Slavonic peoples—a conception he was one of the first to develop —he retained some hostility to Russia. And, indeed, it could hardly be otherwise after all the atrocities perpetrated by the Tsar and his satraps; besides, we

[1] David (d'Angers), Pierre-Jean (1789-1856), must not be confounded with the great painter Louis David. David d'Angers was a celebrated sculptor of republican principles, who executed busts or medallions of most of the eminent men of his day. He was a great friend of Hugo, who wrote of him in *Les Rayons et les Ombres*: 'La forme, ô grand sculpteur, c'est tout et ce n'est rien. Ce n'est rien sans l'esprit, c'est tout avec l'idée!'—(*Translator's Note*.)

were speaking at a time when the terrorism of Nicholas was worse than ever before.

The first thing that surprised me disagreeably was the attitude to him of the Poles, his followers: they approached him as monks approach an abbot, with self-abasement and reverent awe; some of them kissed him on the shoulder. I suppose he was accustomed to these expressions of servile devotion, for he accepted them with the greatest *laisser aller*. To be recognised by people of the same way of thinking, to have influence on them, to see their affection, is desired by every one who is devoted, body and soul, to his cause and lives in it; but external signs of sympathy and respect I should not like to receive—they destroy equality and consequently freedom. Moreover, in that respect we can never compete with bishops, heads of departments, and colonels of regiments.

Hoetsky told me that at the supper he was going to propose a toast 'to the memory of the 24th of February 1848,' that Mickiewicz would respond with a speech in which he would expound his views and the spirit of the new magazine; he wished me as a Russian to reply to Mickiewicz. Not being accustomed to public speaking, especially without preparation, I declined his invitation, but promised to propose the health of Mickiewicz and to say a few words describing how I had drunk his health before in Moscow at a public dinner given to Granovsky in the year 1843. Homyakov had raised his glass with the words, 'To the great Slavonic poet who is absent!' The name (which we dared not pronounce) was not needed; every one got up, every one raised his glass and, standing in silence, drank to the health of the exile. Hoetsky was satisfied. Having thus arranged our *extempore* speeches, we sat down to the table. At the end of the supper, Hoetsky proposed his toast. Mickiewicz got up and began speaking.

His speech was elaborate, clever, and extremely adroit—
that is to say, Barbès[1] and Louis-Napoleon could both
have applauded it with perfect sincerity; it made me
wince. As he developed his thought I began to feel
uneasy and oppressed, and, that not the slightest doubt
might be left, waited for one word, one *name*—it was
not slow to appear!

Mickiewicz worked up to the theme that democracy
was now entering upon a new open campaign, at the
head of which stood France; that it would *again* hasten
to the liberation of all oppressed nationalities under the
same eagles, under the same standards, at the sight of
which all principalities and powers had trembled; and
that it would be led by a member of that dynasty which
has been crowned by the people, and, as it seemed,
ordained by Providence itself to guide revolution by the
well-ordered path of authority and victory.

When he had finished, except for two or three exclamations of his adherents, a general silence followed.
Hoetsky was very well aware of Mickiewicz's blunder,
and, wishing to efface the impression of it as quickly as
possible, came up with a bottle and, as he filled my
glass, whispered to me, 'Well?' 'I am not going
to say a word after that speech.' 'Please do say something.' 'Nothing will induce me.'

The silence continued; some people kept their eyes
fixed on their plates, others scrutinised their glasses, others
fell into private conversation with their neighbours.
Mickiewicz's face changed colour, he wanted to say
something more, but a loud '*Je demande la parole*'
put an end to the painful position. Every one turned
to the man who had risen to his feet. A rather short
man of seventy, with a fine vigorous face, stood with a

[1] Barbès, Armand (1809-1870), called the 'Bayard de la démocratie,' was a people's representative in 1848, imprisoned in 1849,
and set free in 1854.—(*Translator's Note.*)

glass in his trembling hand; anger and indignation were apparent in his large black eyes and his excited face. It was Ramon de la Sagra.[1] 'To the 24th of February,' he said: 'that was the toast proposed by our host. Yes, to the 24th of February, and to the downfall of every despotism, whether of king or emperor, of a Bourbon or a Bonaparte. I cannot share the views of our friend Mickiewicz—he looks at things like a poet, and is right from his own point of view; but I don't want his words to pass without protest in such a gathering'; and so he went on and on, with all the fire of a Spaniard and the authority of an old man.

When he had finished, twenty glasses, among them mine, were held out to clink with his.

Mickiewicz tried to retrieve his position, said a few words of explanation, but they were unsuccessful. De la Sagra did not give way. Every one got up from the table, and Mickiewicz went away.

There could scarcely have been a worse omen for the new journal; it succeeded in existing after a fashion till the 13th of June, and its disappearance was as little noticed as its existence. There could be no unity in the editing of it. Mickiewicz had rolled up half of his imperial banner *usé par la gloire*. The others did not dare to unfurl theirs; hampered both by him and by the committee, many of the contributors abandoned the journal at the end of the month; I never sent them a single line. If the police of Napoleon had been more intelligent, the *Tribune des Peuples* would never have been prohibited on account of a few lines referring to the 13th

[1] Ramon de la Sagra (1798-1871), a Spanish economist, took part in the revolutionary movement of 1848 in France, and wrote advocating the views of Proudhon. In 1854. he returned to Spain, and was several times elected a member of the Cortes. He was, of course, not seventy, as Herzen mistakenly assumes, but fifty, in 1848.—(*Translator's Note*.)

of June. With Mickiewicz's name and devotion to Napoleon, with its revolutionary mysticism and dream of the democracy in arms, with the Bonapartes at its head, the journal might have been a veritable treasure for the President, a clean organ of an unclean cause.

Catholicism, so alien to the Slavonic genius, has a shattering effect upon it. When the Bohemians no longer had the strength to resist Catholicism, they were crushed; in the Poles, Catholicism has developed that mystical exaltation which keeps them perpetually in the world of dreams. If they are not under the direct influence of the Jesuits, they either create some idol for themselves, or give themselves up to the influence of some visionary instead of working for freedom. Messianism, that mania of Wronski's, that delirium of Tovjanski's, had turned the brains of hundreds of Poles, among them of Mickiewicz himself. The worship of Napoleon takes a foremost place in this insanity. Napoleon had done nothing for them; he had no love for Poland, but he liked the Poles who shed their blood for him with the poetic titanic courage displayed in their famous cavalry attack of Sommo Sierra.[1] In 1812 Napoleon said to Narbonne: 'I want a camp in Poland, not a forum. I will not permit either Warsaw or Moscow to open a club for demagogues'—and of him the Poles made a military incarnation of God, setting him on a level with Vishnu and Christ.

Late one winter evening in 1848, I was walking with one of the Polish followers of Mickiewicz along the Place de la Vendôme. When we reached the column the Pole took off his cap. 'Good heavens! . . .' I thought, hardly daring to believe in such idiocy, and meekly asked what was his reason for taking off his cap. The Pole pointed to the bronze figure of the

[1] A mountain chain of Old Castile, where the French defeated the Spanish in 1808.—(*Translator's Note.*)

emperor. How can we expect men to refrain from domineering or oppressing others when it wins so much devotion!

Mickiewicz's private life was gloomy; there was something unfortunate about it, something dark, some 'visitation of God.' His wife was for a long time out of her mind. Tovjanski recited incantations over her, and is said to have done her good; this made a great impression on Mickiewicz, but traces of her illness remained . . . things went badly with them. The last years of the great poet, who outlived himself, were spent in gloom. He died in Turkey while taking part in an absurd attempt to organise a Cossack legion, which the Turkish Government would not permit to be called Polish. Before his death he wrote a Latin ode to the honour and glory of Louis-Napoleon.

After this unsuccessful attempt at journalism I withdrew even more completely into a small circle of friends, enlarged by the arrival of new exiles. At first I had sometimes visited a club, and taken part in three or four banquets, i.e. had eaten cold mutton and drunk sour wine, while I listened to Pierre Leroux or Father Cabet and joined in the Marseillaise. Now I was sick of that, too. With deep pain I watched and recorded the success of the forces of dissolution and the decadence of the republic, of France, of Europe. From Russia came no gleam of light in the distance, no good news, no friendly greeting: my people had given up writing to me; personal, intimate, family relations were suspended. Russia lay speechless, bruised as though dead, like an unhappy peasant-woman at the feet of her master, beaten by his heavy fists. She was then entering upon that terrible five years from which she is emerging now to follow the coffin of Nicholas.[1]

Those five years were for me, too, the most unhappy

[1] Written in 1856.

period of my life; I have no longer such treasures to lose, such convictions to be shattered....

... The cholera raged in Paris; the heavy air, the sunless heat, made one depressed; the sight of the luckless, terrified people, and rows of funeral hearses which raced each other as they drew near the cemeteries —all this was in harmony with the political events.

The victims of the epidemic fell near at hand, at one's side. My mother went to St. Cloud with a friend, a lady of five-and-twenty. As they were coming back in the evening, the lady felt rather unwell; my mother persuaded her to stay the night. At seven o'clock the next morning they came to tell me that she had cholera. I went in to see her, and was aghast. Not one feature was unchanged; she was still handsome; but all the muscles of her face were drawn and contracted, dark shadows lay under her eyes. With some difficulty I succeeded in finding Rayer[1] at the Institute, and brought him home with me. After glancing at the sick woman, Rayer whispered to me: 'You can see for yourself all there is to be done here.' He wrote a prescription and went away.

The sick woman called me and asked: 'What did the doctor say? He did tell you something, didn't he?' 'He sent for some medicine.' She took my hand, and her hand amazed me even more than her face: it had grown thin and angular as though she had been seriously ill for a month: and fixing her eyes upon me full of suffering and horror, she said: 'Tell me, for God's sake, what he said . . . is it that I am dying? . . . You are not afraid of me, are you?' she added. I felt fearfully sorry for her at that moment; that terrible consciousness not only of death, but of the infectiousness of the disease that was rapidly sapping her

[1] Rayer, P. F. O., was a distinguished French physician, and author of numerous medical works.—(*Translator's Note.*)

life, must have been intensely painful. Towards the morning she died.

Ivan Turgenev was about to leave Paris, the lease of his flat was up; he came to us for a night. After dinner he complained of the heat; I told him that I had had a bathe in the morning; in the evening he too went for a bathe. When he came back he felt unwell, drank some soda-water with a little wine and sugar in it, and went to bed. In the night he woke me. 'I am a lost man,' he said; 'it's cholera.' He really was suffering from sickness and spasms; happily, he escaped with ten days' illness.

After burying her friend, my mother went away to the Ville d'Avray. When Turgenev was taken ill, I sent Natalie and the children to her and remained alone with him, and when he was a great deal better I moved there too.

On the morning of June the 12th, Sazonov came to see me there. He was in a very enthusiastic mood: talked of the popular outbreak that was impending, of the certainty of its being successful, of the glory awaiting those who took part in it, and pressed me urgently to join in reaping the laurels. I told him that he knew my opinion of the present position—that it seemed to me stupid, without believing in it, to co-operate with people with whom one had hardly anything in common.

To this the enthusiastic agitator replied that it was of course more safe and peaceful to stay at home and write sceptical articles while others were in the market-place championing the liberty of the world, the solidarity of peoples, and many other good things.

A very despicable feeling, but one which has led and will lead many men into making great mistakes—even committing crimes—impelled me to say: 'What makes you imagine I am not going?'

'I concluded that from what you have just said.'

'No; I said it was stupid, but I did not say that I never do anything stupid.

'That is just what I wanted! That's what I like in you! Well, it's no use losing time; let us go to Paris. This evening the Germans and other refugees are assembling at nine o'clock; let us go first to them.'

'Where are they meeting?' I asked him in the train.

'In the Café Lamblin, in the Palais Royal.'

This was my first surprise.

'In the Café Lamblin?'

'The "reds" usually meet there.'

'For that very reason I should have thought that they ought to meet somewhere else.'

'But they are all used to going there.'

'I suppose the beer is very good!'

Various *habitués* of the revolution were sitting with dignity at a dozen little tables, gloomily and significantly looking about them from under wide-brimmed felt hats and short-peaked caps. These were the perpetual suitors of the revolutionary Penelope, the invariable actors who take part in every popular demonstration and form its *tableau*, its background, and who are as terrifying in the distance as the paper dragons with which the Chinese tried to scare the English.

In the troubled times of social storms and reconstructions in which states move out of their common routine for a long period, a new kind of people spring up who may be called the chorus of the revolution; grown on shifting and volcanic soil, nurtured in an atmosphere of anxiety when every sort of work is suspended, they grow inured from their earliest years to the conditions of political ferment, and like the theatrical setting of it, its impressive and brilliant *mise en scène*. Just as to Nicholas drill was the most important part of tie military art, to them the everlasting banquets, demonstrations, protests, collections, toasts, banners, are the most important part of the revolution.

Among them there are good, valiant people, sincerely devoted and ready to face a bullet; but for the most part they are very unintelligent and extremely pedantic. Immovable conservatives in everything connected with revolution, they stop short at some programme and never advance beyond it.

Discussing all their lives a small number of political ideas, they only know their rhetorical side, so to speak, their ceremonial trappings, *i.e.* the commonplaces which are invariably brought on the scene *à tour de rôle*, like the ducks in a well-known children's toy—in newspaper articles, in speeches, at banquets and in parliamentary sallies.

In addition to the naive people and the revolutionary doctrinaires, unappreciated artists, unsuccessful literary men, students who finished their studies without taking their degree, briefless barristers, actors with no talents, persons of great vanity but of little capacity, with vast pretensions but no perseverance or power of work, are all naturally drawn into this circle. The external authority which guides the human herd in ordinary times is weakened in times of revolution; people, left to themselves, do not know what to do. The younger generation is impressed with the apparent ease with which men attain celebrity in times of revolution, and rushes into futile agitation; this accustoms the young to violent excitements and destroys the habit of work. Life in the clubs and cafés is attractive, full of movement, flattering to vanity and free from restraint. There is no fear of being late, there is no need to work: what is not done to-day may be done to-morrow, or may not be done at all.

The chorus of the revolution, like the chorus of a Greek play, is divided into two halves; the botanical classification may be applied to them: some of them may be called cryptogamous and others phanerogamous. Some become eternal conspirators, are continually changing their lodgings and the shape of their beards. They mysteriously invite one to some extraordinarily important interview, if possible at night, or in some inconvenient place. Meeting their friends in public, they do not like saluting them with a bow, but greet them with a significant glance. Many of them keep their address a secret, never tell one what day they are going away, never say where they are going, write in cypher or invisible ink news which is printed openly in the newspapers.

In the days of Louis-Philippe, so I was told by a Frenchman, E., who had been mixed up in some political affair, was in hiding in Paris. With all its attractions such a life becomes *à la longue* wearisome and tedious. Delessert,[1] a *bon vivant* and a rich man, was at that time prefect; he served in the police not from necessity but for the love of it, and liked at times a festive dinner. He and E. had many friends in common. One day 'between the peas and the cheese,' as the French say, one of them said to him: 'What a pity it is that you persecute poor E.! We are deprived of a capital talker, and he is obliged to hide like a criminal.'

'Upon my soul,' said Delessert, 'his case is completely forgotten! Why is he in hiding?'

His friends smiled ironically.

'I will try to convince him that it is all nonsense — and you, too.'

On reaching home he called one of his chief spies and asked him, 'Is E. in Paris?' 'Yes,' answered the spy. 'Is he in hiding?' asked Delessert. 'Yes,'

[1] Delessert, Gabriel, born 1786, was prefect of police of the town of Paris for twelve years from 1836. — (*Translator's Note*.)

answered the spy. 'Where?' asked Delessert. The spy took out his notebook, looked in it, and read E.'s address. 'Well, then, go to him to-morrow early in the morning and tell him that he need not be anxious, that we are not looking for him, and he can live in peace at his flat.'

The spy carried out his task exactly, and two hours after his visit E. mysteriously informed his friends that he was leaving Paris and would be in hiding in a remote town, because the prefect had found out the place where he was concealed!

Just as the conspirators try to conceal their secret with a transparent veil of mystery and an eloquent silence, the phanerogamous try to display and blurt out all they possess.

They are the permanent tribunes of the clubs and cafés; they are perpetually dissatisfied with everything, they repeat everything—even things that have not happened, while things that have happened are by them squared and cubed and distorted out of all proportion, like the mountains on a relief map. One is so used to seeing them that one unconsciously looks for them in every row in the street, at every demonstration, at every banquet.

. . . The spectacle at the Café Lamblin was still new to me; at that time I was not familiar with the back premises of the revolution. It is true that in Rome I had been in the Café delle Belli Arti and in the square, I had been in the Circolo Romano and in the Circolo Popolare; but the movement in Rome had not then that exotic character which became particularly apparent after the failure of 1848. Ciceruacchio and his friends had a *naïveté* of their own, their southern expressiveness which strikes one as affectation and their Italian phrases which seem to us theatrical; but they were in a period of youthful enthusiasm, they had not yet fully awakened from their three centuries of sleep. *Il popolano* Ciceruacchio was not in the least a political agitator by trade; he liked nothing better than to retire in peace to his little house in Strada Ripetta and to carry on his trade in wood and timber like a *pater familias* and free *civis romanus*.

The men surrounding him were free from all traces of that vulgar, babbling pseudo-revolutionism, of that *taré* character which is so depressingly common in France.

I need hardly say that in speaking of the café agitators and revolutionary lazzaroni I was not thinking of those mighty workers for the emancipation of humanity, of those martyrs for the love of their fellow-creatures and fiery champions of independence whose words could not be suppressed by prison, nor exile, nor banishment, nor poverty—of those creators of events, by whose blood and tears and words a new historical order is established. I am talking about the stagnant margin covered with barren weeds, to whom agitation itself is goal and reward, who like the process of revolution for its own sake, as Tchitchikov's Petrushka[1] liked the process of reading, or as Nicholas liked drill.

There is nothing for reaction to rejoice at in this— it is overgrown with worse weeds and toadstools, not only at the margin but everywhere. In its ranks are whole multitudes of officials who tremble before their superiors, scurrying spies, volunteer assassins ready to murder on either side, officers of every loathsome kind from the Prussian junker to the rapacious French Algerian, from the guard to the *page de chambre*—and that is only touching on the secular side, saying nothing of the mendicant fraternity, the intriguing Jesuits, the priests who act as police, and the other members of the ranks of angels and archangels.

[1] A character in Gogol's *Dead Souls*.—(*Translator's Note*.)

If there are among reactionaries any who resemble our dilettante revolutionaries, they are the courtiers employed for ceremonies, the people who are conspicuous at levees, christenings, royal weddings, coronations, and funerals, the people who exist for the uniform, for gold lace, who make up the aureole and fragrance of power.

In the Café Lamblin, where the desperate *citoyens* were sitting over their *petits verres* and big glasses, I learned that they had no sort of plan, that the movement had no real centre and no programme. They were waiting for inspiration to descend upon them as the Holy Ghost descended upon the heads of the apostles. There was only one point on which all were agreed—*to come to the meeting-place unarmed*. After two hours of empty chatter, we went off to the office of the *True Republic*, agreeing to meet at eight o'clock next morning at the Boulevard Bonne Nouvelle, facing the Château d'Eau.

The editor was not at home: he had gone to the 'montagnards' for instructions. About twenty people, for the most part Poles and Germans, were in the big, grimy, poorly lighted and still more poorly furnished room which served as an assembly hall and a committee room. Sazonov took a sheet of paper and began writing something; when he had written it, he read it aloud to us: it was a protest in the name of the *émigrés* of all nationalities against the occupation of Rome, and a declaration of their readiness to take part in the movement. Those who wished to immortalise their names by associating them with the glorious morrow he invited to sign it. Almost all wished to immortalise their names, and signed it. The editor came in, much dejected, anxious to impress on every one that he knew a great deal but was bound to keep silent; I felt convinced that he knew nothing at all.

'*Citoyens*,' he said, '*la Montagne est en permanence.*' Well, who could doubt its success—*en permanence!*

Sazonov gave the editor the protest of the democracy of Europe. The editor read it through and said: 'That's splendid, splendid! France thanks you, *citoyens*; but; why the signatures? There are so few, that if we are unsuccessful our enemies will vent all their anger upon you.'

Sazonov insisted on the signatures remaining; many agreed with him. 'I won't take the responsibility for it,' said the editor; 'excuse me, I know better the people we have to deal with.' With that he tore off the signatures and delivered the names of a dozen candidates for immortality to the flame of the candle, while he sent the protest itself to the printer.

It was daybreak when we left the office; groups of ragged boys and wretched, poorly dressed women were standing, sitting, and lying on the pavement near the various newspaper offices, waiting for the piles of newspapers—some to fold them, and others to run with them all over Paris. We walked out on to the boulevard: there was absolute stillness; now and then one came upon a patrol of National Guards and police-sergeants, strolling about and looking slyly at us.

'How free from care the city sleeps,' said my comrade, 'with no foreboding of the storm that will waken it to-morrow!'

'Here are those who keep vigil for us all,' I said to him, pointing upwards—that is, to the lighted window of the *Maison d'Or*.

'And very appropriately, too. Let us go in and have an absinthe; my stomach is a bit upset.'

'And I feel empty; it wouldn't be amiss to have some supper too. How they eat in the Capitole I don't know, but in the Conciergerie the food is abominable.'

From the bones left after our meal of cold turkey, no one could have guessed either that cholera was raging in Paris, or that in two hours' time we were going to

AN ABORTIVE RISING

change the destinies of Europe. We ate at the Maison d'Or as Napoleon slept before Austerlitz.

Between eight and nine o'clock, when we reached the Boulevard Bonne Nouvelle, many groups of people had already gathered there, evidently impatient to know what they were to do; their faces showed perplexity, but at the same time something in their aspect betrayed great exasperation. Had those people found real leaders the day would not have ended in a farce.

There was a minute when it seemed to me that something was really going to happen. A gentleman rode on horseback down the boulevard rather slowly. He was recognised as one of the ministers (Lacroix), who was probably taking horse exercise so early not merely for the sake of fresh air. He was surrounded by a shouting crowd, who pulled him off his horse, tore his coat, and then let him go—that is, another group rescued him and escorted him away. The crowd grew; by ten o'clock there may have been twenty-five thousand people. No one we spoke to, no one we questioned, knew anything. Chersosi, a *carbonaro* of old days, assured us that the *banlieu* was coming through the Arc de Triomphe with a shout of '*Vive la République!*'

'Above all,' the elders of the democracy repeated again, 'be unarmed, or you will spoil the character of the whole thing—the all-powerful people ought to show the National Assembly its will peacefully and solemnly so as to give the enemy no occasion to blaspheme.'

At last columns were formed; we foreigners made up a guard of honour immediately behind the leaders, among whom were E. Arago[1] in the uniform of a colonel,

---

[1] Arago, Emmanuel (1812-1896), the son of the more distinguished F. D. Arago, who was one of the members of the Provisional Government formed after the *coup d'état* of 24th February 1848. The others were Ledru-Rollin, Dupont de l'Eure, Garnier-Pagès, Lamartine, Crémieux, Marrast, Flocon, and Louis Blanc.—(*Translator's Note.*)

a former minister, Bastide,[1] and other celebrities of 1848. We moved down the boulevard, shouting various things and singing the Marseillaise. One who has not heard the Marseillaise sung by thousands of voices in that state of nervous excitement and suspense which is inevitable before a struggle can hardly realise the overwhelming effect of the revolutionary hymn.

At that minute there was really something grand about the demonstration. As we slowly moved down the boulevards all the windows were thrown open; ladies and children crowded at them and came out on to the balconies; the gloomy and agitated faces of their husbands, the fathers and proprietors, peeped out from behind them, not observing that in the fourth storeys and attics other heads, those of poor seamstresses and working girls, were thrust out—they waved handkerchiefs, nodded, and greeted us. From time to time as we passed by the houses of well-known people all sorts of shouts were uttered.

In this way we reached the point where the Rue de la Paix joins the boulevards; it was closed by a platoon of the Vincennes Chasseurs, and when our column came up to it the chasseurs suddenly moved apart like the scenery in a theatre, and Changarnier,[2] mounted upon a small horse, galloped up at the head of a squadron of dragoons. With no summons to the crowd to disperse, with no beating of the drums or other legal formalities, he scattered the foremost ranks, cut them off from the others, and, changing the dragoons into open formation,

---

[1] Bastide, Jules (born 1800), a publicist and politician, was minister for foreign affairs in 1848. He had had an eventful career, and for two years took refuge in England after escaping from prison, where he was thrown for taking part in the riots that followed the funeral of Lamarque in 1832.

[2] Changarnier, Nicolas (1793-1877), a prominent politician and general, was exiled at the *coup d'état* of 1851, but lived to serve in the Franco-German War of 1870.—(*Translator's Notes*.)

ordered them to clear the street at full speed. The dragoons with positive zest fell to riding down people, striking them with the flat of their swords and using the edge at the slightest resistance. I hardly had time to take in what was happening when I found myself nose to nose with a horse which was snorting in my face, and a dragoon swearing also right in my face and threatening me with a blow if I did not move away. I retreated to the right, and in one instant was carried away by the crowd and squeezed against the railings of the Rue Basse des Remparts. Of our rank the only one left besides me was M. Strübing. Meanwhile the dragoons pressed upon the foremost ranks with their horses, and the people, unable to get away, were thrust back upon us. E. Arago leaped over into the Rue Basse des Remparts, slipped, and dislocated his leg; Strübing and I jumped down after him. We looked at each other in a sort of frenzied indignation; Strübing turned round and shouted aloud: '*Aux armes! Aux armes!*' A man in a workman's blouse caught him by the collar and, shoving him out of the way, said: 'Have you gone mad? Look there!' A thick brush of bayonets was moving down the street—the Chaussée d'Antin it must have been. 'Get away before they hear you and cut off all escape. All is lost, all!' he added, clenching Ms fist; and, humming a tune as though there were nothing the matter, rapidly walked away. We made our way to the Place de la Concorde. In the Champs-Élysées there was not a single platoon from the *banlieu*; why, Chersosi must have known that there was not. It had been a diplomatic lie to save the situation, though it would perhaps have been fatal if any had believed it.

The shamelessness of attacking an unarmed crowd aroused great resentment. If anything really had been prepared, had there been leaders, nothing would have been easier than for fighting to have begun in earnest.

Instead of showing itself in its full strength, the *Montagne*, on hearing how absurdly the sovereign people had been dispersed by horses, hid itself behind a cloud. Ledru-Rollin carried on negotiations with Guinard.[1] Guinard, the artillery commander of the National Guard, wanted to join the movement, wanted to give men, but would not on any consideration give ammunition—he seems to have wished to act by the moral influence of cannons; Forestier[2] was doing the same with his legion. Whether it helped them much, we saw by the Versailles trial. Every one wanted to do something, but no one ventured; the most foresight was shown by some young men who built their hopes on the new regime—they ordered themselves prefects' uniforms, which they declined to take after the movement failed, and the tailor had to put them up for sale.

When the hurriedly rigged-up government was installed at the *Arts et Métiers*, the workmen, after walking about the streets with inquiring faces and finding neither advice nor leadership, went home, convinced once more of the ineffectiveness of the *Montagnard* fathers of the country; perhaps they gulped down their tears like the man who said to us, 'All is lost!'—or perhaps laughed in their sleeves at the discomfiture of the *Montagne*.

But the dilatoriness of Ledru-Rollin, the pedantry of Guinard—these were the external causes of the failure, and were as *appropriate to the occasion* as decisive characters and fortunate circumstances when they are needed. The internal cause was the poverty of the republican idea in which the movement originated.

[1] Guinard, Auguste-Joseph (born 1799), had been one of the first to proclaim the republic in February 1848, and at the head of the 8th Legion had occupied the Hôtel de Ville.

[2] Forestier, Henri-Joseph (born 1787), was a painter of merit. He was colonel of the 8th Legion of the National Guard.—(*Translator's Notes.*)

An idea that has outlived its day may hobble about the world for years—may even, like Christ, appear after death once or twice to its devotees; but it is hard for it ever again to lead and dominate life. Such ideas never gain complete possession of a man, or gain possession only of incomplete people. If the *Montagne* had been victorious on the 13th of June, what would it have done? There was nothing new they could call their own. It would have been an insipid reproduction of the gloomy Rembrandt or Salvator Rosa picture of 1793 without the Jacobins, without the war, without even the naive guillotine. . . .

After the 13th of June and the attempted rising at Lyons, arrests followed. The mayor came with the police to us at the Ville d'Avray to look for Karl Blind[1] and Arnold Ruge; some of our friends were seized. The Conciergerie was full to overflowing. In one small room there were as many as sixty men; in the middle stood a large slop-bucket, which was emptied once in the twenty-four hours—and all this in civilised Paris, with the cholera raging. Having no desire to spend some two months in such pleasant surroundings, fed on rotten beans and putrid meat, I borrowed a passport from a Moldav-Wallachian and went to Geneva.[2]

Transport in France was in the hands of Laffitte and Calliard in those days. The diligences were put on the railway lines, then taken off—at Châlons, I remember—then put on the rails again. A lean, sunburnt gentleman

---

[1] Karl Blind (born 1826), a writer and revolutionist, was for the part he took in the insurrections in South Germany sentenced to eight years' imprisonment, but was rescued by the mob. He settled in England, where he continued journalistic and propaganda work up to the time of his death.—(*Translator's Note*.)

[2] How well founded my apprehensions were was shown by a police raid on my mother's house at the Ville d'Avray. They seized all the papers, even the correspondence of her maid with my cook. I thought it inopportune to publish my account of the 13th of June at the time.—(*Author's Note*.)

with a clipped moustache and a rather unpleasant appearance got into the carriage with me, and looked at me suspiciously; he had a small travelling-bag, and a sword wrapped up in American leather. He was obviously a police-sergeant in disguise. He scanned me carefully from head to foot, then retreated into the corner and did not utter a single word. At the first station he called up the conductor and told him that he had left behind an excellent map, and would be grateful for a scrap of paper and an envelope. The conductor said they only had three minutes before the bell would ring; the sergeant jumped out, and returning looked at me more suspiciously than ever. For four hours the silence continued: my permission to smoke he even asked without speaking; I answered in the same way with my head and my eyes, and took out a cigar. When it began to get dusk he asked me, 'Are you going to Geneva?' 'No, to Lyons,' I answered. 'Ah!' With that the conversation ended. A little while later the door opened and the conductor with difficulty thrust in a bald-headed, immensely corpulent individual, in a roomy pea-green overcoat and a bright-coloured waistcoat, with a thick stick, a sack, and an umbrella. When this typical figure of the virtuous uncle installed himself between the sergeant and me, I asked him before he had time to recover his breath: '*Monsieur, vous n'avez pas d'objection*?' Coughing, mopping his face, and tying a silk handkerchief round his head, he answered: 'Not in the least, by all means; my son who is in Algiers is always smoking, *il fume toujours*'; and with this good opening he began chatting and telling us stories. Half an hour later, he asked me where I had come from and where I was going. Hearing that I came from Wallachia, he added with characteristic French politeness, '*Ah, c'est un beau pays*,' though he did not know for certain whether it was in Turkey or in Hungary.

My neighbour answered his questions very laconically. *'Monsieur est militaire?'* *'Oui, monsieur.'* *'Monsieur a été en Algérie?'* *'Oui, monsieur.'* 'My eldest son, too, he is there now. In Oran,[1] I suppose?' *'Non, monsieur.'* 'And in your country are there diligences?'

'Between Jassy and Bucharest,' I answered with inimitable assurance. 'Only, with us, diligences are drawn by oxen.'

This greatly astonished my neighbour, and I am sure he would have taken his oath that I was a Wallachian; after this happy detail, even the sergeant was softened and became more conversational.

At Lyons I got out of the diligence and at once went to another booking-office, climbed upon the roof of another diligence, and five minutes later was dashing along the road to Geneva. At the last big town before the frontier, a commissaire of police was sitting with a clerk in the square before the police-station; gendarmes were standing about, and a preliminary examination of passports was held. The description in my passport did not quite fit me, and so, getting down from the knifeboard, I said to the gendarme: *'Mon brave,* where could we quickly get a drink of wine together? Show me; the heat is insufferable.'

'Why, there's my sister's café not two steps away.'

'But what about my passport?'

'Give it here, I'll hand it over to my comrade; he will bring it back to us.'

A minute later the gendarme and I were sitting over a bottle of Beaune in his sister's café, and five minutes later his comrade brought the passport. I offered him a glass, he put his hand to his hat, and we returned to the diligence friends. So far all was well. We reached

---

[1] Oran, a province of Algeria in which the French carried on a successful campaign against Abd-el-Kader in 1847.—(*Translator's Note.*)

the frontier; there was a river, over the river a bridge, and on the other side of the bridge the Piedmontese customhouse. French gendarmes were sauntering in all directions on the bank, looking for Ledru-Rollin, who had crossed the frontier long before, and for Felix Pyat,[1] who would nevertheless cross it later, and like me with a Wallachian passport.

The conductor observed that here they would examine our passports finally, that this would take rather a long time—half an hour—and so he advised us to have something to eat at the posting inn. We went in, and had no sooner sat down than another Lyons diligence drove up; the passengers came in, and foremost among them was my sergeant. Ough! what luck! And I had told him that I was going to Lyons. We bowed frigidly; he, too, seemed surprised; however, he did not say a word.

A gendarme came in, distributed passports; the diligences were already on the other side of the river. 'Kindly cross the bridge on foot, gentlemen.' Now there will be a bobbery, I thought. We went out . . . and here we are on the bridge—no trouble; and now we were over the bridge—still no trouble.

'Ha—ha—ha!' the sergeant laughed nervously. 'So we've got across! Ough! it's like a load off one's back.'

'What?' said I, 'are you . . .'

'Why, you too, it seems?'

'Upon my word,' I answered, laughing heartily, 'I

[1] Pyat, Félix (1810-1889), a journalist, dramatic writer, and communist leader, supported Ledru-Rollin's appeal to the French people in 1849, and on its failure escaped to Switzerland and then to London, where he was a member of the 'European Revolutionary Committee.' He returned to France at the amnesty of 1870, and was in 1871 one of the leaders of the Commune, on the fall of which he again escaped to London. He was condemned to death in his absence, but was again pardoned in 1880.—(*Translator's Note*.)

am straight from Bucharest; came all the way with oxen.'

'It's your luck!' the conductor said to me, holding up his finger.' 'You must be more careful next time. Why did you give two francs to the boy who brought you to the inn? It's a good thing he is *one of us* too; he said to me at once, "He must be a red; he didn't stop a minute at Lyons, and he was so pleased to get a seat that he gave me two francs." "You hold your tongue, it's not your business," I said to him, "or some beast of a gendarme will overhear you and maybe stop him."'

Next day we reached Geneva, the old haven of refuge for the persecuted. 'At the time of the king's death, a hundred and fifty families,' says Michelet in his history of the 16th century, 'escaped to Geneva; a little later, another fourteen hundred. The refugees from France and the refugees from Italy founded the real Geneva, that wonderful sanctuary between three nations; with no support, afraid of the Swiss themselves, it maintained itself by its moral force alone.'

Switzerland was at this time the meeting-place in which the survivors left from European revolutions gathered together from all parts. Representatives of all the unsuccessful risings were shifting about between Geneva and Basle, crowds of the insurgents were crossing the Rhine, others were descending the St. Gothard or coming from beyond the Jura. The cowardly Federal Government did not dare yet to turn them out; the cantons still clung to their ancient holy right of sanctuary.

All the people whose names were on everybody's lips, whom I loved at a distance and was now eager to meet, were passing through Geneva as though on parade at a review, stopping there to rest and going on again. . . .

Chapter 37

A BABEL OF TONGUES—THE GERMAN UMWALZUNGSMÄNNER
—THE FRENCH RED MONTAGNARDS—THE ITALIAN FUORU-
SCITI IN GENEVA—MAZZINI, GARIBALDI, AND ORSINI—THE
ROMAN AND THE GERMAN TRADITIONS—A TRIP ON
'THE PRINCE RADETSKY'

THERE was a time when in a fit of irritation and bitter mirth I thought of writing a pamphlet in the style of Grandville's[1] Illustrations: *Les réfugiés peints par eux-mêmes*. I am glad I did not do it. Now that I look at it more calmly, I am less moved to laughter and indignation. Besides, exile both lasts too long and weighs too heavily on men. . . .

Nevertheless, I do say even now that exile, not undertaken with any definite object, but forced upon men by the triumph of the opposing party, checks development and draws men away from the activities of life into the domain of fantasy. Leaving their native land with concealed anger, with the continual thought of going back to it on the morrow, men make no advance, but are continually thrown back upon the past; hope hinders them from settling down and undertaking any permanent work; irritation and trivial but exasperated disputes prevent their escaping from the familiar circle of questions, thoughts, and memories which make up an oppressive binding tradition. Men in general, and especially men in an exceptional position, have such a passion for formalism, for the coterie spirit, for looking

---

[1] Grandville, Jean-Ignace-Isidore (born 1802), was one of the most celebrated book-illustrators of his time. Perhaps his most famous book is *Les animaux peints par eux-mêmes*. He was deeply interested in animals, insects, and fishes, and drew them wonderfully. He edited *La Caricature*, in which all the most eminent people of his time in Paris are depicted. He died, insane, in 1850.—(*Translator's Note*.)

their part, that they immediately fall into a groove and acquire a doctrinaire stamp.

All exiles, cut off from the living environment to which they have belonged, shut their eyes to avoid seeing bitter truths, and grow more and more used to a narrow, fantastic circle consisting of inert memories and hopes that will never be realised.

Add to this, aloofness from all who are not exiles and an element of exasperation, suspicion, exclusiveness, and jealousy, and this new stiff-necked Israel becomes perfectly comprehensible.

The exiles of 1849 did not yet believe in the permanence of their enemy's triumph; the intoxication of their recent successes had not yet passed off, the applause and songs of the victorious people were still ringing in their ears. They firmly believed that their defeat was a momentary reverse, and did not unpack their trunks. Meanwhile Paris was under police supervision, Rome was falling under the onslaught of the French, the brother of the Prussian King was brutally triumphing in Baden,[1] while Paskevitch in the Russian style had outwitted Görgei[2] in Hungary by bribes and promises. Geneva was full to overflowing with refugees; it became the Coblenz[3] of the revolution of 1848. There were

[1] In 1848 there was an insurrection in Baden, headed by Struve and Hecker, which aimed at establishing a republic. The troops sided with the insurgents, the Grand Duke fled, and in May 1848 a Constituent Assembly was called. After several battles the Grand Duke was by Prussian aid reinstated in July of the same year.

[2] Görgei, Arthur (1818), was commander-in-chief of the Hungarian forces in 1848, was victorious over the Austrians in the spring of that year, but was defeated early in August by the Russian general Paskevitch, and on the 13th of that month surrendered the Hungarian army unconditionally to Rüdiger, another Russian general. He was accused of treachery.

[3] Coblenz was one of the chief centres to which the *émigrés* of the great French revolution flocked from 1790 onwards.—(*Translator's Notes.*)

Italians from all parts; Frenchmen escaping from the Bauchart[1] inquiry and from the Versailles trial; Baden insurgents, who entered Geneva marching in regular formation with their officers and with Gustav Struve; men who had taken part in the rising of Vienna; Bohemians; Poles from Posen and Galicia. All these people were crowded together between the Hotel de Bergues and the Post Office Café. The more sensible of them began to suspect that this exile would not soon be over, talked of America, and went away. It was quite the opposite with the majority, and especially with the French, who, true to their temperament, were in daily expectation of the death of Napoleon and the birth of a republic—some looking for a republic both democratic and socialistic, others for one that should be democratic and not at all socialistic.

A few days after my arrival, as I was walking in Les Paquis, I met an elderly gentleman who looked like a Russian village priest, wearing a low wide-brimmed hat and a *black* white coat, and walking along with a sort of priestly unction; beside him stepped a man of terrific proportions, who looked as though he had been casually put together of immense blocks of human flesh. F. Kapp,[2] the young writer, was with me.

'Don't you know them?' he asked me.

'No; but, if I'm not mistaken, it must be Lot or Noah out for a walk with Adam, who has put on a coat several sizes too large instead of his fig-leaves.'

'They are Struve and Heinzen,' he answered, laughing: 'would you like to make their acquaintance?'

---

[1] The Commission of Inquiry was presided over by Odilon Barrot; the report, drawn up by one Bauchart, is described as a '*monument impérissable de mauvaise foi et de basse fureur.*'

[2] Kapp, Friedrich (1820-1884), a German historian, after the revolution of 1848 went to New York, but returned to Berlin in 1870, and became a Liberal member of the Reichstag.—(*Translator's Notes.*)

'Very much.' He introduced me.

The conversation was trivial. Struve was on his way home, and invited us to come in; we went with him. His small lodging was crowded with exiles from Baden. A tall woman, from a distance very good-looking, with a mass of luxuriant hair flowing loose in an original fashion, was sitting in the midst of them; this was his wife, the celebrated Amalie Struve.

Struve's face made a strange impression on me from the very first; it expressed that moral rigidity which superstitious bigotry gives to fanatics and dissenters. Looking at his strong, narrow forehead, at the untroubled expression of his eyes, at his uncombed beard, his slightly grizzled hair, and his whole figure, I could have fancied that this was either a fanatical pastor of the army of Gustavus Adolphus who had forgotten to die, or a Taborite[1] preaching repentance and the sacrament under two aspects. There was a surly coarseness about the appearance of Heinzen,[2] that Sobakevitch of the German revolution; full-blooded and clumsy, he kept looking angrily from under his brows, and was sparing of words. He wrote later on that it would be sufficient to *massacre* two millions of the inhabitants of the globe and the cause of revolution would go swimmingly. Anybody who had once seen him would not be surprised at his writing this.

I cannot refrain from relating an extremely funny incident which occurred to me in connection with this

[1] The more thoroughgoing of the followers of John Huss were called Taborites, from their headquarters at Mt. Tabor in Bohemia.

[2] Heinzen, Karl Peter (1827-1880), wrote for the *Leipziger Allgemeine Zeitung* and the *Rheinische Zeitung*, and his articles led to the suppression of these two papers. He published an attack on the government, 'Die prussische Bureaucratie,' for which he was prosecuted. In 1848 he was one of the leaders of the Baden revolution. Later on he escaped to America, where he edited *The Pioneer*. —(*Translator's Notes*.)

cannibalistic project. There was, and indeed still is, living in Geneva a Dr. R., one of the most good-natured men in the world and one of the most constant and platonic lovers of the revolution, the friend of all the refugees; he doctored them gratis as well as giving them food and drink. However early one might arrive at the Café de la Poste, the doctor would already be there and already reading his third or fourth newspaper; he would beckon one mysteriously and murmur in one's ear: 'I fancy it will be a hot day in Paris to-day.' 'Why so?' 'I can't tell you from whom I heard it, but it was a man in close relations with Ledru-Rollin; he was here on his way through. . . .' 'Why, you were expecting something yesterday and the day before yesterday too, weren't you, Doctor? ''Well, what of that? *Stadt Rom war nicht in einem Tage gebaut.*'

So it was to him as a friend of Heinzen's that I appealed in the very same café when the latter published his philanthropic programme. 'Why,' I said to him, 'does your friend write such pernicious nonsense? The reaction is making an outcry, and indeed it has every reason to: he's a regular Marat in a German setting! And how can one ask for two million heads?'

R. was confused, but did not like to give his friend away. 'Listen,' he said at last: 'you have lost sight of one fact, perhaps: Heinzen is speaking of the whole human race; in that number there would be at least *two hundred thousand Chinese*.' 'Oh, well, that's a different matter; why spare them?' I answered; and for long afterwards I could never think of this reassuring fact without bursting into laughter.

Two days after our meeting in Les Paquis, the *garçon* of the Hôtel de Bergues, where I was staying, ran up to my room and announced with an air of importance: 'General Struve and his adjutants.' I imagined either that some one had sent the *garçon* up as a joke, or that he had made some blunder; but the door opened and—

> 'Mit bedächtigem Schritt
> Gustav Struve tritt . . .'

and with him four gentlemen: two were in the military uniform worn in those days by German students, and had in addition red armlets adorned with various emblems. Struve presented his suite to me, democratically referring to them as 'brothers in exile.' I learnt with delight that one of them, a young man of twenty, who looked like a *Bursch* who had recently emerged from the '*fuchs*'[1] stage, was now successfully filling the post of minister of home affairs *per interim*.

Struve at once began instructing me in his theory of the seven scourges, *die sieben Geissel*—Popes, priests, kings, soldiers, bankers, etc.—and of the establishment of some new democratic and revolutionary religion. I observed that if it depended upon us whether to establish a new religion or not, it would be better not to establish any, but to leave it to the will of God, as, from the very nature of the case, it was more His concern. We argued. Struve made some remark about the *Weltseele*; I observed that in spite of Schelling's having so clearly defined the world-soul by calling it *das Schwebende*, I found great difficulty in grasping it.

He jumped up from his chair and, coming as close to me as possible, with the words, 'Excuse me, allow me,' began tapping my head with his fingers, and pressing it with them, as though my skull had been composed of the keys of a concertina. 'Yes, indeed,' he commented, addressing his four brothers in exile, '*Bürger Herzen hat kein, aber auch gar kein Organ der Veneration!*' All were

---

[1] Undergraduates in their first year were called 'foxes' in German universities.—(*Translator's Note*.)

satisfied with the lack of the 'bump of reverence' in me, and I was equally so.

Hereupon he informed me that he was a great phrenologist, and had not only written a book on Halle's system but had even selected his Amalie from it, after first feeling her skull. He assured me that the bump of the passions was completely absent in her, and that the back part of the skull where they are located was almost flat. On these grounds, sufficient for a divorce, he married her.

Struve was a very queer fish: he ate nothing but Lenten food, with the addition of milk, drank no wine, and kept his Amalie on a similar diet. This was not enough for him: he went every day to bathe with her in the Arve, the water of which scarcely reaches the temperature of eight degrees in the middle of summer, as it flows so swiftly from the mountains that it has not time to get warm.

Later on it often happened that we talked of vegetarianism. I raised the usual objections: the formation of the teeth, the great loss of energy in the digestion of vegetable fibre, and the lower development of the brain in herbivorous animals. He listened blandly without losing his temper, but stuck to his opinion. In conclusion, apparently wishing to impress me, he said: 'Do you know that a man always nourished on vegetarian diet so purifies his body as to be quite free from smell after death?' 'That's very pleasant,' I replied; 'but what advantage will that be to me? I won't be sniffing myself after death.' Struve did not even smile, but said to me with serene conviction: 'You will speak very differently one day!' 'When my bump of reverence develops,' I added.

At the end of 1849 Struve sent me the calendar he had newly devised for 'free' Germany. The days, the months, everything had been translated into an ancient German jargon difficult to understand; instead of saints' days, every day was dedicated to the memory of two celebrities—for instance, to Washington and Lafayette; but, on the other hand, every tenth day was devoted to the memory of the enemies of mankind—for instance, Nicholas and Metternich. The holidays were the days when particularly great men such as Luther and Columbus were commemorated. In this calendar Struve had the gallantry to replace Christmas on the twenty-fifth of December by the festival of Amalie!

Meeting me one day in the street, he said among other things that we ought to publish in Geneva a journal common to all the exiles, in three languages, which would carry on the struggle against the 'seven scourges' and maintain the 'sacred fire 'of the peoples, now crushed by the reaction. I answered that it would, of course, be a very good thing. The publishing of papers was at that time an epidemic disease: every two or three weeks new schemes were started, specimen copies appeared, prospectuses were sent about, then two or three numbers would come out—and would all disappear, leaving no trace. People who were incapable of anything considered themselves competent to edit a paper, scraped together a hundred francs or so, and spent them on the first and last number. So I was not in the least surprised at Struve's intention; but I was very much surprised by his calling upon me at seven o'clock the next morning. I thought some misfortune had happened, but Struve, after calmly settling himself in a chair, brought a sheet of paper out of his pocket and, preparing to read it, said: '*Bürger*, since we agreed yesterday as to the necessity of publishing a journal, I have come to read you the prospectus of it.'

When he had read it he informed me that he was going to Mazzini and many others to invite them to meet at Heinzen's for deliberation on the subject. I, too, went to Heinzen's: he was sitting with a ferocious air at the table, holding a manuscript in one gigantic paw; the other he held out to me, muttering thickly, '*Bürger, platz.!*'

Some eight persons, French and German, were present. Some ex-representative of the people in the French National Assembly was making an estimate of the cost, and writing something in slanting lines. When Mazzini arrived, Struve proposed reading the prospectus that had been written by Heinzen. Heinzen cleared his throat and began reading it in German, although the only language common to all was French.

Since they had not the faintest shadow of a new idea, the prospectus was only the thousandth variation of those democratic lucubrations which are the same sort of rhetorical exercise on revolutionary texts as church sermons are on those of the Bible. Indirectly guarding himself from a charge of socialism, Heinzen said that the democratic republic would of itself solve the economic question to the general satisfaction. The man who did not flinch at the demand for two million heads was afraid that his organ would be considered communistic.

I urged some objection to this when the reading was finished, but from his abrupt replies, from Struve's intervention, and from the gestures of the French deputy, I perceived that we had been invited to the council to accept Heinzen's and Struve's prospectus, not to deliberate upon it; it was in strict harmony with the theory held by Elpidifor Antiohovitch Zurov, the military governor of Novgorod.[1]

Mazzini listened with a melancholy air, but agreed, and was almost the first to subscribe for two or three shares. '*Si omnes consentiunt ego non dissentio,*' I thought *à la* Schufterle in Schiller's *Robbers*, and I too subscribed.

But the subscribers appeared to be few in number;

[1] See Vol. II. Chapter 27.

however often the French deputy added and subtracted, the sum subscribed was insufficient.

'Gentlemen,' said Mazzini, 'I have thought of a way of getting over the difficulty: publish the journal at first only in French and German; as for the Italian translation, I shall put all articles of *interest* in my *Italia del Popolo*—that will save you one-third of the expenditure.'

'To be sure! what could be better!' Mazzini's proposition was accepted by all. He grew a little more cheerful. I was awfully amused, and very eager to show him that I had seen the trick he had played. I went up to him and, watching for a moment when no one was near us, I said: 'How capitally you got out of the journal!'

'Well,' he observed, 'an Italian part is really superfluous, you know.'

'So are the two others!' I added.

A smile glided over his face and vanished as quickly as though it had never been there.

That was the second time of my seeing him. Mazzini, who knew of my stay in Rome, wanted to make my acquaintance. One morning I went with L. Spini to see him in Les Paquis.

When we went in Mazzini was sitting dejectedly at the table listening to what was being said by a rather tall, graceful, and handsome young man with fair hair. This was the daring companion-in-arms of Garibaldi, the defender of Vascello, the leader of the Roman legionaries, Giacomo Medici. Another young man with an expression of melancholy preoccupation sat plunged in thought, paying no attention to what was going forward—this was Mazzini's colleague in the triumvirate, Marco Aurelio Saffi.

Mazzini got up and, looking me straight in the face with his piercing eyes, held out both hands in a friendly way. Even in Italy a head so severely classical, so elegant in its gravity, is rarely to be met with. At moments the expression of his face was harshly austere, but it quickly grew soft and serene. An active, concentrated intelligence sparkled in his melancholy eyes; there was an infinity of persistence and strength of will in them and in the lines on his brow. All his features showed traces of long years of anxiety, of sleepless nights, of past storms, of powerful passions, or rather of one powerful passion, and also some element of fanaticism—perhaps of asceticism.

Mazzini is very simple and amiable in his manner, but the habit of rule is apparent, especially in argument; he can scarcely conceal his annoyance at contradiction, and sometimes does not conceal it. He knows his strength, and genuinely despises all the external trappings of dictatorial authority. His popularity was at that time immense. In his little room, with the everlasting cigar in his mouth, Mazzini at Geneva, like the Pope in the old days at Avignon, held in his hands the threads that like a spiritual telegraph system brought him into living communication with the whole peninsula. He knew every heart-throb of his party, felt the slightest tremor in it, promptly responded to everything, and with amazing tirelessness gave general guidance to everything and every one.

A fanatic and at the same time an organiser, he covered Italy with a network of secret societies connected together and devoted to one object. These societies branched off into arteries that defied detection, split up, grew smaller and smaller, and vanished in the Apennines and the Alps, in the regal palazzi of aristocrats and the dark alleys of Italian towns into which no police can penetrate. Village priests, diligence conductors, the *principe* of Lombardy, smugglers, innkeepers, women, bandits, all were made use of, all were links in the chain that was bound to him and that was subject to him. From the times of Menotti[1] and the brothers Bandiera,[2] enthusiastic youths, vigorous men of the people, vigorous aristocrats, sometimes old men, come forward in constant succession . . . and follow the lead of Mazzini, consecrated by the elder Buonarotti, the comrade and friend of Gracchus Babeuf,[3] and advance to the unequal combat, disdainful of chains and the block, and sometimes at the point of death adding to the shout of '*Viva l'Italia!*' that of '*Viva Mazzini!*'

There has never been such a revolutionary organisation anywhere, and it would hardly be possible anywhere but in Italy, unless in Spain. Now it has lost its old unity and old strength, it is exhausted by the ten years of martyrdom, it is worn out by loss of blood and the anguish of suspense, its thought has grown older; and yet what outbursts, what heroic examples, there are still: Pianori, Orsini, Pisacane!

I do not think that by the death of one man a country could be raised from such degradation as France has fallen into now.[4]

[1] The 'Bolognese insurrection' began on 2nd February 1831 at the house of Ciro Menotti at Modena. There thirty-one conspirators surprised by the ducal troops held the soldiers at bay for hours.

[2] Attilio and Emilio Bandiera, two young Venetians, lieutenants in the Austrian navy, attempted an insurrection in 1843. On its failure they escaped Corfu; to Cortu; but, misled by false information, landed in Calabria with twenty companions, were caught and shot at Cosenza in July of the same year. Their letters to Mazzini in London had been opened by the English authorities, who then resealed them and sent the information so gained to the Austrian Government. Sir James Graham and Lord Aberdeen were principally responsible.

[3] Babeuf, Françis-Émile, nicknamed Gracchus (1760-1797), conspired against the Directoire, was condemned to death, but stabbed himself. He advocated a form of communism called *babouvisme*.

[4] The reference is to Orsini's attempt to assassinate Napoleon III. on 14th January 1858.—(*Translator's Notes*.)

I do not justify the plan on which Pisacane made his attempt;[1] it seemed to me as ill-timed as the two previous risings in Milan: but that is not the point. I only mean to speak here of the way in which it was actually carried out. These men overwhelm one with the grandeur of their tragic poetry, their terrible strength, and silence all blame and criticism. I know no instance of greater heroism, among either the Greeks or the Romans, among the martyrs of Christianity or of the Reformation!

A handful of vigorous men sail to the luckless shore of Naples, bearing a challenge, an example, a living witness that all is not yet dead in the people. The handsome young leader is the first to fall, with the flag in his hand—and after him the rest fall, or worse still are caught in the clutches of the Bourbon. The death of Pisacane and the death of Orsini were like two fearful thunderclaps in a sultry night. Latin Europe shuddered —the wild boar,[2] terrified, retreated to Caserta and hid himself in his lair.

Pale with horror, the man who was driving France in her funeral hearse to the graveyard trembled in his seat.

Pisacane's attempt might well be described among the people in these poetical lines:—[3]

> Sceser con I 'armi, e a noi non fecer guerra,
> Ma s' inchinaron per bacciar la terra:

---

[1] 'In 1857 Pisacane seized the *Cagliari* steamer, freed the political prisoners in the island of Ponza, and with a small force effected a landing on the Neapolitan coast at Sapri, hoping to join others of the republican party. Met by overwhelming numbers, he fell at the head of his men, most of them falling with him.'

[2] The 'wild boar' meant is, of course, Ferdinand 11. of Naples, nicknamed Bomba because of the cruel bombardment of Naples and other cities during the suppression of the insurrection.—(*Translator's Notes*.)

[3] Here is a poor prose translation of these wonderful lines, which have passed into a popular legend:—

'They gathered with weapons in their hands, but they did not

Ad uno ad uno li gardai nel viso:
Tutti aveano una lagrima e un sorriso,
Li disser ladri usciti dalle tane,
Ma non portaron via nemmeno un pane;
E li sentii mandare un solo grido:
Siam venuti a morir pel nostro lido—
Eran trecento, eran giovani e forti:
        E sono morti!

Con gli occhi azzuri, e coi capelli d'oro
Un giovin camminava innanzi a loro.
Mi feci ardita, e, presol per la mano,
Gli chiesi: Dove vai, bel capitano?
Guardommi e mi rispose: O mia sorella,
Vado a morir per la mia patria bella!
Io mi sentii tremare tutto il core;
Nè potei dirgli: V' aiuti'l Signore;
Eran trecento, eran giovani e forti:
        E sono morti!

. . . .
(L. Mercantini, *La Spigolatrice di Sapri.*)

In 1849 Mazzini was a power, and it was not for nothing that the governments feared him; his star was then in its full brilliance—but it was already setting. It might have maintained itself for long years yet, grow-

---

war with us; they threw themselves on the earth and kissed it, the tear quivered in their eyes, and all wore a smile. We were told they were robbers who had come out of their dens; but they took nothing, not even a crust of bread, and we heard from them one cry only: "We have come to die for our country!" They were three hundred, they were young and strong! And they are dead!

'At their head came a young leader with golden hair and blue eyes. . . . I made so bold I took him by the hand and asked: "Whither goest thou, splendid leader?" He looked at me and said: "My sister, I go to die for my country!" and my heart ached; I had not strength to say: "God be thy help!"

'They were three hundred, they were young and strong! And they are dead!'

And I knew the *bel capitano*, and more than once talked with him of the fortunes of his distressful country.—(*Author's Note.*)

ing paler little by little; but after repeated failures and desperate efforts, it began to decline rapidly.

Some of Mazzini's friends allied themselves with Piedmont, others with Napoleon. Mazzini went his revolutionary bypath, the party split up into factions, the federal character of the Italians showed itself more conspicuously.

Garibaldi himself, in spite of his own feelings, pronounced a severe criticism on Mazzini, and, influenced by the enemies of the latter, published a letter in which he indirectly blamed him.

.   .   .   .   .   .

This is what has turned Mazzini grey and made him old, this is what has given a look of bitter intolerance, even exasperation, to his face, to his glance. But such men do not give in, do not yield; the worse things go with them, the higher they hold the flag. If Mazzini loses friends and money, and barely escapes one day from chains and the gallows, on the next he takes his stand more obstinately and resolutely than ever, collects fresh money, seeks fresh friends, denies himself everything, even sleep and food, ponders whole nights over new plans and every time actually creates them, flings himself again into the conflict, and, again beaten, sets to work once more with feverish ardour.

In this unyielding steadiness, in this faith which runs far ahead of facts, in this inexhaustible activity which failure only incites and provokes to fresh effort, there is something of grandeur, and, if you like, something of madness. Often it is just that grain of madness which is the essential condition of success. It acts on the people's nerves and carries them away. A great man acting directly is bound to be a great maniac, especially with such enthusiastic people as the Italians, who, moreover, preserve the religious conception of nationality. Only the sequel can show whether Mazzini has lost his magnetic power over the Italian masses through his ill-timed and unsuccessful attempts. It is not reason, it is not logic that leads nations, but faith, love, and hatred.

The Italian refugees were not superior to the other refugees either in talent or education. The greater number of them knew nothing, indeed, but their own poets and their own history. But they were free from the stereotyped, commonplace stamp of the rank and file of French democrats (who argue, declaim, and feel exactly the same thing in herds, all going into ecstasies at once), as well as from the uncouth, coarse, pothouse character typical of the German refugees. The ordinary French democrat is a bourgeois *in spe*; the German revolutionary, like the German *Bursch*, is just the philistine over again in a different stage of development. The Italians are more original, more individual.

The French are turned out ready-made by thousands on the same pattern. The present government was not originally responsible for this curtailment of individuality, but it has grasped the secret of it. Absolutely in the French spirit, it has organised public education—that is, all education, for there is no home education in France. In every town of the empire the same thing is being taught on the same day, at the same hour, from the same books. At all examinations the same questions are asked, the same examples set; teachers who make any departure from the text, or make any change in the syllabus, are promptly removed. This soulless uniformity of education has only put into a compulsory hereditary form what existed unformulated in men's minds already.

It is the conventional democratic notion of equality applied to intellectual development. There is nothing of the sort in Italy. The Italian, a federalist and an artist by temperament, flies with horror from every sort of barrack discipline, uniformity and geometrical regularity. The Frenchman is innately a soldier; he loves discipline, command, the uniform; he loves to inspire terror. The Italian, if it comes to that, is rather a bandit than a soldier, and by that I do not mean anything at all to his discredit. He prefers at the risk of capital punishment to kill his enemy at his own impulse rather than to kill by order; but it is without throwing any responsibility on others. He prefers a meagre livelihood in the mountains, concealing smugglers, to honoured service in the gendarmerie, discovering them.

The educated Italian, like us, is developed of his own accord by life, by his passions, by the books that have happened to come into his hands, and so attains to understanding of one sort or another. This is why there are gaps, discords, both in his culture and in ours. Our culture, like his, is in many respects inferior to the specialised finish of the French and the theoretical learning of the Germans; but, on the other hand, the colour is more brilliant both in us and in the Italians.

We even have the same defects as they. The Italian has the same tendency to laziness as we: he does not think of work as an enjoyment; he does not like the worry of it, the weariness of it, the lack of leisure. Industry in Italy is almost as backward as among us; the Italians, like us, have treasures lying under their feet and they do not dig them up. Manners in Italy have not been influenced by the modern bourgeois tendency to the same degree as in France and in England.

The history of the Italian petty-bourgeois is quite unlike the development of the bourgeoisie in France and in England. The wealthy bourgeois, the descendants *del popolo grasso,* have more than once successfully rivalled the feudal aristocracy, have been rulers of cities, and therefore they have been not further from but nearer to the plebeians and *contadini* than the rapidly enriched vulgarians of other lands. The bourgeoisie in the

French sense is represented in Italy by a special class which has come into existence since the first revolution, and which might be called, as in geology, the Piedmont strata. It is distinguished in Italy as in the whole continent of Europe by being invariably liberal in *many* questions, though in *all* afraid of the people and of indiscreet talk about labour and wages, and, what is more, by always giving way to the enemy above and never to their followers below.

The Italian exiles were drawn from every possible stratum of society. There were all sorts to be found about Mazzini, from the old names that occur in the chronicles of Guicciardini and Muratori to which the people's ear has been accustomed for centuries, such as Litti, Borromeo, del Verme, Belgiojoso, Nani, Visconti, to some half-savage runaway Romeo from the Abruzzi with his dark olive-coloured face and irrepressible rashness! Here were clericals too, like Sirtori, the heroic priest who, at the first firing in Venice, tucked up his cassock, and all through the siege and defence of Marghera fought, gun in hand, in the foremost ranks under a shower of bullets; here, too, were the brilliant staff of Neapolitan officers, such as Pisacane, Cosenz, and the brothers Mezzocappa. Here, too, were peasants from Trasteverina, faithful and hard as steel in privation, stern, austere, dumb in calamity, modest and indomitable like Pianori; and beside them, Tuscans, effeminate even in pronunciation, but ready for the struggle too. Lastly, there were Garibaldi, a figure taken straight out of Cornelius Nepos, with the simplicity of a child and the daring of a lion; and Felice Orsini, whose beautiful head has so lately rolled from the steps of the scaffold.

But at their names I must pause.

I made Garibaldi's acquaintance in 1854 when he sailed from South America as the captain of a ship and stayed in the West India Docks; I went to see him accompanied by one of his comrades in the Roman war, and by Orsini. Garibaldi, in a thick, light overcoat, with a bright-coloured scarf around his neck and a cap on his head, struck me as more of a genuine sailor than as the glorious leader of the Roman legion, statuettes of whom in fantastic costume were being sold all over the world. The good-natured simplicity of his manner, the absence of all affectation, the cordiality with which he received us, all disposed me in his favour. His crew consisted almost entirely of Italians; he was their head and chief, and I am sure he was a strict one, but they all looked happily and affectionately at him; they were proud of their captain. Garibaldi gave us lunch in his cabin, regaling us with specially prepared oysters from South America, dried fruits, port—when suddenly he leaped up, saying, 'Wait a bit! We will drink a different wine with you,' and ran up on deck; then a sailor brought in a bottle; Garibaldi looked at it with a smile and filled our glasses. . . . One might have expected anything from a man who had crossed the ocean, but it was nothing more nor less than a bottle with the label of his native town Nice, which he had brought with him to London from America.

Meanwhile, in his simple and unceremonious talk one was more and more conscious of the presence of strength; without phrases and commonplaces, the people's leader, who had amazed all old soldiers by his valour, was revealed, and it was easy to recognise in the ship-captain the wounded lion who, fighting at every step, retreated after the taking of Rome and, as he lost his followers, gathered together again at San Marino, at Ravenna, in Lombardy, in the Tyrol, in Tessino, soldiers, peasants, bandits, any one of any sort to strike back at the foe—and all this beside the body of his wife, who had succumbed to the hardships and privations of the march.

In 1854 his opinions were widely divergent from those of Mazzini, although he was on good terms with him. He told him in my presence that Piedmont ought not to be irritated, that the chief aim now was to shake off the Austrian yoke, and he greatly doubted whether Italy was as ready for union and a republic as Mazzini imagined. He was entirely opposed to all projects and attempts at insurrection.

When he was about to sail for coal to Newcastle-on-Tyne and was from there setting off to the Mediterranean, I told him how immensely I liked his seafaring life, and that of all the exiles he was the one who had chosen the better part.

'And who forbids them doing the same?' he replied with warmth. 'This was my cherished dream; you may laugh at it if you like, but I cherish it still. I am known in America: I could have three or four such boats under my command. I could take all the refugees on them: the sailors, the lieutenants, the workmen, the cooks, might all be exiles. What can they do now in Europe? Grow used to slavery and be false to themselves, or go begging in England. Settling in America is worse still—that's the end, that's the country "of forgetting the fatherland": it is a new fatherland, there are new interests, everything is different; men who have settled in America fall out of the ranks. What is better than my idea?' (his face beamed): 'what could be better than gathering together round a few masts and floating over the ocean, hardening ourselves in the rough life of sailors, in conflict with the elements and with danger? A floating revolution, ready to land on any shore, independent and unassailable!'

At that moment he seemed to me a hero of antiquity, a figure out of the *Æneid* . . . who—had he lived in other ages—would have had his legend, his 'Arma virumque cano!'

Orsini was a man of quite a different type. He showed to the full his wild strength and terrific energy on the 14th of January 1858, in the rue Lepelletier; they won him a great name in history, and brought his head under the knife of the guillotine at thirty-six. I made the acquaintance of Orsini at Nice in 1851; at times we were even very intimate, then drifted apart, came together again, and in the end 'a grey cat ran between us' in 1856, and, though we were reconciled, we never felt the same to each other again. Such types as Orsini are only developed in Italy; on the other hand, they appear there at all times, in all ages: they are conspirators and artists, martyrs and adventurers, patriots, *condottiere,* Teverina and Rienzi, anything you like, but not vulgar, petty, commonplace, bourgeois. Such characters stand out vividly in the chronicles of every Italian city. They amaze us by their goodness, they amaze us by their wickedness, and they impress us by the strength of their passions and by the strength of their will. The yeast of restlessness is fermenting in them from early years— they must have danger, they must have laurels, glory, fame; they are purely southern natures, with hot blood in their veins, with passions almost beyond our understanding, ready for any privation, for any sacrifice, from a sort of thirst of enjoyment. Self-denial and devotion in them go hand in hand with revengefulness and intolerance; they are simple in many ways and cunning in many ways. Reckless as to the means they use, they are reckless, too, of danger; descendants of the Roman patricians and children in Christ of the Jesuit fathers, reared on classic memories and the traditions of mediaeval turmoils, a mass of ancient virtues and catholic vices are fermenting in their souls. They set no value on their own lives nor on the lives of others either; their terrific persistence is on a level with Anglo-Saxon obstinacy. On the one hand there is a naive love of the external, an *amour propre* bordering on vanity, a voluptuous desire to have their fill of applause, of glory; on the other, all the Roman heroism in face of privation and death.

People of this energy can only be checked by the guillotine. Scarcely do they escape from the gendarmes of Sardinia before they begin hatching plots in the very claws of the Austrian hawk; and the day after a miraculous rescue from the dungeons of Mantua they begin, with hands still bleeding from the leap to freedom, to sketch a plan of grenades, then, face to face with danger, fling them under a carriage. In the hour of failure they rise to titanic heights, and by their death deal a blow more powerful than a bursting grenade. . . .

As a young man Orsini had fallen into the hands of the secret police of Pope Gregory XIV.; he was condemned for taking part in the movement in Rome and sentenced to the galleys, and remained in prison till the amnesty of Pius IX. From this life with smugglers, with bravoes, with survivors of the Carbonari, he gained a temper of iron and an immense knowledge of the national spirit. From these men, who were daily in conflict with the society which oppressed them, he learnt the art of self-control, the art of being silent not only before a judge but even with his friends.

Men of Orsini's stamp have a great influence on others: people are attracted by their reserved character and at the same time are not at home with them; one looks at them with the nervous pleasure, mingled with uneasiness, with which one admires the graceful movements and velvety gambols of a panther. They are children, but not good children. Not only Dante's hell is 'paved' with them, but all the later centuries nurtured on his sinister poetry and the malignant wisdom of Machiavelli are full of them. Mazzini, too, belongs to their family, in the way that Cosimo Medici did; Orsini, in the way that Giovanni Procida did. One cannot even exclude from them the great 'adventurer of the sea,' Columbus, nor the still greater 'bandit' of later days, Napoleon Buonaparte.

Orsini was strikingly handsome; his whole appearance, elegant and graceful, could not but attract attention; he was quiet, spoke little, gesticulated less than his fellow-countrymen, and never raised his voice. The long black beard, as he wore it in Italy, made him look like some young Etruscan priest. His whole head was extraordinarily beautiful, only a little marred by the irregular line of the nose.[1] And all the same there was something in Orsini's features, in his eyes, in his frequent smile and his gentle voice, that checked intimacy. It was evident that he was holding himself in, that he never fully let himself go and was wonderfully self-controlled; it was evident that not one word fell from those smiling lips without intention, that there were depths behind those inwardly shining eyes, that, where we should hesitate and step back, he would smile and without a change of face or tone of voice, would go forward, remorseless and undoubting.

In the spring of 1852 Orsini was expecting very important news in regard to his family affairs: he was worried at not getting a letter; he told me so several times, and I knew in what anxiety he was living. At dinner-time one day, when two or three outsiders were present, the postman came into the entry: Orsini sent to ask if there was a letter for him; it appeared that there was; he glanced at it, put it in his pocket, and went on with the conversation. An hour and a half later, when we were alone with him, Orsini said to us: 'Well,

[1] Napoleon, so the newspapers wrote, ordered Orsini's head to be steeped in sulphuric acid that it might be impossible to take a death mask from it. What progress in humanity and chemistry since the days when the head of John the Baptist was given on a golden dish to the daughter of Herod!—(*Author's Note*.)

thank God, at last I have got the answer, and it is all very good news.' We, knowing that he was expecting a letter, had not guessed that this was it, with so unconcerned an air had he opened it and then put it into his pocket. A man like that is a born conspirator. And he was one, indeed, all his life.

And what was accomplished by him with his energy, by Garibaldi with his daring, by Pianori with his revolver, by Pisacane and the other martyrs whose blood is not yet dry? Italy will be delivered from the Austrians, if at all, by Piedmont; as it was from the Bourbon of Naples by fat Murat, both under the protection of a Buonaparte. Oh, *divina Commedia*?—or simply *Commedia*! in the sense in which Pope Chiaramonti[1] said it to Napoleon in Fontainebleau. . . .

I became very intimate later on with the two men of whom I spoke when describing my first meeting with Mazzini.

Medici was a Lombard. In his early youth, unhappy at the hopeless position of Italy, he went to Spain, afterwards to Monte Video and to Mexico; he served in the ranks of the Cristinos[2]—was, I believe, a captain—and at last returned to his native place after the election of Mastai Ferretti.[3] Italy was showing signs of life; Medici threw himself into the movement. He performed miracles of valour at the head of the Roman legionaries during the siege; but the French hordes entered Rome all the same over the bodies of many noble victims— over the dead body of Laviron, who, as though to atone

[1] Pope Pius vii. signed the Concordat of 15th July 1801 with Napoleon, was forced by the latter to come to Paris to consecrate him as Emperor in 1804, was later on kept prisoner in Fontainebleau, and only returned to Rome in 1814.

[2] The Cristinos were the supporters of the Spanish Queen Regent Cristina against the Carlists.

[3] Cardinal Mastai Ferretti, elected Pope in 1846, known as Pius IX.—(*Translator's Notes*.)

for the crime of his country, was fighting against it, and fell, struck down by a French bullet at the gates of Rome.

One would imagine a tribune and warrior like Medici as a *condottiero* bronzed by gunpowder and the tropical sun, with bold features, with abrupt words and vigorous gesticulation. Pale, fair, with soft features, eyes full of gentleness, and elegant manners, Medici was more like a man who has spent his whole life in the society of ladies than a guerilla chieftain and an agitator. A poet, a dreamer, at that time passionately in love—everything about him was elegant and attractive.

The few weeks spent with him at Geneva did me a great deal of good. It was the very blackest period for me, in 1852, six weeks after the burial of my wife. I was utterly shattered: every signpost, every guiding clue was lost; I do not know whether I was even then like one demented, as Orsini said in his diary, but I was certainly in a bad way. Medici was sorry for me; he did not say so, but late in the evening, at twelve o'clock, he sometimes knocked at my door and came in to talk with me, sitting on my bed. (Once when we were chatting like this we caught a scorpion on the quilt.) He would sometimes knock, too, between six and seven in the morning, saying, 'It's a lovely day, let us go to Albaro'—that was where the Spanish beauty lived with whom he was in love. He had no hope of a speedy change of circumstances; before him was a prospect of years of exile, everything was growing worse and gloomier; but there was something youthful, gay, sometimes naïve, about him. I have noticed the same thing in almost all characters of that mould.

On the day of my departure several friends came to dine with me—Pisacane, Mordini, and Cosenz.[1] . . .

[1] Cosenz (born 1820) was an Italian general who defended Venice against the Austrians in 1848, joined Garibaldi in 1859, was minister

'Why is it,' I asked in jest, 'that our friend Medici, with his fair hair and northern aristocratic face, reminds me more of a Vandyck cavalier than of an Italian?' 'That's natural,' Pisacane went on, still in jest: 'Giacomo is a Lombard, he is descended from some German Ritter.' 'Fratelli,' said Medici, 'there is not a single drop of German blood in these veins!' 'It's all very well for you to talk; no, you must bring proofs, explain why you have the features of a northerner,' the former went on. 'Oh, well,' said Medici,' if I have the features of a northerner, I suppose one of my ancestresses must have forgotten herself with a Pole!'

Saffi had the purest and most candid nature that I have met in a man not Russian. The men of Western Europe are often not very intelligent, and so seem simple and slow-witted; but gifted natures are rarely simple. In Germans one meets with the disgusting simplicity of immaturity in practical life; among the English the simplicity that is due to slowness of mind, to their always seeming half asleep and not being able to wake up properly. On the other hand, the French are for ever taken up with *arrière-pensées*, and absorbed in playing their part. Together with the lack of simplicity they have another defect: they are all very poor actors, and do not know how to conceal their little game. Affectation, boasting, and a habit of fine phrases have so entered into their flesh and blood that men have perished, have paid with their lives, for the part they were playing, and yet their sacrifice has been all falsity. These are terrible things, and many are indignant at their being put into words, but it is still more terrible to deceive oneself. That is why it is so comforting, so easy to breathe, when in this jostling crowd of pretentious mediocrities and

of war under the latter's dictatorship in Naples, later on was several times elected to the Chamber of Deputies, and was a senator after 1872.—(*Translator's Note.*)

insufferable, affected, and self-glorifying talents one meets a strong man free from the slightest artificiality, free from pretentiousness, free from the vanity that jars like a knife scratching on a plate. It is like coming out of a stuffy theatre-corridor lighted by lamps, after an afternoon performance, into the sunshine—breathing fresh, wholesome air and seeing real lime trees after cardboard magnolias and sailcloth palm trees. Saffi is one of these men. Mazzini, old Armellini, and he were the triumvirate in the time of the Roman Republic. Saffi was in charge of the ministry of home affairs, and, up to the end of the struggles with the French, was in a foremost place, and that meant then under the bullets and cannon-shot.

He returned from exile and once more crossed the Apennines; he made this sacrifice with no faith in it, from a sense of duty, from a feeling of great devotion, that he might not wound some, that his absence might not be a bad example. He spent some weeks in Bologna, where he would have been shot within twenty-four hours if he had been caught; his task was not simply to conceal himself—he had to act, to prepare for action, whilst awaiting news from Milan. I never heard from him about the details of this part of his life. But I did hear about it, a great deal about it, from a man who might well be a good judge of deeds of daring, and I heard it at a time when their personal relations were greatly strained. Orsini had accompanied him across the Apennines; he used to tell me with enthusiasm of the even, calm serenity, of the light, almost gay, mood of Saffi at the time when they were going down the mountains on foot; with the enemy almost within sight, Saffi would carelessly sing folk-songs and repeat verses of Dante. . . . I imagine he would have gone to the stake with the same verses and the same songs on his lips, with no thought at all of his heroism.

In London, at Mazzini's or at his friends', Saffi was mostly silent; he rarely took part in argument, sometimes grew eager for a minute and then subsided again. They did not understand him, that was clear to me, *il ne savait pas se faire valoir* . . . but I never heard from one of the Italians who fell away from Mazzini one word, one slightest hint, against Saffi.

One evening an argument sprang up between Mazzini and me about Leopardi.

There are poems of Leopardi with which I am passionately in sympathy. Much of his work, like Byron's, is spoilt by theorising, but sometimes a line of his, like one of Byron's, stabs, hurts, wrings the heart. There are such words, such lines, in Lermontov; there are some in the iambics of Barbier.[1]

Leopardi was the last book read, looked at before her death, by Natalie. . . .

To men of action, to agitators who move the masses, these bitter hesitations, these heartrending doubts are incomprehensible. They see in them nothing but profitless lamentation, nothing but feeble despondency. Mazzini could not like Leopardi — that I knew beforehand; but he attacked him with a sort of exasperation. I felt very much vexed; of course, he was angry with him for being of no use for propaganda. In the same way Frederick II. might have been angry with him . . . I do not know . . . well, for instance, because he would be of no use as a soldier. It is the revolting desire to restrict the free play of personality, to force men into categories and ranks — as though political activity were like serf-labour to which the bailiffs drive weak and strong, willing and unwilling alike, without consulting their wishes. Mazzini was angry. Half in jest and half in earnest, I said to him: 'I believe you have a grudge

---

[1] Barbier, Henri-Auguste (1805-1882), a French poet, was the author of a volume of verses called *Iambes*. — (*Translator's Note*.)

against poor Leopardi for not having taken part in the Roman revolution; but you know he has an excellent reason to urge in his defence—you keep forgetting it!'

'What reason?'

'Why, the fact that he died in 1836.'

Saffi could not resist defending the poet whom he loved even more than I did and of course understood even more deeply: he analysed him with that æsthetic, artistic feeling in which a man rather reveals aspects of his spirit than 'thinks.'

From this conversation, and from a few more like it, I saw that their path was not really the same. The thought of one is seeking means, concentrated on means alone—that is, in a sense running away from doubt; it thirsts for nothing but practical activity, and that is in a way indolence. To the other, objective truth is precious and his mind is working; moreover, to an artistic nature art is precious in itself, apart from its relation to reality.

Leaving Mazzini, we talked for a long time yet of Leopardi. His poems were in my pocket; we went into a café and read several of my favourite ones.

That was sufficient. When men are in sympathy, in the finer shades, they need not speak of many things— it is clear that they are at one about vivid colours and deep shadows.

Speaking of Medici, I mentioned a deeply tragic figure, Laviron. My acquaintance with him was brief; he flashed by me and vanished in a cloud of blood. Laviron was an engineer and an architect who had completed his studies at the Polytechnique. I made his acquaintance in the very heyday of the revolution, between the 24th of February and the 15 th of May (he was then a captain in the National Guard). The vigorous, stern where necessary, and gay, good-natured Gallo-Frankish blood of the' nineties coursed unmixed in his veins. I imagine that the architect Kleber was of the same stamp when he carried earth in a wheelbarrow with the young actor Talma clearing a space for the festival of the Federation. Laviron belonged to the small number of men who were not intoxicated by the victory of the 24th of February and the proclamation of a republic. He was at the barricades when they were fighting, and in the Hotel de Ville when those who had not fought were electing dictators: when a new government came into the town-hall like a *deus ex machina*, he loudly protested against its composition, and, together with a few vigorous men, asked where it had come from, why it was the government? With perfect consistency, on the 15th of May Laviron burst with the Parisian populace into the bourgeois assembly and, with an unsheathed sword in his hand, forced the president to admit the orators of the people to the tribune. The cause was lost and Laviron was forced into hiding. He was judged and condemned *par contumace*. The ace. reaction was drunk with success; it felt strong for combat and soon strong for conquest—then came the June days, proscriptions, exiles, the *Blue* terror. It was just at that period that I was sitting one evening on the boulevard in front of Tortoni's in a crowd of all sorts of people, and, as is always the case in Paris—under constitutional and unconstitutional monarchy, under the republic and under the empire—spies were scattered about everywhere amongst them. Suddenly—I could not believe my eyes—Laviron walked up to me. 'How are you?' he said. 'What madness is this?' I answered in an undertone, and taking him by the arm I walked away from Tortoni's. 'How can you expose yourself like this, and especially just now?'

'If only you knew how dreary it is to sit shut up in hiding! it's enough to drive one crazy. . . . I sat thinking and thinking, and then went out for a walk.'

'But why on the boulevard?'

'That makes no difference. I am less known here than on the other side of the Seine, and who would dream of my walking about by Tortoni's? I am going away, though. . . .'

'Where?'

'To Geneva. Everything is so dreary and sickening; we have terrible calamities ahead of us. Everywhere there is change for the worse, and pettiness is everywhere and in everything. Well, good-bye—good-bye; and may our next meeting be a more cheerful one.'

In Geneva Laviron worked as an architect, and was building something when suddenly war was declared 'for the Pope' against Rome. The French made their treacherous attack on Città Vecchia, and were approaching Rome. Laviron threw down his calipers and galloped off to Rome. 'You need an engineer, an artilleryman, a soldier. I am a Frenchman. I am ashamed of France, and go to fight against my countrymen,' he said to the triumvirs, and joined the ranks of the Romans as a sacrifice of atonement for his country. With gloomy daring he headed the advance; when everything was lost he still fought on, and fell at the gates of Rome, shot down by a French bullet.

The French newspapers greeted his death with a shower of abuse, claiming that it was the judgment of God on an infamous traitor to his country! . . .

When a man who has long been watching black curls and black eyes suddenly turns to a fair-haired woman with light-coloured eyebrows, pale and nervous, his eyes always receive a shock and cannot at once get over it. The difference of which he has not been thinking, which he has forgotten, produces an involuntary physical effect upon him.

Exactly the same thing happens when one turns quickly from the Italian circles to the German.

Undoubtedly the Germans are more developed on the theoretical side than any other people, but they have not gained much by it so far. From Catholic fanaticism they have passed to the Protestant pietism of transcendental philosophy and the romance of philology, and are now gradually making the transition to exact science; the German 'studies diligently at all his stages,' and his whole history is summed up in that, and he will get marks for it on the Day of Judgment. The common people of Germany, who have studied less, have suffered a great deal; they bought the right to Protestantism by the Thirty Years' War, the right to an independent existence—that is, to a colourless existence under the supervision of Russia—by the struggle with Napoleon. The emancipation in 1814 and 1815 was the complete victory of the reaction; and when, in place of Jerome Buonaparte, *der Landesvater* appeared in a powdered wig and an old-fashioned uniform long laid by, and announced that next day was fixed, let us say, for the forty-fifth parade (the one before, the forty-fourth, had taken place before the revolution), then all the emancipated people felt as though they had suddenly lost touch with the present and gone back to another age, and every one felt his head to see if he had grown a pigtail with a ribbon on it. The people accepted this with simple-hearted foolishness, and sang Körner's songs. Science and learning advanced. Greek tragedies were performed in Berlin, there were dramatic triumphs for Goethe in Weimar.

The most radical men among the Germans remain philistines in their private life. Bold as they are in logic, they feel no obligation to be consistent in practice, and fall into glaring contradictions. The German mind, in matters revolutionary as well as in everything else, accepts the general idea in its unconditional—of course, that is, unreal—significance, and is satisfied with working it out intellectually, imagining that a thing is done when it is understood, and that the fact as easily follows the thought as the meaning of the fact is grasped by the consciousness.

The English and the French are full of prejudices, while a German is free from them; but both French and English are more consistent in their lives—the rule they follow is perhaps absurd, but it is what they have accepted. The German accepts nothing except reason and logic, but he is ruled in many things by *other considerations*— this is selling the soul for bribes.

The Frenchman is not morally free: though rich in initiative in practical life, he is poor in abstract thought. He thinks in received conceptions, in accepted forms; he gives a fashionable cut to commonplace ideas, and is satisfied with them. It is hard for him to take in anything new, although he does rush at it. The Frenchman oppresses his family and believes it is his duty to do so, just as he believes in the 'Legion of Honour' and the authority of the law-courts. The German believes in nothing, but takes advantage of public prejudices where it suits him. He is accustomed to trivial comfort, to *Wohlbehagen*, to peace and quiet, and, as he goes from his study to the *Prunkzimmer* or his bedroom, sacrifices his free thought to his dressing-gown, to his peace and quiet, and to his kitchen. The German is a great Sybarite, though this characteristic is not noticed in him, because his poor and narrow luxury and petty mode of life are not very much to look at; but the Eskimo who is ready to sacrifice everything for fish-fat is as much epicurean as Lucullus. Moreover, the German, lymphatic by temperament, soon grows heavy and sends down a thousand roots into his familiar mode of life; anything that might disturb him in his habits terrifies his philistine temper.

All the German revolutionaries are cosmopolitans,

sie haben überwunden den Standpunkt der Nationalität, and are filled with the most touchy, most obstinate patriotism. They are ready to accept an all-world republic, to abolish the frontiers between states, but Trieste and Danzig must belong to Germany. The Vienna students were not above setting off for Lombardy under the command of Radetsky; they even, under the leadership of some professor, took a cannon, which they presented to Innsbrück. With this conceited and martial patriotism, Germany has, from the time of the first revolution and up to this day, looked with horror to the right and with horror to the left. On this side, France with standards unfurled is crossing the Rhine; on that side, Russia is crossing the Niemen, and the people numbering twenty-five millions finds itself utterly forlorn and deserted, is scolding with terror, full of hatred from terror, and to comfort itself proving theoretically from authentic sources that the existence of France is no longer existence, while the existence of Russia is not yet existence.

The 'council of war' assembled in St. Paul's Church in Frankfort, and consisting of various worthy doctors, theologians, chemists, philologists, and professors, *sehr ausgezeichneten in ihrem Fache*, applauded the Austrian soldiers in Lombardy and oppressed the Poles in Posen. The very question of Schleswig-Holstein (*stammverwandt!*) was only a subject of interest to them from the point of view of '*Teutschtum.*' The first free word, uttered after centuries of silence by the representatives of emancipated Germany, was in opposition to weak and depressed nationalities. This incapacity for freedom, these awkwardly revealed inclinations to retain what had been unjustly acquired, provoke irony: one forgives insolent pretensions only when accompanied by vigorous actions, and those were absent.

The revolution of 1848 had everywhere the character of hastiness and precipitate action, but there was scarcely anything absurd about it in France and in Italy; in Germany, however, everywhere except in Vienna, it had a farcical character, incomparably more comic than the humour of Goethe's wretched farce, *Der Bürgergeneral*.

There was not a town, not a spot in Germany where at the time of the rising there was not an attempt at a 'committee of public safety' with all its principal characters: with a frigid youth as Saint-Just, with gloomy terrorists, and a military genius representing Carnot. I knew two or three Robespierres personally: they always put on clean shirts, washed their hands, and had clean nails. On the other hand, there were also dishevelled Collots d'Herbois; and if there happened to be a man in the club fonder of beer than the rest and more openly given to dangling after *Stubermädchen*—he was the Danton, *eine schweigende Natur*!

French weaknesses and defects are partly dissipated by their light and fugitive character. In the German the same defects assume a more solid and fundamental character, and hence are more striking. One must see for oneself these German efforts to play *so einen burschikosen Kamin de Paris* in politics in order to do them justice. I was always reminded of the playfulness of a cow when that excellent and respectable animal, adorned with all the domestic virtues, takes to frisking and galloping in the meadow, and with a serious face kicks up her two hind legs or gallops sideways chasing her own tail.

After the Dresden affair, I met in Geneva one of the agitators who had taken part in it, and began at once questioning him about Bakunin. He lauded him up to the skies, and began describing how he had himself commanded a barricade under his instructions. Inflamed by his own narrative he went on: 'A revolution is a thunderstorm; in it one must listen neither to the dictates of the heart nor to considerations of ordinary justice. . . . One must oneself have taken part in such events fully to understand the Montagne of 1794. Only imagine: we suddenly observe a vague movement in the royalist party, false reports were intentionally circulated, suspicious-looking men appeared. I reflected and reflected, and at last resolved to *terrorise* my street. "*Männer!*" I said to my company, "under pain of court-martial, which may at once sentence you to death in case of disobedience, I command you to seize every one, regardless of sex, age, or calling, who attempts to cross the barricade, and to bring him under close guard to me." This was kept up for more than twenty-four hours. If the *Bürger* who was brought to me was a good patriot, I let him go; but if he was a suspicious character, then I gave the signal to the guard.'

'And,' I said with horror, 'and they?'

'And they accompanied him home,' the terrorist replied with pride and satisfaction.

I will add another anecdote illustrating the character of the German champions of freedom.

The youth whom I mentioned, when describing my visit to Gustav Struve, as filling the post of minister of home affairs wrote me a note a few days later in which he asked me to find him work of some sort. I suggested that he should copy for the press the manuscript of my *Vom anderen Ufer* from the handwriting of Kapp, to whom I had dictated it in German from the Russian original. The young man accepted the proposal. A few days later he told me that he was so uncomfortably lodged with several students that he had neither space nor quiet to work, and asked leave to copy it in Kapp's room. Even there the work made little progress. The minister *per interim* arrived at eleven o'clock in the morning, lay on the sofa, smoked cigars, drank beer . . . and went off in the evenings to gatherings and consultations at Struve's. Kapp, a man of the greatest delicacy, was ashamed of him. A week or more passed in this way. Kapp and I said nothing, but the ex-minister broke the silence: he wrote me a note asking me for *a hundred francs in advance* for the work. I wrote him that he was working so slowly that I could not give him such a sum in advance, but that since he was in great need of money I was sending him twenty francs, although he had not yet done ten francs' worth of copying.

In the evening the minister appeared at the gathering at Struve's and reported on my anti-civic action and my misuse of my fortune. The worthy minister considered that socialism consisted not in a social organisation, but in a senseless partition of senselessly acquired property!

In spite of the amazing chaos prevailing in Struve's brains, he did, being an honest man, consider that I was not altogether to blame, and that it might be better for the *Bürger und Bruder* to copy more and ask less money in advance. He persuaded him not to make a great outcry over the story.

'Well, then, I shall send him back the money—*mit Verachtung,*' said the minister.

'What nonsense!' cried a student. 'If the *Bruder und Bürger* does not care to take the money, I suggest that we spend it on beer and send out for some at once to drink to the perdition *der Besitzenden.*'

'Do you agree?'

'Yes, yes, we all agree—bravo!'

'We will drink,' cried the orator, 'and pledge ourselves not to bow to the Russian aristocrat who has insulted the *Bruder.*'

'Yes, yes, we must not bow to him.'

And so they drank the beer and gave up bowing to me.

All these absurd failings, together with the peculiar *Plumpheit* of the Germans, jar upon the southern nature of the Italians and excite a physical, racial hatred in them.

The worst of it is that the good side of the Germans, that is, their philosophical culture, is either of no interest to the Italian or beyond his ken; while the vulgar, ponderous side is always conspicuous. The Italian often leads the most frivolous and idle life, but with a certain artistic, rhythmic grace about it, and that is why he can least put up with the bear-like joking and clumsy familiarity of the jovial German.

The Anglo-Germanic race is far coarser than the Franco-Roman. There is no help for that: it is its physical characteristic; it is absurd to be angry with it. The time has come to accept once for all that the different races of mankind, like different species of animals, have their different characteristics and are not to blame for them. No one is angry with the bull for not having the beauty of the horse or the swiftness of the stag; no one reproaches the horse because its flesh is not so good to eat as that of the ox: all that we can ask of them in the name of animal brotherhood is to graze peaceably in the same field without kicking or goring each other. In nature, everything attains to whatever it is capable of attaining to, is formed as chance determines, and so takes its generic *pli*: training goes some distance, corrects one thing and develops another; but to expect beefsteaks from horses, or horses' paces from bulls, is nevertheless absurd.

To grasp concretely the difference between the two opposite traditions of the European races, one has but to glance at the street-boys in Paris and in London; I take them as an example because they are absolutely spontaneous in their rudeness.

Look how the Parisian *gamins* jeer at any queer Englishman, and how the London street-boys mock at a Frenchman; in this little instance the two opposite types of two European races are sharply defined. The Parisian *gamin* is insolent and persistent, he can be insufferable: but, in the first place, he is witty, his mischief is limited to jests, and he is as amusing as he is annoying; and, in the second, there are words at which he blushes and at once desists, there are words which he never uses; it is difficult to stop him by roughness, and if the victim lifts his stick I would not answer for the consequences. It must be noted, too, that the French boys need something to attract their attention: a red waistcoat with blue stripes, a brick-coloured coat, a strange-looking muffler, a flunkey carrying a parrot or a dog, things only done by Englishmen and, take note, only outside England. To be simply a foreigner is not enough to make them mock and run after you.

The wit of the London street-boys is simpler. It begins with guffawing at the sight of a foreigner,[1] if only he has a moustache, a beard, or a wide-brimmed hat; then they shout some twenty times: '*French pig! French dog!*' If the foreigner turns to them with some reply, the neighings and bleatings are redoubled; if he walks away, the boys run after him — then all that is left is the *ultima ratio* of lifting a stick, and sometimes bringing it down on one of them. After that the boys run away full speed, dropping oaths and sometimes throwing mud or a stone from a distance.

In France, a grown-up workman, shopman, or woman selling wares in the street never takes part with the *gamins* in the pranks they play upon foreigners; in London, all the dirty women, all the grown-up shopmen grunt like pigs and abet the boys.

In France there is one shield which at once checks the most persistent boy — that is, poverty. In the country that knows no word more insulting than the word *beggar*, the foreigner is the more persecuted the poorer and more defenceless he is. One Italian refugee, who

[1] All this has greatly changed since the Crimean War (1866). — (*Author's Note.*)

had once been an officer in the Austrian cavalry and had left his country after the war, completely destitute, when winter came, wore his greatcoat of a military officer. This excited such a sensation in the market-place through which he had to pass every day, that the shouts of 'Who's your tailor?' roars of laughter, and finally tugging at his collar, forced the Italian at last to give up his greatcoat and, shivering to the marrow of his bones, to go about in his jacket.

This coarseness in street mockery, this lack of delicacy and tact in the common people, helps to explain how it is that women are nowhere beaten so often and so badly as in England,[1] how it is that an English father is ready to cast dishonour on his own daughter and a husband on his wife by taking legal proceedings against them.

The rude manners of the English streets are a great offence at first to the French and the Italians. The German, on the other hand, receives them with laughter and answers with similar rudeness; an interchange of abuse is kept up, and he is very well pleased with it. They both take it as a civility, a pleasant joke. 'Bloody dog!' the proud Briton shouts at him, grunting like a pig. 'Beastly John Bull!' answers the German, and each goes on his way.

This behaviour is not confined to the streets: one has but to look at the polemics of Marx, Heinzen, Ruge, *et consorts*, which were unceasing from 1849, have never ceased, and are still kept up on the other side of the Atlantic Ocean. We are unaccustomed to see in print such expressions, such accusations: nothing is spared, no respect is paid to personal honour, to the privacy of the family or the inviolability of a secret.

---

[1] *The Times*, two years ago, reckoned that on an average in every police district in London (there are ten) there were two hundred cases of assaults on women and children per annum; and how many assaults never lead to proceedings?—(*Author's Note*.)

Among the English, coarseness disappears as we rise higher in the scale of intelligence or aristocratic breeding; among the Germans it never disappears. The greatest poets of Germany (with the exception of Schiller) fall into the most uncouth vulgarity.

One of the reasons of the *mauvais ton* of Germans is that breeding in our sense of the word does not exist in Germany at all. Germans are taught, and taught a great deal, but they are not educated at all, even in the aristocracy, in which the manners of the barracks, of the *Junker*, are predominant. They are completely lacking in the aesthetic sense in daily life. The French have lost it, just as they have lost the elegance of their language; the Frenchman of to-day rarely knows how to write a letter free from legal or commercial expressions —the counter and the barrack-room have distorted their manners.

To conclude this comparison, I will describe an incident in which I saw with my own eyes and face to face the gulf which separates the Italians from the *Tedeschi*, and which there will be no bridging for years to come by any number of amnesties or manifestoes of the brotherhood of nations.

I was travelling with Tessier du Mothe, in 1852, from Genoa to Lugano. We reached Arona by night, and, inquiring when the steamer started, learned that it was at eight o'clock next morning, and went to bed. At half-past seven the porter came to take our trunks, and by the time we reached the landing-stage they were already on deck. But in spite of that we looked at each other with some perplexity instead of going on board.

A huge white flag with the two-headed eagle on it was fluttering over the hissing and swaying steamer, and on the stern was painted the name, *Fürst Radetsky*. We had forgotten to ask overnight what steamer was going, whether an Austrian or a Sardinian. Tessier had at the Versailles trial been condemned *in contumaciam* to deportation. Though Austria had nothing to do with that, yet surety it would seize the opportunity to keep him in prison for six months, at any rate, while making inquiries. The example of Bakunin showed what they were capable of doing with me. By agreement with Piedmont, the Austrians had not the right to demand passports from those who without landing on the Lombard shore went to Mogadino, which belongs to Switzerland; but I imagine they would not, if opportunity arose, disdain so simple a means of seizing Mazzini or Kossuth.

'Well,' said Tessier,' to go back is absurd!'

'Well, let's go ahead, then!' and we went on deck.

Just before starting, the passengers were surrounded by a detachment of soldiers armed with guns—what for? I do not know. Two small cannon, fastened in a special way, stood on the steamer. When the steamer set off the soldiers were dismissed. On the cabin walls hung regulations: among them was the statement that those passengers who were not going to Lombardy need not show their passports; but it was added that if any one of such persons were guilty of any offence against the K.K. (Kaiserlich Königlichen) police regulations he must be judged according to the laws of Austria. *Or donc*, wearing a Calabrian hat or a tricolor cockade was a crime against Austria. Only then I fully appreciated what clutches we were caught in. However, I am far from regretting my trip; nothing special happened during our journey, but I gathered a rich store of observations.

Several Italians were sitting on deck; they were smoking cigars in gloomy silence, looking with concealed hatred at the fair-haired officers dressed in white jackets who were bustling about on all sides without the slightest necessity. I must observe that among them were lads of twenty, and they were mostly young men; I can hear now the jarring, guttural, barrack-room voices, the insolent laughter that was like coughing, besides the loathsome Austrian accent in speaking German. I repeat that there was nothing dreadful about it, but I felt that for their manner of standing and turning their backs in our very faces, giving themselves airs and showing off, 'We are the victors—our side has won,' they ought to have been flung into the water; and even more, I felt that I should have been delighted to have seen it done, and would eagerly have helped.

Any one who had taken the trouble to look for five minutes at these two groups of men could not fail to understand that there can be no talk of reconciliation, that in the very blood of these people there lies a hatred for each other which it will take centuries to dissipate, to soften and to reduce to an inoffensive racial difference. After midday some of the passengers went down to the cabin, others asked to have lunch on deck. Here the racial difference was still more strikingly apparent. I looked at them with amazement—not a single gesture was the same. The Italians ate little, with the innate natural grace with which they do everything. The officers tore off pieces, chewed them loudly, threw down the bones, shoved their plates; some, bending right down to the table, with peculiar agility and extraordinary rapidity splashed the soup from the spoon into their mouths; others ate butter *from a knife*—without bread or salt. I looked at these performers and, glancing at an Italian, smiled—he understood me at once, and, responding with a sympathetic smile, betrayed his intense disgust. Another observation: while the Italians asked with a smile and gentle manner for a plate or for wine, every time thanking the waiter with a nod or a glance, the Austrians treated the attendants with revolting rudeness, just as retired Russian cornets and lieutenants treat their serfs in the presence of strangers.

By way of a finishing touch, a lanky young officer with pale yellowish hair called up a soldier, a man of fifty, who looked like a Pole or a Croat, and began abusing him for some negligence. The old man stood at attention and, when the officer had finished, tried to say something; but he had scarcely brought out 'Your honour,' when 'Hold your tongue and be off!' the pale yellow youth shouted at him in a husky voice. Then, turning to his comrades as though nothing had happened, he fell to drinking beer again. With what object was all this done before us? And was it not all done expressly for our benefit?

When we landed at Mogadino our long-suffering hearts could be restrained no longer, and, turning towards the steamer, which had not moved away, we shouted, '*Viva la Republic a!*'—while one Italian, shaking his head, repeated, '*E brutissimi, brutissimi!*'

Is it not premature to talk so rashly of the solidarity and brotherhood of the nations, and will not any artificial covering up of their hostility be a mere hypocritical truce? I believe that national peculiarities will lose their offensive character just so far as they have lost it in cultivated society; but for such breeding to permeate the depths of the masses needs time. When I look at Folkestone and Boulogne, at Dover and Calais, then I feel full of dread and want to say—many centuries.

Chapter 38
Switzerland—James Fazy and the Refugees— Monte Rosa

THE agitation in Europe was still so violent in 1849 that it was difficult, living in Geneva, to fix the attention on Switzerland alone. Moreover, political parties are rather like the Russian Government in the skill with which they divert the attention of the traveller. If he falls under their influence, he sees everything, but sees it all not simply but from a certain angle; he cannot get out of an enchanted circle. His first impression is prearranged, suborned, and does not belong to himself. The prejudiced view of the party catches him unawares, unprepared, indifferent, and, so to say, disarmed, and before he has taken his bearings it becomes his view. In 1849 I knew only Radical Switzerland, that Switzerland which brought about a democratic revolution, which in 1847 suppressed the *Sonderbund*.[1] Then more and more surrounded by the refugees, I shared their indignation with the cowardly Federal Government and the pitiful part it was playing in the face of its reactionary neighbours.

I learnt more about Switzerland and got to understand it better on later visits, and most of all in London. In the dreary leisure of the years 1853 and 1854 I learnt a great deal, and formed a different view of many things that I had experienced or seen in the past.

Switzerland was passing through a difficult ordeal. Among the ruins of the whole world of free institutions, among the fragments of foundering civilisations grinding each other into dust, amidst the destruction of all conditions of human life, of all political forms, for the benefit

[1] The *Sonderbund* was the alliance of the seven Catholic cantons of Switzerland, which aimed at separation from the Federal Government. It was dissolved after a brief civil war.—(*Translator's Note*.)

of a brutal despotism, two countries remained as they were—one behind its sea, the other behind its mountains, both mediaeval republics, both firmly rooted in the soil by the traditions of ages.

But what a difference of power and position between England and Switzerland! If Switzerland, too, is like an island behind her mountains, her position, shut in by other countries, and her national spirit compel her to steer her course with care, and also make her politics far from simple. In England the common people do not stir, they are three centuries behindhand. Activity in England is confined to a certain class: the majority of the people are outside any movement; they are scarcely stirred by Chartism, and even that is confined exclusively to the town workmen. England stands aside, flings its inflammable material across the ocean as it accumulates, and there it grows triumphantly. Ideas do not crowd upon her from the Continent, but enter slowly, adapted to her manners and translated into her language.

It is utterly different in Switzerland: she has no ruling caste, nor even striking differences between the town and country. The patriarchal patricians of the cantons could not hold out against the first pressure of democratic ideas. Every doctrine, every idea passes backwards and forwards across Switzerland, and they all leave their traces on her: she speaks three languages. Calvin preached there; the tailor Weitling [1] preached there; there Voltaire laughed and Rousseau was born. That land in which every man from the ploughman and the workman upwards has a hand in the government,

[1] Weitling, Wilhelm (born 1808), got into touch with communists in Paris and Switzerland during his wanderings as a journeyman tailor, was prosecuted for propaganda of his ideas in Germany, escaped to America, where he became the head of a communist colony in the state of Iowa, wrote *Das Evangelium des armen Sünders, Garantien der Harmonie und Freiheit* (1842), and *Die Menschheit wie sie ist und wie sie sein sollte* (1845).—(*Translator's Note.*)

which is oppressed by powerful neighbours, has no standing army, no bureaucracy, and no dictatorship, remains after the storms of revolution and the saturnalia of reaction the same free republican federation as before.

I should very much like to know how conservatives explain the fact that the only countries in Europe that are tranquil are those in which personal freedom and freedom of speech are the least restricted. While the Austrian Empire, for instance, is kept up by a series of *coups d'état* with the stimulant of galvanic shocks and administrative revolutions, and the French throne is only maintained by terrorism and the abolition of all legality, in Switzerland and England even the absurd and antiquated forms that have grown up with their freedom are preserved unshaken under its mighty canopy.

The behaviour of the Federal Council in regard to political refugees, whom they turned out at the first request from Austria and from France, was disgraceful. But the responsibility for it falls exclusively on the Government; questions of foreign policy are by no means so near the heart of the people as domestic problems. In reality all nations are only interested in their own affairs; everything outside is confined to a remote preference or simply a rhetorical exercise, sometimes sincere, but even then rarely affecting practice. The nation which has gained a reputation by its humane sympathy with all and everything knows less geography than any and is more than any tainted with insufferably susceptible patriotism. Moreover, the Swiss is by nature itself not drawn to distant horizons: he is confined to his native valley by his mountains, as the dweller by the sea to its shore, and as long as he is not interfered with in it he says nothing.

The right, assumed by the Federal Government, of dealing with the refugees did not really belong to the Swiss central government at all; according to its law, the question of the exiles was in the jurisdiction of each canton. The Swiss Radicals, carried away by French theories, tried to strengthen the central government in Berne, and made a great mistake. Fortunately, the attempts at centralisation, except in those instances in which its practical benefit is obvious, such as the organisation of the post and maintenance of roads and currency, were not at all popular in Switzerland. Centralisation may do a great deal for order and for various public undertakings, but it is incompatible with freedom. It easily brings a nation to the position of a well-tended flock, or a pack of hounds cleverly kept in order by a huntsman.

That is why the Americans and the English hate it as much as the Swiss.

Numerically weak, uncentralised Switzerland is a many-headed hydra, a Briareus; you cannot vanquish her at one blow. Where is her head? Where is her heart? Moreover, one cannot imagine a king without a capital city. A king is as great an absurdity in Switzerland as the grades of the Russian civil service in New York. The mountains, republicanism, and federalism have reared and preserved in Switzerland a mighty, vigorous breed of men, as sharply differentiated from each other as the soil is by the mountains, and as united by them as it is.

It is worth seeing the representatives of various cantons gathered together at some federal shooting competition, with their several standards, in their several costumes, with carbine on shoulder. Proud of their separate individuality and of their unity, coming down from their native mountains, they greet each other with brotherly shouts and salute the federal standard (which is kept in the town where the last competition was held), and yet remain distinct.

In these festivals of a free people, in the military games,

free from the offensive *étalage* of monarchy and the gorgeous setting of gold-embroidered aristocracy and dazzling guards, there is something impressive and powerful. On all sides speeches are delivered, home-made wine flows, there are sounds of shouting, singing, and bands; and all are conscious that there is no leaden weight, no oppressive burden of authority, on their shoulders. . . .

In Geneva soon after my arrival a banquet was given at the end of the term to the pupils of all the schools. James Fazy, the president of the canton, invited me to this fête. A big pavilion had been put up in an open space in Carouge. The council and all the leading figures in the canton were present, and dined with the children. A number of citizens, those whose turn it was, in uniform and carrying guns, had been summoned for a guard of honour. Fazy delivered a speech of a thoroughly radical character, congratulated the prize-winners, and proposed the health of 'The future citizens!' to the strains of music and the firing of cannon. After this the children filed past him, two by two, to the field where various sports had been prepared, air-balloons, acrobatic performances, and so on. The armed citizens —that is, the fathers, uncles, and elder brothers of the school-children—formed an avenue, and as the head of the column passed they presented arms. . . . Yes! presented arms before their sons and the orphans brought up at the expense of the canton. . . . The children were the honoured guests of the town, its 'future citizens.' All this was strange to such of us as had been present at Russian school anniversaries and similar ceremonies.

It seems strange to us, too, that all the workmen, all the grown-up peasants, the waiters in restaurants as well as the restaurant-keepers, those who live in mountains and those who live in marshes, have a very good knowledge of the affairs of the canton, take an interest in them, and belong to one or other party. Their language, their degree of culture, is very different; and if a Geneva workman sometimes reminds one of a member of some Lyons club, while the simple mountaineer is to this day like the men who surrounded Schiller's William Tell, that does not prevent their both taking the warmest interest in public affairs. In France there are offshoots and branches of political and social societies in the towns; their members are interested in the revolutionary question, and incidentally know something of the actual government. But, on the other hand, those who are outside these associations, and especially the peasants, know nothing and care nothing either for the affairs of France or for the affairs of the department.

Lastly, both we Russians and the French are struck by the absence of all sorts of trappings and vestments, all the operatic setting of a government. The president of a canton, the president of the Federal Assembly, the state secretaries (*i.e.* the ministers), and the federal colonels go to the café like simple mortals, dine at the common table, discuss public affairs, argue with workmen and argue before them among themselves, and they all drink the same wine and *kirsch*.

From the beginning of my acquaintance with James Fazy, I was impressed by this democratic simplicity, and it was only later on that I perceived that in all matters relating to the law the government of the canton was anything but weak, in spite of its lack of wardrobe grandeur, of stripes on trousers, of plumage, of beadles with staves, of sergeants with moustaches, and all the other gewgaws and superfluities of the royal *mise en scène*.

In the autumn of 1849 the persecution of refugees who had sought shelter in Switzerland began; the government was in the weak hands of doctrinaires, the federal ministers lost their heads. The intimidated Confederation, which had once refused Louis-Philippe's request for the deportation of Louis-Napoleon, now at the command of the latter turned out those who sought a refuge, and performed the same gracious act for Austria and Prussia. Of course, the Federal Government had on this occasion to deal not with a fat old king who disliked extreme measures, but with men whose hands were wet with blood and who were in the fury of savage reprisals. But what was the Federal Assembly afraid of? If it had been capable of looking beyond its mountains, it would have perceived how much secret alarm lay hidden under the insolence and menaces of the neighbouring governments. Not one of them had in 1849 a sufficiently stable position and sense of its own power to begin a war. The Confederation need only have shown its teeth and they would have desisted; the doctrinaires preferred timid submission, and began a petty, unworthy persecution of men who had nowhere to go to.

For a long time some of the cantons, and among them that of Geneva, maintained their opposition to the Federal Assembly, but at last even Fazy was drawn, *nolens volens*, into persecuting the refugees.

His position was very unpleasant. The transition from being a conspirator into being a member of the government, however natural it may be, has its comic and vexatious sides. In reality, it must be said that it was not Fazy who went over to the government, but the government who went over to Fazy; nevertheless, the former conspirator was not always at one with the president of the canton. He had to strike at his own people, or at times openly to disregard the Federal decrees, or to take measures against which he had been declaiming for the last ten years. He followed the one or the other course as the caprice took him, and so excited the hostility of both sides.

Fazy was a man of great energy and of great administrative abilities, but too much of a Frenchman not to like hard-and-fast measures, centralisation, authority. He had spent his whole life in the political struggle. As a young man we meet him on the Paris barricades of 1830, and then in the Hotel de Ville among the young people who, in opposition to Lafayette and the bankers, demanded the proclamation of a republic. Périer[1] and Laffitte[2] considered that the 'best republic' was the Duc d'Orléans; he was made king, while Fazy threw himself into the extreme republican opposition. Then he was associated with Godefroy Cavaignac[3] and Marrast,[4] with the Société des Droits de l'Homme and with the Carbonari, was mixed up with Mazzini's Savoy expedition, and published a journal which after the French fashion was suppressed by successive fines. . . .

Convinced at last that there was no doing anything in France, he bethought himself of his native land, and

[1] Périer, Casimir-Pierre (1777-1832), was a wealthy banker who supported the Liberal opposition under Charles x., and after the Paris revolution of 1830 became Minister of the Interior under Louis-Philippe, in which capacity he vigorously suppressed risings in Paris and Lyons.

[2] Laffitte, Jacques (1767-1844), was a French financier who took an active part in bringing about the revolution of 1830, and was at first the most influential minister of Louis-Philippe's government. He was dismissed by the king because he wished the French to go to the assistance of Italy in her effort to throw off the Austrian yoke, and was succeeded by Périer.

[3] Cavaignac, Godefroy (1801-1845), the eldest son of J. B. Cavaignac, the member of the Convention, took a leading part in the July revolution of 1830, was tried and acquitted, again arrested in 1834, and escaped to England. In 1841 he returned to France and became one of the most active editors of *La Réforme*. His popularity greatly favoured the rise of his brother, Louis-Eugène, the general, who, though he put down the June rising in 1848, remained under a cloud under Napoleon III. because he refused to take the oath of allegiance.

[4] Marrast, Armand (1801-1852), a journalist, was a member of the Provisional Government of 1848, and then mayor of Paris and president of the National Assembly.—(*Tranlator's Notes*.)

transferred all his energy and all the experience he had gained as a politician, a journalist, and a conspirator to the advancement of his ideas in the canton of Geneva. He thought out a radical revolution in it, and carried it through. Geneva rose up against its old government. Debates, attack and counter-attack, passed from private rooms and newspapers into the market-place, and Fazy appeared at the head of the rebellious part of the town. While he was organising and stationing his armed friends, a grey-headed old man looked out of a window and, having been an officer by profession, could not resist giving advice where to station a cannon or a company. Fazy obeyed him. The advice was excellent—but who was this officer? Count Osterman-Tolstoy, commander-in-chief of the allied armies at Kulm, who had left Russia on the accession of Nicholas and had lived afterwards almost permanently at Geneva.

During this revolution Fazy showed that he possessed to the full not merely tact and judgment, but also the audacity which Saint-Just considered necessary in a revolutionary. Having vanquished the Conservatives almost without bloodshed, he appeared before the Grand Council and informed it that it was dissolved. The members wanted to arrest him, and asked with indignation: 'In whose name dare he speak like that?'

'In the name of the people of Geneva, who are sick of your bad government and are with me,' and thereupon Fazy pulled back the curtain on the council-room door. A crowd of armed men filled the hall, ready at Fazy's first word to lower their guns and fire. The old 'patricians' and peaceful Calvinists were disconcerted. 'Go, while there is yet time!' observed Fazy, and they meekly trudged home, while Fazy sat down at the table and wrote a decree or *plébiscite* announcing that the people of Geneva, having dissolved the old government, were assembling to elect a new one and to frame a new democratic code, and in the meantime were entrusting the executive power to James Fazy. This was his eighteenth of Brumaire for the benefit of democracy and the people. Though he did elect himself dictator, the choice was undoubtedly a very good one.

From that time—that is, from the year 1846—he had been governing Geneva. Since, in accordance with the constitution, the president is elected for a period of two years and cannot be elected twice in succession, the people of Geneva appointed every two years some inconspicuous adherent of Fazy's, and in this way he remained *de facto* president, to the great distress of the Conservatives and Pietists, who always remained in the minority.

Fazy displayed new abilities during the period of his dictatorship. Administration, finance, everything made rapid progress; the resolute way in which radical principles were put into practice won the attachment of the people: Fazy showed himself as vigorous in organisation as he had been in destruction. Geneva flourished under his rule. This I was told not only by his friends but by people completely disinterested, among others by the celebrated victor of Kulm, Osterman-Tolstoy.

Abrupt and irritable, hasty and intolerant by disposition, Fazy always had despotically republican leanings; as he grew used to authority, the despotic *pli* sometimes got the upper hand. Moreover, events and ideas after 1848 caught Fazy unawares; he was perplexed on the one hand and circumvented on the other. Here it was the republic of which he had dreamed with Godefroy Cavaignac and Armand Carrel . . . and yet there was something wrong about it. His old comrade Marrast, as president of the National Assembly, observed to him that he had made an incautious reference to Catholicism 'at lunch in the presence of the secretary,' and told him that religion must be respected in order that the priests might not be incensed; when the ex-editor of the *Nationale* passed from room to room in the president's house, two sentries saluted him. Another friend and *protégé* of Fazy's went further still: he became himself president of the republic, but would not recognise his old comrade, and aimed at being a Napoleon.

'Was the republic in danger?' And meanwhile the workers and the leading men were not interested in it; they were all talking of socialism. So that was what was to blame—and with obstinacy and exasperation Fazy fell upon socialism. That meant that he had reached his limit, his *Kulminationspunkt*, as the Germans say, and was going downhill.

Mazzini and Fazy, who had been socialists in the days before socialism, became its enemies when it began to pass from general tendencies into a new revolutionary force. Many a lance I have broken with both of them, and I have seen with surprise how little can be done by logic when a man does *not want* to be convinced. If in both these men it was policy, a concession to the necessity of the times, what need had they to get so hot about it? What need had they to play their parts so well even in private conversation? No, there was something else in it, a sort of grudge against a doctrine formulated *outside* their own circle: there was a spite against the very name. I once suggested to Fazy that in our conversations I should call socialism Cleopatra, that he might not be angered by the word and prevented from understanding by the sound of it. Mazzini's *brochures* against socialism later on did the famous agitator far more harm than did Radetsky,—but that is not the point under discussion here.

One day on reaching home I found a note from Struve—he informed me that Fazy was turning him out, and very abruptly. The Federal Government had long before decreed the deportation of Struve and Heinzen; Fazy had confined himself to communicating the fact to them. What new incident had occurred?

Fazy did not want Struve to publish his 'international' journal in Geneva; he was afraid—and perhaps he was right—that Heinzen and Struve would publish such dangerous nonsense as to provoke again threats from France, to raise a howl from Prussia, and set Austria gnashing its teeth. How a practical man could imagine that the journal would come into existence I do not know; anyway, he offered Struve the choice of giving up the journal or of leaving Geneva. To give it up when Struve was fanatically dreaming that by means of his journal he would finally vanquish 'the seven scourges of mankind' was too much for the Baden revolutionary. Then Fazy sent a policeman to him with the order to leave the canton at once. Struve received the policeman frigidly, and announced that he was not yet ready for departure. Fazy resented the treatment of the policeman, and ordered the police to turn Struve out. To enter a house without a legal warrant was impossible; the measures taken in Berne had been by the police and not by a legal tribunal (what the French call *mesures de salut publique*). The policeman knew that, but, wishing to oblige Fazy, and probably to pay Struve back for his rude reception, got a carriage ready and sat down with a comrade under a lime-tree not far from Struve's house.

Struve, secretly delighted that the era of persecution and martyrdom was beginning again, and convinced beforehand that nothing of importance would be done to him, sent notes concerning the proceedings to all his acquaintances. While awaiting their fervent sympathy and ardent indignation he could not resist going out to visit his friend Heinzen, who had received a similar polite *billet-doux* from Fazy. As Heinzen lived close by, Struve, *ganz gemüthlich*, went off to him wearing his indoor clothes and slippers. He had scarcely reached the lime-tree behind which the crafty son of Calvin was concealed, when the latter barred his way and, showing the order of the Federal Council, asked Struve to follow him. Two policemen reinforced the urgency of his invitation. The astonished Struve, cursing Fazy and putting him on the list of the 'seven scourges,' got into the carriage and was driven off with the policeman to the canton of Vaud.

Since Fazy had been dictator, nothing of the sort had happened in Geneva. There was something coarse, unnecessary, and even clownish about it. I was returning home between eleven and twelve that evening, boiling with indignation: at the Pont des Bergues I met Fazy; he was walking along in excellent spirits, accompanied by a few Italian refugees.

'Ah, good evening; any news?' he said, seeing me.

'A great deal,' I answered with elaborate frigidity.

'Why, what?'

'Why, here for instance in Geneva, just as in Paris, men are seized in the street, carried off by force; *il n'y a plus de séicurité dans les rues*—I am afraid to walk about. . . .'

'Oh, you are referring to Struve. . .' answered Fazy, already so angry that his voice began to break. 'What is one to do with these nonsensical people? I am tired of them: I'll show these gentry what it means to treat the law with contempt, to be openly disobedient to the orders of the Federal Council. . . .'

'A right,' I observed, smiling, 'which you reserve for yourself alone.'

'Am I to expose the canton and myself to danger for the sake of every lunatic broken out of Bedlam, and to do it under present circumstances too? And, what's more, one gets no thanks but only rudeness from them. Only fancy, gentlemen: I sent a *commissaire* of the police to him, and lie all but kicked him out—it's beyond anything! They don't understand that an official (*magistrat*) coming in the name of the law must be treated with respect, mustn't he?'

Fazy's companions nodded their heads affirmatively.

'I don't agree,' I said, 'and see no reason at all to respect a man for being a policeman and for coming to announce some nonsense written by Fourrère or Drouey[1] in Berne. There is no need to be rude, but why should one lavish civilities on a man who comes to one as an enemy, and, what's more, an enemy supported by force?'

'I never heard such things in my life,' remarked Fazy, shrugging his shoulders and flashing a withering glance at me.

'It's new to you because you have never thought about it. To imagine that officials are sacred personages is something thoroughly monarchical.'

'You refuse to see the difference between respect for the law and slavish servility, because with you the Tsar and the law are the same thing—*c'est parfaitement russe!*'

'But how is one to see it when your respect for the law means respect for a constable or a police-sergeant?'

'Are you aware, sir, that the *commissaire* of police whom I sent is not merely a very honest man, but one of the most devoted patriots? I have seen him in action....'

'And an exemplary father of a family,' I went on; 'only, that has nothing to do with either me or Struve; we are not acquainted with him, and he came to Struve not as a model citizen but as the instrument of an oppressive power....'

'Why, upon my soul,' observed Fazy, growing more

[1] Drouey (1799-1855) led the revolution in his canton in 1845, in 1849 was elected vice-president of the Swiss Federal Union, and in 1850 president.—(*Translator's Note*.)

and more irate, 'what do you care for that Struve? Only yesterday you were laughing at him yourself. . . .'

'I should not laugh to-day if you were to hang him.'

'Do you know what I think——?' He paused. 'It's my opinion that he is simply a Russian spy.'

'Oh, Lord, what nonsense!' I said, bursting into laughter.

'Nonsense, indeed!' shouted Fazy still more loudly; 'I tell you that in earnest!'

Knowing the unbridled hastiness of my Geneva tyrant, and knowing that with all his irritability he was in reality a hundred times better than his words and not an ill-natured man, I might perhaps have let his shouting pass; but there were other people listening. Besides, he was president of the canton, and I was just such another vagrant without a passport as Struve himself, and therefore I responded in a stentorian voice:

'Do you imagine because you are president that, if you say a thing, that's enough for every one to believe it?'

My shouting produced its effect: Fazy lowered his voice, but, mercilessly beating his fist against the parapet of the bridge, he observed: 'Why, there was his uncle too, Gustav Struve, a Russian attorney in Hamburg.'

'That's as good as "The Wolf and the Lamb." I had better be going home. Good-bye!'

'Yes, indeed, we had better go to bed instead of arguing, or we shall end by quarrelling,' observed Fazy with a forced smile.

I went to the Hôtel des Bergues; Fazy and the Italians crossed the bridge. We had been shouting so excitedly that several of the windows of the hotel had been opened, and an audience consisting of waiters and tourists had been listening to our discussion.

Meanwhile the policeman and very honest citizen who had carried Struve off returned, not alone but still accompanied by Struve. A very amusing incident had occurred in the first little town in the canton of Vaud, near Coppet, where Madame de Staël and Madame Récamier once lived. The prefect of the police, an ardent republican, hearing how Struve had been seized, declared that the Geneva police had acted illegally, and not only refused to send him on further, but turned him back.

The fury of Fazy may be imagined when, to put the finishing touch to our conversation, he heard of Struve's safe return. After exchanging abuse with the 'tyrant' by letter and by word of mouth, Struve departed to England with Heinzen; there the latter formulated his demand for two million heads, and then peacefully sailed off with his Pylades to America, at first with the object of founding a *school for young girls*, afterwards to edit in St. Louis *The Pioneer*, which is sometimes too strong for elderly men to stomach.

Five days after our conversation on the bridge I met Fazy in the Café de la Poste.

'Why is it I have not seen you for so long?' he asked; 'surely you are not still angry? Well, I must own all this business with the refugees is enough to drive one out of one's mind! The Federal Council keeps bombarding me with one note after another, and here the accursed *sous-préfet* of Gex is simply staying here on purpose to see whether the French are interned. I try to satisfy every one, and for that my own people are angry with me. Here's a new trouble now, and a very nasty one; I am sure they 'll abuse me, and what am I to do?' He sat down at my little table and, dropping his voice, went on: 'This is not a question of talk: it's not socialism, it's simply robbery!'

He handed me a letter. Some German feudal prince complained that when his little town had been taken by the students various objects of value had been seized by them, and among other things some ancient vessel of rare workmanship; that it was in the possession of the late commander of the legion, Blenker; [1] and as it had come to the knowledge of his highness that Blenker was living in Geneva, he asked for the co-operation of Fazy in recovering the stolen articles.

'What do you say?' asked Fazy in a solemn voice.

'Nothing. Lots of things happen in war-time.'

'What ought I to do, do you think?'

'Take no notice of the letter, or write to the fool that you are not his detective in Geneva. What have you to do with his crockery? He ought to be glad Blenker did not hang him, and here he is worrying about his goods.'

'You are a very dangerous sophist,' said Fazy, 'and you don't think what discredit such things cast on our party.... We can't leave it like that.'

'I don't know why you take it to heart so much. Far worse things are done in the world. As for the party and its honour, I dare say you will say again that I am a sophist—but think for yourself, will you do any good by giving publicity to the matter? Don't take any notice of the German prince's accusation and it will be taken as a calumny; but if people add to the rumour about it that you sent to make a police search—what is more, if by ill-luck anything is found—then it

---

[1] Blenker, Ludwig (born 1812), served in 1832 in Greece in the Bavarian legion of King Otto, and was afterwards a wine merchant in Worms. In 1848 he became a prominent figure of the revolutionary party in Rheingessen, and as a leader of the insurgents took Worms and stormed Landau. When the Baden rising was suppressed he escaped to Switzerland, whence he was expelled, and then went to America, where during the Civil War in 1861 he collected a troop of German *Jäger* and saved Washington from the enemy, became a general, but afterwards for some negligence in the commissariat was forcibly retired with M'Clellan, and spent the rest of his days peacefully on his farm.—(*Translator's Note.*)

will be difficult to exonerate Blenker and the whole party'

Fazy was genuinely amazed at the Russian irregularity of my views. The Blenker affair ended most fortunately. He was not in Geneva: on the arrival of the police and investigating magistrates, his wife calmly showed all their possessions and their money, described where they had got them from, and, hearing about the vessel, found it herself—it was a very ordinary silver vessel. It had been taken by some young men in the legion and brought to their colonel as a souvenir of the victory.

Later on, Fazy apologised to Blenker, admitting that he had been over hasty in the matter. The immoderate passion for discovering the truth, for going into every detail in criminal cases, for pursuing the guilty with fury and crushing them, is a purely French failing. The judicial process is for them a bloodthirsty sport like bull-baiting for the Spaniards; the prosecutor, like a skilful toreador, is humiliated and mortified if the baited beast escapes unharmed. In England there is nothing of the kind: the judge looks with cool unconcern at the prisoner in the dock, shows no zeal, and is almost pleased when the jury acquit him.

The refugees, on their side, tormented Fazy and poisoned his existence. That was all very natural, and one must not be too severe upon it. The passions unloosed during revolutionary movements are not appeased by failure, and, having no other outlet, find a vent in peevish restlessness of spirit. These men had a mortal longing to speak just when they had to hold their tongues, to keep in the background, to efface and concentrate themselves; they, on the contrary, were trying not to disappear from the footlights, but to advertise their existence by every means in their power. They wrote pamphlets, wrote to the newspapers, talked at meetings, talked in cafés, spread false news, and frightened the foolish governments by expectations of an immediate insurrection. The majority of them belonged to the class of very harmless persons who make up the chorus of revolution; but the terrified governments with equal senselessness believed in their power, and, unaccustomed to free, bold speech, made an outcry about the inevitable danger, the menace to religion, the throne, and the family, and insisted that the Federal Council should expel these terrible advocates of disorder and destruction.

One of the first measures taken by the Swiss Government was the removal from the French frontier of those of the refugees who were specially disliked by Napoleon. It was particularly disagreeable to Fazy to carry out this measure; he was personally acquainted with almost all of them. After informing them of the order to leave Geneva, he did his best not to know who had gone and who had not. Those who remained had to keep away from the principal cafés, from the Pont des Bergues, and that was the very concession they would not make. This led to ludicrous scenes, suggestive of a boarding-school, scenes in which the performers on the one side were the representatives of the people, grey-headed men, well-known literary men over forty, and on the other, the president of a free canton and the police agents of the servile neighbours of Switzerland.

Once, in my presence, the *sous-préfet* of Gex asked Fazy in an ironical tone: 'Tell me, M. le président, is So-and-so in Geneva?' 'He has been gone a long time,' Fazy answered abruptly. 'I am very glad to hear it,' said the *sous-préfet*, and went on his way. And Fazy, clutching my arm convulsively and pointing furiously at a man who was calmly smoking a cigar: 'There he is! there he is! Let us move to the other side, so as not to meet the villain. This is hell—there is no other word for it!'

I could not help laughing. Of course, it was a refugee

who had been expelled, and he was promenading up and down the Pont des Bergues, which is for Geneva what the Tverskoy Boulevard is for Moscow.

I stayed in Geneva till the middle of December. The measures which the Russian Government was stealthily beginning to take against me compelled me to go to Zurich to try to save my mother's property, upon which the Tsar 'of eternal memory' was beginning to lay his Imperial claws.

This was a terrible period of my life. A lull between two thunderclaps, an oppressive, painful, but not eventful calm. . . there were menacing omens, but I still, even then, turned away from them. Life was troubled, inharmonious, but there were bright days in it; for those I was indebted to the grand natural scenery of Switzerland.

Remoteness from men, and beautiful natural surroundings have a wonderfully healing effect. From experience I wrote in *A Wreck*:—

'When the soul bears within it a great grief, when a man has not mastered himself sufficiently to grow reconciled with the past, to grow calm enough for understanding, he needs distance and mountains, the sea and warm mild air. He needs them that sadness may not pass into bitterness and despair, that he may not grow hard. . . .'

I was longing for a rest from many things even then. A year and a half spent in the centre of political upheavals and dissensions, in continual irritation, in the midst of bloody sights, terrible downfalls, and petty treacheries, had left much bitterness, misery, and weariness at the bottom of my soul. Irony began to take a different character. Granovsky wrote to me after reading *From the Other Shore*, which I wrote just at that time: 'Your book has reached us. I read it with joy and a feeling of pride . . . but, for all that, there is something of fatigue about it; you stand too much alone, and perhaps you will become a great writer, but what was in Russia living and attractive to all in your talent seems to have disappeared on foreign soil. . . .' Then Sazonov, who, just before I left Paris in 1849, read the beginning of my story, *Duty before Everything*, written two years previously, said to me:' You won't finish that story, and you will never write anything more like it. Your bright laughter and good-natured jesting are gone for ever.'

But could a man pass through the ordeal of 1848 and 1849 and remain the same? I was myself conscious of the change. Only at home, when no outsiders were present, there were sometimes moments as of old, not of 'bright laughter' but of bright sadness; recalling the past and our friends, recalling recent scenes of our life in Rome, beside the cots of our sleeping children or watching their play, the soul was attuned to the mood of old days—there came a breath of freshness, of youthful poetry, of gentle harmony, there was peace and content in the heart, and under the influence of such an evening life was easier for a day or two.

These minutes were not frequent; a wretched, depressing distraction prevented them. The number of visitors kept increasing about us, and towards evening our little drawing-room in the Champs-Élysées was full of strangers. For the most part, these were newly arrived refugees, good and unfortunate people, but I was intimate with only one man. . . . And why was I intimate with him! . . .

I was delighted to leave Paris, but in Geneva we found ourselves in the same society, though the persons in it were different and it was on a narrower scale. In Switzerland everything at that time had rushed into politics; everything—*tables d'hôte* and coffee-houses, watchmakers and women—all were divided into parties.

An exclusive preoccupation with politics, particularly in the painful stagnation which always follows unsuccessful revolutions, is extremely wearisome with its arid barrenness and monotonous censure of the past. It is like summer-time in big cities where everything is hot, dusty, airless, where through pale trees the walls and the hot paving-stones reflect the glaring sun. A living man craves for air which has not been breathed over a thousand times, free from the smell of the refuse of life, from the sound of discordant jangling, from the dirty, putrid stench and everlasting noise.

Sometimes we did in fact tear ourselves away from Geneva, visit the shores of Lake Léman and the foot of Mont Blanc; and the frowning, gloomy beauty of mountain scenery with its intense shadows screened all the vanity of vanities from one's eyes, refreshing soul and body with the cold breath of its everlasting glaciers.

I do not know whether I should like to stay for ever in Switzerland. We dwellers in the plains and prairies after a time feel the mountains a restriction; they are too immense and too close, they hem us in, limit us; but sometimes it is good to stay a while in their shadow. Moreover, a pure and good-hearted race live in the mountains, a race of people poor but not unfortunate, with few wants, accustomed to a life of sturdy independence. The froth of civilisation, its verdigris, has not settled on these people; historical changes have passed like clouds beneath their feet, scarcely touching them. The Roman world still persists in Graubünden, the times of the peasant wars have scarcely passed in Appenzell. Perhaps in the Pyrenees, in the Tyrol, or other mountains, the same sturdy type of population may be found, but it no longer exists in Europe as a whole.

In the north-east of Russia, however, I have seen something like it. In Perm and Vyatka I have come upon people of the same stamp as in the Alps.

Exhausted by the long, unbroken climb step by step up the mountain, my companion and I, travelling to Zermatt, stopped to give our horses a rest, and went into a small inn a little above St. Niklaus, if I remember right. The hostess, a tall, thin, but muscular old woman, was all alone in the house. Seeing guests, she bustled about, complaining of the scantiness of her stores, and, after rummaging here and there, brought out a bottle of *kirsch*, some bread hard as a stone (bread is not a simple matter in the mountains; it is brought up from the villages on asses), some smoked mutton (also very dry), some cheese and goat's milk, and then proceeded to make us a sort of sweet omelette which I could not eat; but the mutton, the cheese, and the *kirsch* were very good. The woman regaled us as though we were invited guests, put choice morsels before us with a good-natured air, and kept apologising. Our guides, too, ate and drank *kirsch*. As I was going away I asked her what we owed her. The woman pondered for a long time, even went into the other room to collect her thoughts, and then, after some preliminary remarks about the dearness of provisions and the difficulty of transport, ventured to say *five francs*. 'What!' I commented, 'with the horses' food, too?' She did not understand what I meant, and made haste to add: 'Well, four will be enough.'

When I was being taken from Perm to Vyatka, in a village where we changed horses I asked a woman who was sitting on a log beside her hut for some *kvass*. 'It's dreadfully sour,' she answered; 'but here, I'll bring you some home-made beer; it's left from the holiday, you see.' A minute later she brought me an earthenware jug wrapped in a rag, and a dipper. The gendarme and I drank to our hearts' content. As I handed the dipper back to the old woman I gave her ten or fifteen kopecks, but she would not take the coin, saying: 'God bless you! to think of taking from a travelling man, and you going as you are,' glancing at the gendarme.' But why should we drink your good beer for nothing, auntie? Take it for cakes for the children.' 'No, kind sir, don't you think it; but if you've money to spare, give it to the poor or put up a candle to God.'

Another similar incident happened to me on the Great River near Vyatka. I had gone to look at the curious procession in which the *ikon* of St. Nicholas of Hlynov is taken down the river to pay a visit. On the way back, I went with my driver into a hut where he got some oats. The people of the house and three pilgrims were sitting down to dinner; there was a strong smell of cabbage soup, and I asked for some for myself. A young woman brought me a wooden bowl of soup, a hunk of bread, and a huge salt-cellar. When I had eaten I gave the master of the house a quarter-rouble. He looked at me and scratched the back of his head, saying: 'That won't do, you know; here you 've eaten two-ha'porth and given me a quarter-rouble; it's not right for me to take it—it's a sin before God and a shame before men.'

I remember I have somewhere mentioned the Perm peasant habit of putting a piece of bread with *kvass* or milk outside the window at night, in case an *unfortunate*—that is, an exile—should be making his way back from Siberia and be afraid to knock, so that he might find nourishment without making a noise. I have found a like custom on the Swiss mountains; only, not being near Siberia, there it is done simply for the benefit of travellers. On the rather high peaks, where life is scanty, where the rock stands out like the skull of a man beginning to grow bald, and an icy-cold wind blows on the vegetation, as dried and withered as the herbs in a chemist's shop—there I came upon huts, empty, but with unlocked doors, that a traveller who had lost his way or had been overtaken by bad weather might find hospitality even without a host. All sorts of peasant wares were there, and, on the table, cheese, bread, and goat's milk. Some after eating leave a coin on the table, others leave nothing, but evidently nobody steals. Of course, very few strangers reach them, but nevertheless these unlocked doors amaze a townsman.

Since I am talking of mountains and heights, I will describe my visit to Monte Rosa. How can I better finish my chapter on Switzerland than on a height of seven thousand feet?

From the hut of the old woman who was ashamed to take five francs for feeding four men and two horses, including a whole bottle of *kirsch*, we were climbing till late evening up a narrow pass, in places hardly more than a yard wide, to Zermatt; on the rocky and uneven little path the accustomed horses moved carefully at a walking pace, picking out the spot to put their hoof on. The guides were continually reminding us not to touch the reins, but to let the horse go as it would. On one side was a steep precipice, some three thousand feet or more. At the bottom below, the Visp roared and raced along with a sort of senseless haste, as though trying to find a more open channel to break away from its narrow, stony bed. Its foaming and whirling surface could be seen here and there; on its mountainous banks there were regular pinewoods which looked like moss from the height on which we were moving. On our other side there was a bare, stony height here and there hanging over our heads. For whole hours one goes on and on . . . the hoofs ring on the stone, the horse slips, the Visp roars, and still there are the same rocks on one side, beyond which nothing can be seen, and on the other the abyss below already growing dim with the twilight — it produces a feeling of dreariness, of nervous fatigue; I should not care to repeat that journey often.

Zermatt is the highest spot on which several families are living: it stands as though in a cauldron; huge masses of mountains surround it. One of the people there takes in the few travellers; we found in his house a Scotsman, a geologist. It got quite dark while they were setting our supper; the nearness of the mountains made the evening twice as dark. Between ten and eleven our hostess, listening at the window, said: 'Why, there's the sound of hoofs, and I can hear the shout of the guides . . . who would care to travel at night-time on such a path?' The tramp of hoofs came slowly nearer; the hostess took a lantern and went out with it to the entrance. I followed her; something began to stand out against the black darkness, figures appeared in the streak of light from the lantern, and at last two horses came up to the entrance. On one horse sat a tall, middle-aged woman, on the other a boy of fourteen. The lady alighted from the horse as calmly as though she had returned from a ride in Hyde Park, and went into the common room. She had met the Scotsman before, and so began talking to him at once. After asking for something to eat, she sent her son to find out from the guides how long the horses must rest. They said that two hours would be enough. 'Surely you are not going on without waiting for daylight?' asked the Scotsman. 'One can't see an inch before one's face, and you'll be going down by a new road.'

'This is the time I've allowed for it.'

Two hours later the Englishwoman and her son began the descent on the Italian side, and we went to bed for two or three hours. At dawn we took as a third guide a botanist who knew all the paths and whistled the Alpine airs in a wonderful way, and began our ascent of one of the nearer peaks, climbing towards a sea of ice and the Matterhorn.

At first a greyish mist hid everything and wetted us

with a fine rain; we went up and up and it sank lower; soon it became glaringly bright and the air became extraordinarily pure and clear.

Hugo describes somewhere 'what can be heard on the mountains'; his mountain could not have been a high one. I was struck, on the contrary, by the complete absence of sound; there was absolutely nothing to be heard except the light, intermittent grinding from the slipping avalanches, and that only at rare intervals . . . as a matter of fact, the stillness is deathly, *transparent*—I use the word intentionally,—an extraordinary rarefaction of the air seems to make *visible*, audible, this absolute dumbness, this eternal, inanimate, elemental sleep [1] of primeval ages.

Life is noisy—but everything living is below and hidden in the clouds. Here are no plants, only grey rough lichen is found here and there upon the stones. Higher still it is even fresher, and the region of never-melting frost begins: here there is the dividing line, here is nothing; only the most inquisitive of all animals crosses it to peep for a minute at that desert of emptiness, to look at the highest outposts of the planet, and hastens to descend to his own domain, full of vanities, of trivial bustle—where he is at home.

We halted before that sea of snow and ice which lay stretched between us and the Matterhorn; ringed round by mountains that were bathed in sunshine, dazzlingly white, it looked like the frozen arena of some titanic coliseum. Hollowed out in places by the winds into the form of waves, it seems to have grown stiff at the very moment of movement; the curves of the billows are frozen before they have had time to sink.

I got off my horse and lay down on a granite boulder moored to the shore by the snowy billows . . . mute,

[1] Here I seem to have justified the famous 'I hear the silence!' of the Moscow police-master.

motionless whiteness, boundless on all sides . . . a light wind lifted a fine white powder, wafted it away, set it whirling . . . it fell, and all again passed into stillness; but twice the avalanches breaking away with a hollow reverberation rolled down in the distance, clinging to the rocks, clashing against them and leaving a cloud of snow behind them. . . .

A man feels strange in this setting—a visitor, superfluous, an outsider; and on the other hand he breathes more freely, and as though from the colour surrounding him grows whiter and purer within . . . earnest and full of a sort of devout gravity! . . .

What melodramatic rhetoric I should be charged with if I concluded this picture of Monte Rosa by saying that in that world of whiteness, freshness, and silence, of the two travellers stranded on that height, reckoning each other dear friends, one was plotting black treachery against the other!

Yes, life sometimes plays us melodramatic tricks—it has its *coups de théâtre* which are very artificial.

Appendix II

(*From 'West European Sketches — Notebook II.'*)

I

IL PIANTO

AFTER the days of June, I saw that the revolution was vanquished, but I still believed in the vanquished, in the fallen, I believed in the wonder-working powers of the relics, in their moral strength. In Geneva I began to understand more and more clearly not only that the revolution was vanquished, but that it was bound to be vanquished.

My head was dizzy with my discoveries, an abyss was opening before my eyes, and I felt that the ground was giving way under my feet.

It was not the reaction that vanquished the revolution. The reaction showed itself everywhere densely stupid, cowardly, in its dotage; everywhere it shamefully retreated into safety before the onrush of the popular tide, furtively biding its time in Paris, in Naples, in Vienna, and in Berlin. The revolution fell, like Agrippina, under the blows of her own children, and, what was worst of all, without their being conscious of it; there was more heroism, more youthful self-sacrifice, than good judgment; and the pure, noble victims fell, not knowing why. The fate of the survivors was almost more grievous. While absorbed in dissensions among themselves, in personal disputes, in melancholy self-delusion, and consumed by unbridled vanity, they kept dwelling on their unexpected days of triumph, and were unwilling to take off their faded laurels or wedding garments, though it was not the bride who had deceived them.

Misfortunes, idleness, and poverty induced intolerance,

VOLUNTARY MARTYRS

obstinacy, nervous irritability. . . . The exiles broke up into little groups, rallying not round principles but round names and hatreds. The fact that their thoughts continually turned to the past, and that they lived in an exclusive, narrow circle, began to find expression in speech and thought, in manners and in dress; a new class—the class of refugees—was formed, and grew as stiff and rigid as the rest. And just as once St. Basil the Great wrote to St. Gregory Nazianzen that he 'gloated over fasting and revelled in privations,' so now there were voluntary martyrs, victims by vocation, unhappy as a profession, and among them were very conscientious people; and indeed St. Basil was quite sincere when he wrote to his friend of his orgies of mortifying the flesh and of the voluptuous ecstasy of persecution. With all that, ideas did not move a step forward, thought slumbered. . . . If these people had been awakened by the blast of a new trumpet and a new call to battle, they would, like the nine sleeping maidens, have been the same as on the day on which they fell asleep.

These bitter truths made my heart sink with despondency; I had to live through a hard stage of my education.

I was sitting mournfully one day in my mother's dining-room in gloomy, disagreeable Zurich; it was at the end of December 1849. I was going next day to Paris. It was a cold, snowy day; two or three logs smoking and crackling burned reluctantly on the hearth. All were busy with packing. I sat utterly alone. My life in Geneva floated before my mind; the whole future looked dark, I felt afraid of something, and I was so insufferably miserable that if I could I would have fallen on my knees and wept and prayed; but I could not, and instead of prayer I wrote my *curse*—my *Epilogue* to 1849.

'Disillusionment, fatigue, *Blasiertheit*!' The democratic critics said of those lines, wrung out of me by pain. Yes, disillusionment! Yes, fatigue! . . . Disillusionment is a vulgar, hackneyed word, the veil under which the sloth of the heart, egoism posing as love, the noisy emptiness of vanity with pretensions to everything and strength for nothing, lie hidden. All these exalted, misunderstood characters, thin with envy and miserable with superciliousness, have wearied us for years past, both in life and in novels. All that is perfectly true; but is there not something real, characteristic of our times, at the bottom of these spiritual sufferings which degenerate into absurd parody and vulgar masquerade?

The poet who found words and voice for this malady was too proud to pose and to suffer for the sake of applause; on the contrary, he often uttered his bitter thought with so much humour that simple-hearted readers were convulsed with merriment. Byron's disillusionment was more than caprice, more than a personal mood; Byron was shattered because life deceived him. And life deceived him not because his demands were unreal, but because England and Byron were of different ages, were of different educations, and met just at the epoch when the mist was being dissipated.

This divergence has existed in the past, but in our age it has come to consciousness; in our age the impossibility of any conviction bridging the gulf has become more and more evident. After the Roman break-up came Christianity; after Christianity—the belief in civilisation, in humanity. Liberalism is the *latest religion*, though its church is not of the other world but of this. Its theology is political theory; it stands upon the earth and has no mystical conciliations, it aims at conciliation in real life. Triumphant and then defeated liberalism has revealed the rift in all its nakedness; the painful consciousness of this is expressed in the irony of the modern man, the scepticism with which he sweeps away the fragments of his shattered idols.

Irony gives expression to the vexation aroused by the fact that logical truth is not the same as the truth of history, that apart from dialectical development it has its own development through chance and passion, that apart from reason it has its romance.

Disillusionment[1] in our sense of the word was not known before the Revolution; the eighteenth century was one of the most religious periods of history. I am not speaking now of the great martyr Saint-Just or of the apostle Jean-Jacques; but was not the pope Voltaire, blessing Franklin's grandson in the name of God and Freedom, a fanatic of his religion of humanity?

Scepticism was proclaimed together with the republic of the 22nd of September 1792.

The Jacobins and revolutionaries in general belonged to a minority, separated from the life of the people by their culture: they formed something like a secular clergy ready to shepherd their human flocks. They represented the *highest* thought of their time, its *highest but not its common consciousness*. not the *thought of all*.

This new clergy had no means of coercion, neither physical nor supernatural: from the moment that the governing power dropped out of their hands, they had only one weapon—conviction. But for conviction to be *right* is not enough; their whole mistake lay in supposing so; something more was necessary—*mental equality*.

So long as the desperate conflict lasted to the strains of the hymn of the Huguenots and the hymn of the Marseillaise, so long as men were burnt at the stake and blood was flowing, this inequality passed unobserved. But at last the oppressive edifice of feudal monarchy fell, and slowly the walls were shattered, the locks torn off

---

[1] As a matter of fact, our scepticism was not known in the last century; England and Diderot alone are the exceptions. In England scepticism has been at home for long ages, and Byron follows naturally on Shakespeare, Hobbcs, and Hume.—(*Author's Note*.)

the gates . . . one more blow struck, and the brave men advance, the gates are flung open and the crowd rushes in. But it was not the crowd they expected. Who are these men; to what age do they belong? These are not Spartans, not the great *populus Romanus*. *Davus sum, non Œdipus*! An overwhelming wave of filth flooded everything. The inner horror of the Jacobins was expressed in the Terror of 1793 and 1794: they saw their fearful mistake, tried to correct it with the guillotine; but, however many heads they cut off, they still had to bow their own before the might of the class of society that was rising to the top. Everything gave way before it; it overpowered the Revolution and the Reaction, it filled up the old forms and submerged them because it made up the one effective majority of its day. Sieyès was more right than he thought when he said that the petty-bourgeoisie *was everything*.

The petty-bourgeois were not produced by the Revolution; they were ready with their codes and their traditions, in a different way discordant with the revolutionary idea. The aristocracy had held them down and kept them in the background; set free, they passed over the dead bodies of those who had freed them and established their own regime. The minority were either crushed or swallowed up among the bourgeois.

A few men of each generation were, in spite of events, left the obstinate guardians of the idea; these Levites, or perhaps Aztecs, are unjustly punished for their monopoly of exclusive culture, for the mental superiority of the well-fed caste, the leisured caste that had time to work not only with muscles.

We are angered, moved to fury, by the absurdity, by the injustice of this fact. As though some one (apart from ourselves) had promised us that everything in the world should be just and beautiful and go easily. We have marvelled enough at the abstract wisdom of nature and of historical development; it is time to perceive that in nature as in history there is a great deal that is fortuitous, stupid, unsuccessful, and confused. Reason, fully developed thought, comes last. Everything begins with the foolishness of the newborn child; possibility and striving are innate in him, but before he reaches development and consciousness he is exposed to a series of external and internal influences, checks and obstacles. One has water on the brain, another falls and flattens his skull—both remain idiots; the third does not fall nor die of scarlet fever—and becomes a poet, a military leader, a bandit, or a judge. We know as a rule far more of the successes in nature, in history, and in life: we are only now beginning to feel that all the cards are not so well shuffled as we thought, because we are ourselves a losing card, a failure.

It mortifies us to find that the idea is impotent that truth has no compelling force over the world of actuality. A new sort of Manichæism takes possession of us, we are led, *par dépit*, to believe in rational (that is, purposive) evil, as we did believe in rational good—that is the last tribute we pay to idealism.

The anguish will pass with time; its tragic and passionate character will be softened: it scarcely exists in the new world of the United States. That young people, enterprising and more practical than intelligent, is so occupied in the organisation of its own life that it knows nothing at all of our agonies. Moreover, there are not two cultures there. The persons who make up the classes in that society are incessantly changing, they rise and fall with the bank account of each. The sturdy race of English colonists is multiplying terribly; if it gets the ascendency, people will not be the happier for it, but they will be more comfortable. That comfort will be duller, poorer, more arid than that which floated in the ideals of romantic Europe; but with it there will be neither Tsar nor centralisation, and perhaps there will be no hunger either. Any one, who can put off the old Adam of Europe from himself and be born again a new Jonathan, had better take the first steamer to some place in Wisconsin or Kansas; there he will certainly be better off than in decaying Europe.

Those who *cannot*, remain to live out their lives, representatives of the fair dream with which men lulled themselves to sleep. They have lived too much in fantasies and ideals to fit into the age of American good sense.

There is no great loss in that; we are not many, and we shall soon be extinct.

But how is it men grow up so out of harmony with their environment? . . .

Imagine a hothouse-reared youth—the one, for instance, who has described himself in *The Dream*; imagine him face to face with the most boring, with the most tedious society, face to face with the monstrous Minotaur of English life, uncouthly welded together of two beasts— the one sinking into decrepitude, the other knee-deep in filthy mire, weighed down like the Caryatides whose everlastingly strained muscles leave not a drop of blood to spare for the brain. If he could have adapted himself to this life, he would, instead of dying at thirty in Greece, by now have been Lord Palmerston or Lord John Russell. But since he could not, there is nothing surprising in his saying, like his Harold to his ship:

> 'Nor care what land thou bearest me to,
> But not again to mine.'

But what awaited him in the distance? Spain devastated by Napoleon, Greece sunk back into barbarism, the general resurrection after 1814 of all the stinking Lazaruses; there was no getting away from them in Ravenna or in Diodati. Byron could not be satisfied like a German with theories *sub specie æternitatis*, nor like a Frenchman with political chatter; he was crushed, but crushed like a menacing Titan, flinging his scorn in men's faces and not troubling to soften the blow.

This discordance and disharmony, of which Byron as a poet and a genius was conscious forty years ago, has, after a succession of painful experiences, after the filthy transition from 1830 to 1848, and the infamous one from 1848 to the present, overwhelmed many of us to-day. And we, like Byron, do not know what to do with ourselves, where to lay our heads.

The realist Goethe, like the romantic Schiller, knew nothing of this rending of the spirit. The one was too religious, the other too philosophical. Both could find peace in abstract spheres. When the 'spirit of negation 'appears as such a jester as Mephistopheles, then the disharmony is not yet tragic; his mocking and for ever contradictory nature is still blended in the higher harmony, and in its own due time will chime in with everything—*sie ist gerettet*. Lucifer in *Cain* is very different; he is the gloomy angel of darkness, on whose brow shines with dim lustre the star of bitter thought, full of inner discords which can never be harmonised.

He does not jest with negation, he does not amuse with the impudence of his infidelity, he does not allure by sensuality, he does not procure simple maidens, wine, and diamonds, but calmly impels to murder, by some inexplicable force, like the lure of still moonlit water, that promises nothing but death in its comfortless, cold, glimmering embraces.

Neither Cain nor Manfred, neither Don Juan nor Byron, has any deduction, any solution, any 'moral.' Perhaps from the point of view of dramatic art this is a defect, but it gives a stamp of sincerity and shows the depths of the gulf. Byron's epilogue, his last word, if you like, is *The Darkness*; that is the logical conclusion of a life that begins with *The Dream*. Complete the picture for yourselves.

Two enemies, hideously disfigured by hunger, are dead, they are devoured by some crab-like monsters . . . a ship is rotting—the tarred rope sways in the muddy waters in the darkness, there is fearful cold, the animals are dying out, history has already perished and the place is cleared for new life: our period will be reckoned as the fourth formation—that is, if the new world arrives at being able to count up to four.

Our historical vocation, our work, lies in the fact that by our disillusionment, by our sufferings, we reach resignation and humility in face of the truth, and spare following generations from these troubles. With us humanity is regaining sobriety, with us recovering from its drunken orgy; we are its birth-pangs. If the birth-agony ends well, all is for the best; but we must not forget that the child or mother, or maybe both, may die by the way, and then—well, then history, like the Mormon it is, will begin the process over again. . . . *E sempre bene*, friends!

We know how Nature disposes of the individual: whether sooner or later, whether without sacrifice or over the bodies of the dead, she cares not; she goes her way, or goes any way that chances. Ten thousands of years she builds up a coral reef, every spring abandoning to death the foremost ranks. The polypi die without suspecting that they have served the *progress* of the reef.

We, too, shall serve something. Entering into the future as an element in it does not mean that the future will fulfil our ideals. Rome did not carry out Plato's idea of a republic nor the Greek idea in general. The Middle Ages were not the development of Rome. Modern Western thought will pass into history and be incorporated in it, will have its influence in its place, just as our body passes into the composition of grass, of sheep, of cutlets, and of men. We do not like that kind of immortality, but what is there to be done about it?

Now I am accustomed to these thoughts, they no longer terrify me. But at the end of 1849 I was overwhelmed by them; and in spite of the fact that every event, every meeting, every contact, every person seemed bent on tearing away the last green leaves, I still frantically and obstinately sought a *way of escape*.

That is why I prize now so highly the courageous thought of Byron. He saw that there is *no escape*, and proudly said so.

I was unhappy and perplexed when these thoughts began to haunt me; I tried by every means to run away from them. . . like a lost traveller, like a beggar, I knocked at every door, stopped every one I met and asked my way, but every meeting and every event led to the same result—to *humility* in the face of the *truth*, to meek acceptance of it.

Three years ago I sat by Natalie's sick-bed and saw death drawing her mercilessly, step by step, to the grave; that life was all that was precious to me. About me all was darkness; I sat alone in dull despair, but did not comfort myself with hopes, did not betray my grief for one moment by the narcotic thought of meeting beyond the grave.

So it is hardly likely that I should be false to myself over the impersonal problems of life.

II

Post Scriptum

I know that my outlook on Europe will meet with a bad reception at home. We for our own comfort *want* a different Europe and believe in it as Christians believe in Paradise. Dissipating dreams is always a disagreeable thing to do, but some inner force which I cannot overcome makes me tell the truth even when it does me harm.

As a rule we know Europe from school, from literature — that is, we do not know it, but judge it *à livre ouvert*, from books and pictures, just as children judge the real world from their *Orbis pictus*, imagining that all the women in the Sandwich Islands hold their hands above their heads with a sort of tambourine, and, wherever there is a naked negro, there is sure to be standing five paces from him a lion with a dishevelled mane or a tiger with fierce eyes.

Our *classic* ignorance of the Western European will be productive of a good deal of harm; race hatreds and bloody collisions will develop from it later on.

In the first place, we know nothing but the top, *cultured* layer of Europe, which conceals the heavy substratum of popular life formed by the ages, and evolved by instincts and by laws that are little understood in Europe itself. European culture does not penetrate into those foundations in which, as in the works of the Cyclops, the hand of man is indistinguishable from that of nature and history passes into geology. The European states are welded together of two different peoples whose special characteristics are maintained by utterly different educations. There is here none of the Oriental unity which makes the Turk who is a Grand Vizier and the Turk who hands him his pipe just like each other. Masses of the country population have, since the religious wars and the peasant risings, taken no active part in events; they have been swayed by them to right and left like growing corn, never for a minute leaving the ground in which they are rooted.

Secondly, that stratum with which we do become acquainted, with which we do enter into contact, we only know historically, not as it is to-day. After spending a year or two in Europe we see with surprise that the men of the West do not correspond as a rule with our conception of them, that they are *greatly inferior* to it.

Elements of truth enter into the ideal we have formed, but either these no longer exist or they have completely changed their character. The valour of chivalry, the elegance of aristocratic manners, the stern decorum of the Protestants, the proud independence of the English, the luxurious life of Italian artists, the sparkling wit of the Encyclopedists and the gloomy energy of the Terrorists—all that has been melted down and transmuted into one dead level of universally predominant *bourgeois manners*. They make up a complete whole— that is, a finished, self-contained outlook upon life with its traditions and rules, with its own good and evil, with its own manners and its own morality of a lower order.

As the knight was the leading type of the feudal world, so the merchant has become the leading type of the new world; feudal lords are replaced by employers. The merchant in himself is a colourless intermediate figure; he is the middle-man between the producer and the consumer; he is something of the nature of a means of communication, of transport. The knight was more in himself, more of a person, and kept up his dignity as he understood it, which made him in reality not dependent either on wealth or on position; his personality was what mattered. In the petty-bourgeois the personality is concealed or does not stand out, because it is not what matters; what matters is the ware, the produce, the thing, what matters is *property*.

The knight was a terrible ignoramus, a bully, a duellist, a bandit and a monk, a drunkard and a pietist, but he was open and genuine in everything: moreover, he was always ready to lay down his life for what he thought right; he had his moral tradition, his code of honour— very arbitrary, but one from which he did not depart without loss of his own respect or the respect of his peers.

The merchant is a man of peace and not of war, stubbornly and persistently sticking to his rights, but weak in attack; calculating, parsimonious, he sees trade in everything, and, like the knight, enters into single combat with every one he meets, but measures himself with him in cunning. His ancestors—mediæval townsmen—were forced to be sly to save themselves from violence and robbery; they purchased peace and wealth by evasiveness, by secretiveness and pretence, keeping themselves close and holding themselves in check. His ancestors, cap in hand and bowing low, cheated the knight; shaking their heads or sighing, they talked to their neighbours of their poverty, whilst they secretly buried their hoards in the earth. All this has naturally passed into the blood and brains of their descendants, and has become the physical characteristic of a special human species known as the *middle class*.

While it was in a difficult position and joined with the enlightened aristocracy in defending its faith, in fighting for its rights, it was full of greatness and poetry. But this was not for long, and Sancho Panza, having gained his place and lolling simply at his ease, let himself go and lost his peasant honour, his commonsense; the vulgar side of his nature got the upper hand.

Under the influence of petty-bourgeoisie everything is changed in Europe. Chivalrous honour is replaced by the honesty of the book-keeper, elegant manners by propriety, courtesy by stiff decorum, pride by a readiness to take offence, parks by kitchen gardens, palaces by hotels, open to *all* (that is, all who have money).

The old, out-of-date, but consistent conceptions of relations between men have been shaken, while no new recognition of the *true* relations between men has appeared. This chaotic void has greatly contributed to the develop-

A MEDLEY OF MORAL PRINCIPLES 143

ment of all the bad and petty sides of bourgeoisie under the all-powerful influence of unbridled acquisitiveness.

Analyse the moral principles current for the last half-century, and what a medley you will find! The Roman conception of the state together with the Gothic division of powers, Protestantism and political economy, *salus populi* and *chacun pour soi*, Brutus and Thomas a Kempis, the Gospel and Bentham, the balancing of income and expenditure and Jean-Jacques Rousseau. With such a hotch-potch in the head and with a magnet in the breast, for ever attracted by gold, it was not hard to arrive at the absurdities reached by the foremost countries of Europe.

The whole of morality has been reduced to the duty of him who has not by every possible means to acquire, and of him who has to preserve and to increase his property; the flag which they run up in the market-place when trading begins has become the banner of a new society. The man has *de facto* become the appurtenance of property; life has been reduced to a perpetual struggle for money.

The political question since 1830 is becoming exclusively the petty-bourgeois question, and the age-long struggle is expressed in the passions and tendencies of the ruling class. Life is reduced to a gamble on the Stock Exchange; everything—the publication of newspapers, the elections, the legislative chambers—all have become money-changers' shops and markets. The English are so used to putting everything into shop language that they call their old English Church the *Old Shop*.

All parties and shades of opinion in the petty-bourgeois world have gradually divided into two camps: on one hand the bourgeois property-owners, obstinately refusing to abandon their monopolies; on the other the petty-bourgeois who have nothing, who want to tear the wealth out of the others' hands but have not the power—that is, on the one hand *avarice*, on the other hand *envy*. Since there is no real moral principle in all that, the part taken by any individual on one or the other side is determined by external conditions of fortune and social position. One wave of the opposition after the other triumphs—that is, attains to property or position—and passes naturally from the side of envy to the side of avarice. Nothing can be more favourable for this transition than the fruitless swing backwards and forwards of parliamentary parties—it gives movement and sets limits to it, provides an appearance of *doing something*, and an external show of public interest in order to attain their private ends.

Parliamentary government, not as it follows from the popular foundations of the Anglo-Saxon *Common Law*, but as it has taken shape in the law of the state, is simply the wheel in a squirrel's cage, and the most colossal one in the world. Could a show of a triumphant march forward whilst remaining majestically in the same spot be possibly achieved more perfectly than it is by the two English Houses of Parliament?

But just that maintenance of the show is the great point. Upon everything belonging to contemporary Europe, two characteristics obviously derived from the shop are deeply imprinted: on one hand, hypocrisy and secretiveness; on the other, ostentation and *étalage*. It is all window-dressing, buying at half-price, passing off rubbish for the real thing, show for reality, concealing some condition, taking advantage of a literal meaning, seeming instead of being, behaving properly instead of behaving well, keeping up external *Respektabilität* instead of inner dignity.

In this world everything is so much a stage sham that even the coarsest ignorance assumes an air of education. Which of us has not blushed for the ignorance of Western

European society? I am not here speaking of men of learning, but of the people who make up what is called society. There can be no serious theoretical education; it takes too much time and is too distracting from *business*. Since nothing that lies outside trading operations and the 'exploitation' of their social position is essential in the petty-bourgeois world, their education is bound to be limited. That is what accounts for the absurdity and slowness of mind which we see in the bourgeois, whenever he has to step off the common beaten track. Cunning and hypocrisy are by no means so clever and so far-sighted as is supposed; their range is poor, and they are soon out of their depth.

The English are aware of this, and so do not leave the beaten track, and put up with the not merely burdensome but, what is worse, absurd inconveniences of their mediævalism through fear of any change.

The French petty-bourgeois have not been so prudent, and for all their slyness and duplicity have fallen headlong into an empire.

Full of confidence in their victory, they proclaimed universal suffrage as the basis of their new regime. This arithmetical standard suited their taste; the truth is determined by addition and subtraction, it could be reckoned up and put down in figures.

And what did they put to the decision of the votes of all in the present state of society? The question of the existence of the republic. They wanted to crush it by means of the people, to make of it an empty word, because they did not like it. Is any one who respects the truth going to ask the opinion of the first stray man he meets? What if Columbus or Copernicus put America or the movement of the earth to the vote?

It was shrewdly conceived, but in the end the good souls overshot their mark.

The gap between the *parterre* and the actors, covered

at first by the faded carpet of Lamartine's eloquence, has grown wider and wider; the blood of June has washed the channel deeper; and then the question of the president was put to the irritated people. As answer to the question, Louis-Napoleon, rubbing his sleepy eyes, stepped out and took everything into his hands—that is, even the petty-bourgeois, who fancied, from memory of old days, that he would reign and they would govern.

What you see on the great stage of political events is repeated in microscopic form on every hearth. The corruption of petty-bourgeoisie has crept into all the secret places of the family and private life. Never has Catholicism, never have the ideas of chivalry, been impressed on men so deeply, so many-sidedly, as the bourgeois ideas.

Noble rank had its obligations. Of course, since its rights were partly fantastic, its obligations were fantastic too, but they did provide a certain mutual security between equals. Catholicism laid still more obligations. Feudal knights and believing Catholics often failed to carry out their obligations, but the consciousness that, by so doing, they were guilty of a breach of the social bonds recognised by themselves prevented them from being free in their lapses and from justifying their behaviour. They had their holiday attire, their official setting which was not false but rather their ideal.

We are not now concerned with the nature of those ideals. They were tried and their cause was lost long ago. We only want to point out that petty-bourgeoisie on the contrary involves no obligations, not even the obligation to serve in the army, so long as there are volunteers; or rather, its only obligation is *per fas et nefas* to have property. Its gospel is brief: 'Heap up wealth, multiply thy riches till they are like the sands of the sea, use and misuse thy financial and moral capital, without ruining thyself, and in comfort and honour thou wilt attain length of years, marry thy children well, and leave an honoured memory behind thee.'

The destruction of the feudal and Catholic world was essential, and was the work not of the petty-bourgeois but simply of free men—that is, of men who had set themselves free from all wholesale classification. Among them were knights like Ulrich von Hutten, gentlemen like Voltaire, watchmakers' apprentices like Rousseau, army doctors like Schiller, and merchants' sons like Goethe. The petty-bourgeois took advantage of their work and showed themselves emancipated, not only from monarchs and slavery but from all social obligations, except that of contributing to the hire of the government who guarded their security.

Of Protestantism they made *their own* religion, a religion that reconciles the conscience of the Christian with the practice of the usurer, a religion so bourgeois that the common people, who shed their blood for it, have abandoned it. In England the working class goes to church less than any.

Of the Revolution they tried to make their own republic, but it slipped between their fingers, just as the civilisation of antiquity slipped away from the barbarians—that is, with no place in real life, but with hope for *instaurationem magnam*.

The Reformation and the Revolution were both so terrified by the emptiness of the world which they had come into that they sought salvation in two forms of monasticism—the cold, dreary bigotry of Puritanism and the frigid, artificial civic morality of republican formalism.

Both the Quaker[1] and the Jacobin forms of intolerance were based on the fear that the ground was not

[1] Here Herzen ignorantly uses the word 'Quaker' as equivalent to 'Nonconformist,' or perhaps 'Puritan.' It is needless to point out that tolerance is one of the most prominent principles of the Society of Friends.—(*Translator's Note*.)

firm under their feet; they saw that they needed to take strong measures, to persuade men in the one case that this was the church, in the other that it was freedom.

Such is the general atmosphere of European life. It is most oppressive and insufferable where the modern Western system is most developed, where it is most true to its principles, where it is most wealthy and most *cultured*—that is, most industrial. And that is why it is not so unendurably oppressive to live in Italy or Spain as it is in England or France. . . . And that is why poor, mountainous, rustic Switzerland is the only corner of Europe into which one can retreat in peace. [1]

[1] These fragments, printed in vol. iv. of *The Polar Star*, ended with the following dedication, written before the arrival of Ogaryov in London and before the death of Granovsky:

'. . . Accept this skull—it belongs to you by right'(*Pushkin*).

Here for the time we will stop. Some day I shall publish the chapters I have omitted and shall write others, without which my narrative remains unintelligible, incomplete, perhaps useless, and in any case will not be what I meant. But all that must be later, much later. . . .

Now let us part; and one word at leave-taking, to you friends of my youth.

When everything had been buried, when even the clamour partly provoked by me, partly spontaneous, had subsided about me, and people had dispersed to their living, I lifted up my head and looked around me; I had nothing living, nothing akin to me but my children. Wandering among strangers, watching them more closely, I gave up seeking *friends* and held aloof—not from men but from intimacy with them.

It is true, at times it seems that I have still feelings in my heart, words which it is a pity not to utter, which might do good or at least bring comfort to the listener, and one is sorry that it must all be smothered and lost in the soul, as the eye loses itself in the empty distance . . . but that is the rapidly fading glow of sunset, the reflection of the retreating past.

It is to that that I have turned back. I have left the world alien to me and have come back to you; and again we have been living together as in old times, are meeting every day, and nothing is changed, no one has grown older, no one is dead—and I am as at home with you, and it is as clear that I have no other standpoint than ours, no vocation but that to which I dedicated myself from childhood.

My story of the past is, maybe, dull and feeble, but you, friends, will give it a warm reception; this work has helped me to live through a terrible period, it has lifted me out of the idle despair in which I was perishing, it has brought me back to you. With it I enter upon my winter, not *gaily* but *calmly* (in the words of the poet whom I love beyond measure):—

'*Lieta no . . . ma sicura!*' said Leopardi of death in his *Ruysch e le sui mummie*.

So all unwittingly you have saved me: accept this skull—it belongs to you by right.

ISLE OF WIGHT, VENTNOR,
    Octber 1, 1855.

Chapter 39
MONEY and POLICE—THE EMPEROR JAMES ROTHSCHILD
AND THE BANKER NICHOLAS ROMANOV—POLICE
AND MONEY

IN the December of 1849 I learnt that the authorisation for the mortgage of my estate sent from Paris and witnessed at the Embassy had been destroyed, and that after that an injunction had been laid on my mother's fortune. There was no time to be lost, and, as I have mentioned in a previous chapter, I at once left Geneva and went to my mother's.

It would be hypocritical to affect to despise property in our time of financial disorganisation. Money is independence, power, a weapon.

And no one flings away a weapon in time of war, though it may have come from the enemy or be ever so rusty. The slavery of poverty is awful; I have studied it in all its aspects, living for years with men who have escaped from political shipwrecks in the clothes they stood up in. And so I thought it right and necessary to take every measure to snatch what I could from the bear's claws of the Russian Government.

Even so, I was not far from losing everything. When I left Russia I had no definite plan; I only wanted to remain abroad as long as possible. The Revolution of 1848 arrived and drew me into its whirlpool before I had done anything to secure my property. Worthy persons have blamed me for throwing myself headlong into political movements and leaving the future of my family to the will of the gods. Perhaps it was not altogether prudent; but if, living in Rome in 1848, I had sat at home considering ways and means of saving my property while revolting Italy was surging before my windows, then I should probably not have remained in foreign countries, but have returned to Petersburg, have entered the service again, might have become a vice-governor, have sat at the head prosecutor's table, and should have addressed my secretary with insulting familiarity and my minister as 'Your High Excellency.'

I had no such self-restraint and good sense, and I am infinitely thankful for it now. My heart and my memory would be the poorer if I had missed those bright moments of faith and enthusiasm! What could have made up to me for the loss of them? Indeed, why speak of me? What would have made up for it to her whose broken life was nothing afterwards but suffering that ended in the grave? How bitterly would my conscience have reproached me if, from prudent caution, I had robbed her of almost the last minutes of untroubled happiness! And after all I did succeed in saving almost all our property except the Kostroma estate.

After the June days my position was becoming dangerous. I made the acquaintance of Rothschild, and asked him to change for me two Moscow Bank bonds. Business then was not flourishing, of course; the exchange was in a very bad way; his terms were not good, but I at once accepted them, and had the satisfaction of seeing a faint smile of compassion on Rothschild's lips —he took me for a reckless *prince russe* who had run into debt in Paris, and so fell to calling me *Monsieur le Comte*.

On the first bonds the money was promptly paid; but on the later ones for a much larger sum, though the payment was made, Rothschild's representative informed him that an injunction had been laid on my capital— luckily I had withdrawn it all.

And so I found myself in Paris with a large sum of money in the midst of general upheaval, without experience or knowledge what to do with it. Yet everything was fairly well arranged. As a rule, the less excitement, uneasiness, and anxiety there is in financial matters, the better they succeed. Greedy money-grubbers and financial cowards are as often ruined as spendthrifts.

By the advice of Rothschild, I bought myself some American shares, a few French ones, and a small house in the Rue Amsterdam, tenanted by the Havre Hôtel.

One of my first revolutionary steps, which cut me off from Russia, plunged me into the respectable class of conservative idlers, brought me acquainted with bankers and notaries, taught me to look at the Stock Exchange news—in fact, turned me into a West European *rentier*. The disharmony between the modern man and the environment in which he lives brings a dreadful confusion into private behaviour. We are in the very middle of two currents in conflict with each other; we are flung and shall continue to be flung first in one and then in the other direction, until one or the other finally overpowers us, and the stream, still restless and turbulent but flowing in one direction only, makes things easier for the swimmer by carrying him along with it.

Happy the man who knows how to steer so that, yielding to the waves and swaying with them, he still swims his own course!

On the purchase of the house I had the opportunity of looking more closely into the business and bourgeois world of France. The bureaucratic pedantry over completing a purchase is not inferior to ours in Russia. The old notary read me several documents, the statute concerning the reading of them *main levée*, then the actual statute itself—all of this making up a complete folio volume. In our final negotiation concerning the price and the legal expenses, the owner of the house said that he would make a concession and take upon himself the very considerable expenses of the legal conveyance, if I would immediately pay the whole sum to him personally. I did not understand him, since from the very first I had openly stated that I was buying it for ready money. The notary explained to me that the money must remain in his hands for at least three months, during which its sale would be advertised and all creditors who had any claims on the house would be called upon to state their case. The house was mortgaged for seventy thousand, but there might be further mortgages in other hands. In three months' time, after inquiries had been made, the *purge hypothécaire* would be handed to the purchaser and the former owner would receive the purchase money.

The owner declared that he had no other debts. The notary confirmed this. 'Your honour and your hand on it,' I said to him—'you have no other debts which could be secured by the house?'

'I will readily give you my word of honour.'

'In that case, I agree, and will come here to-morrow with Rothschild's cheque.'

When I went next day to Rothschild's, his secretary flung up his hands in horror: 'They are cheating you! This is impossible; we will stop the sale if you like. It's something unheard of, to buy from a stranger on such terms.'

'Would you like me to send some one with you to look into the business?' Baron James himself suggested.

I did not care to play the part of an ignorant boy, so said that I had given my word, and took the cheque for the whole sum. When I reached the notary's I found there, besides the witnesses, the creditor who had come to receive the seventy thousand francs. The deed of purchase was read over, we signed it, the notary congratulated me on being a Parisian house-owner—there was nothing left to do but to hand over the cheque. . . .

'How vexing!' said the house-owner, taking it from my hands; 'I forgot to ask you to draw it in two cheques. How can I pay out the seventy thousand now?'

'Nothing is easier: go to Rothschild's, they'll give it you in two cheques; or, simpler still, go to the bank.'

'I'll go if you like,' said the creditor; the house-owner frowned and answered that that was his business, that he would go.

The creditor frowned. The notary good-naturedly suggested that they should go together.

Hardly able to refrain from laughter, I said to them: 'Here's your receipt; give me back the cheque, I will go and change it.'

'You will infinitely oblige us,' they said with a sigh of relief; and I went.

Four months later the *purge hypothécaire* was sent me, and I gained ten thousand francs by my rash trustfulness.

After the 13 th of June 1849, the Prefect of Police, Rébillaud, made some report against me; probably in consequence of his report, strange steps were taken by the Petersburg Government in regard to my estate. It was these steps, as I have said, that compelled me to go with my mother to Paris.

We travelled through Neufchâtel and Besançon. Our journey began with my forgetting my greatcoat in the posting-station yard at Berne; as I had a warm overcoat and warm overshoes with me, I did not go back for it. All went well till we reached the mountains, but in the mountains we were met by knee-deep snow, eight degrees of frost, and the cursed Swiss *bise*. The diligence could not go on, the passengers were transferred by twos and threes into small sledges. I do not remember having ever suffered so much from cold as on that night. My legs were simply in agony. I stuffed them into the straw; then the post driver gave me a collar of some sort, but that was not much help. At the third station I bought from a peasant woman her shawl for fifteen francs, and wrapped myself in it; but by that time we were already on the descent, and with every mile it grew warmer.

This road is magnificently fine on the French side; the vast amphitheatre of immense mountains, so varied in outline, accompanies one up to Besançon itself; here and there on the crags stand the ruins of fortified feudal castles. In this landscape there is something mighty and austere, resolute and morose; gazing at it, a peasant boy grew up and was formed, the descendant of old country stock, Pierre Joseph Proudhon. And indeed one may say of him, though in a different sense, what was said by the poet of the Florentines:

>'E tiene ancor del monte e del macigno.'

Rothschild agreed to take my mother's bond, but would not cash it in advance, on account of Gasser's letter. The Board of Trustees did in fact refuse the payment. Then Rothschild instructed Gasser to demand an interview with Nesselrode and to inquire of him what was wrong. Nesselrode replied that though there was no doubt about the bonds and Rothschild's claim was valid, the Tsar had commanded that the money should be retained on secret political grounds.

I remember the amazement in Rothschild's office on the reception of this reply. The eye involuntarily glanced to the bottom of the statement for the sign of Alaric or the seal of Genghis Khan. Rothschild had not expected such a trick even from so celebrated a master of despotic action as Nicholas. 'It is little matter for wonder to me,' I said to him, 'that Nicholas should try to carry off my mother's money to punish me, or to catch me with it as a bait; but I could not have imagined that your name would have so little weight in Russia. The bonds are yours and not my mother's; when she signed them she gave them to bearer (*au porteur*), but since you endorsed them that *porteur*[1] is you; and you are insolently answered, "The money is yours, but the master has told me not to pay it."'

My words produced their effect. Rothschild began to lose his temper, and walking about the room said: 'No, I won't allow myself to be treated like that; I will bring an action against the bank; I will insist upon a definite answer from the Minister of Finance!'

'Well,' thought I, 'Vrontchenko won't understand this gentleman. A "confidential" reply would have been a favour, but a "definite" one is too much!'

'Here you have a sample of how familiarly and *sans gêne* the autocracy, upon which the reaction is building such hopes, disposes of property. The communism of the Cossack is almost more dangerous than that of Louis Blanc.'

'I will think what to do,' said Rothschild; 'we can't put up with this.'

Three days after this conversation, I met Rothschild on the boulevard.

'By the way,' he said, stopping me, 'I was speaking of your business yesterday to Kisselyov. [2] You must excuse me, but I ought to tell you that he expressed a very unfavourable opinion of you, and does not seem willing to do anything for you.'

'Do you often see him?'

'Sometimes at evening parties.'

'Be so good as to tell him that you have seen me to-day, and that I have the worst possible opinion of him, but that at the same time I don't think it would be fair to rob his mother on that account.'

---

[1] This endorsement is done for security in sending cheques in order that no one else should be able to receive the money.

[2] This was not P. D. Kisselyov, who was in Paris later, the well-known minister of crown property, a very decent man; but the other one. afterwards transferred to Rome.—(*Author's Notes.*)

Rothschild laughed; I think that from that time he began to surmise that I was not a *prince russe*, and he took to addressing me as Baron; he elevated me to this rank, I imagine, to make me worthy of conversing with him.

Next day he sent for me; I went at once. He handed me an unsigned letter to Gasser, and added: 'Here is our proposed letter; sit down and read it attentively, then tell me whether you are satisfied with it. If you want to add or change anything, we will do so at once. Meanwhile, allow me to go on with my work.'

First I looked about me. Every minute a small door opened and one Bourse agent after another came in, uttering a number in a loud voice; Rothschild, still reading, muttered without raising his eyes: 'Yes,—no,—good,—perhaps,—enough,—' and the number walked out. There were various persons in the room, capitalists of the common sort, members of the National Assembly, two or three exhausted tourists with youthful moustaches and elderly cheeks, those everlasting figures that are seen drinking wine at watering-places and presenting themselves at courts, the feeble and lymphatic scions of effete aristocratic families, who yet presume to pass from the gaming table to the Bourse. They were all talking together in undertones. The Jewish autocrat sat calmly at his table, looking through papers and noting something down on them, probably millions, or at least hundreds of thousands.

'Well,' he said, turning to me, 'are you satisfied?'

'Perfectly,' I answered.

The letter was excellent, curt and emphatic as it should be when one power is addressing another. He wrote to Gasser that the latter must at once demand an audience with Nesselrode and the Minister of Finance; that he must tell them that Rothschild is not interested to know to whom the bonds did belong; that he has bought them and insists on payment, or a clear legal statement of the reason why payment is deferred; that, in case of refusal, he would put the matter before the legal authorities, and he advised them to weigh carefully the consequences of a refusal, which seemed particularly strange to him when the Russian Government was negotiating through him for the conclusion of a new loan. Rothschild wound up by saying that in case of further delay he would be impelled to give the matter publicity through the newspapers to warn other capitalists. He recommended Gasser to show this to Nesselrode.

.   .   .   .   .   .

We were interrupted. . . . Schomburg asked me to look in half an hour later.

When half an hour later I was mounting the staircase of the Winter Palace of Finance in the Rue Laffitte, the rival of Nicholas was coming down it.

'Schomburg has told me,' said His Majesty, smiling graciously, and holding out his own august hand, 'the letter has been signed and sent off. You will see how they will come round. I'll teach them to play tricks with me.'

I felt inclined to drop on my knees and to offer an oath of allegiance together with my gratitude, but I confined myself to saying: 'If you feel perfectly certain of it, allow me to open an account, if only for half of the sum.'

'With pleasure,' answered the gracious autocrat, and went his way into the Rue Laffitte.

I made my obeisance to His Majesty, and, being so near, went into the *Maison d'Or*.

Within a month or six weeks Nicholas Romanov, that Petersburg merchant of the first guild, who had been so reluctant to pay up, terrified by the prospect of a meeting of creditors and the publication in the newspapers, did at the Imperial command of Rothschild pay up the illegally detained money, together with the interest and the interest on the interest, apologising for his ignorance of the law, which he certainly could not be expected to know in his social position.

From that time forth I was on the best of terms with Rothschild. He liked in me the field of battle on which he had beaten Nicholas; I was for him something like Marengo or Austerlitz, and he several times described the details of the business in my presence, smiling faintly, but magnanimously sparing his vanquished opponent.

While this business was going on—and it occupied about six months—I was staying at the Hotel Mirabeau, Rue de la Paix. One morning in April I was told that a gentleman was waiting for me in the hall and particularly wished to see me. I went out. An abject old individual who looked like a government clerk was standing in the hall.

'The Commissaire of Police of the Tuileries Arrondissement So-and-so.'

'Pleased to see you.'

'Allow me to read you the decree of the Ministry of Home Affairs, communicated to me by the Prefect of Police, and relating to you.'

'Pray do so; here is a chair.'

'We, the Prefect of Police:[1]—In accordance with paragraph seven of the law of the 13 th and 21st of November and 3rd of December of 1849, giving the Ministry of Home Affairs the power to expel (*expulser*) from France any foreigner whose presence in France may be subversive of order and dangerous to public tranquillity, and in view of the ministerial circular of the 3rd of January 1850,

'Do command as follows:

'The here-mentioned'(*le N—— é*, that is, *nommé,* but this does not mean 'aforesaid 'because nothing has been

[1] I translate it word for word.—(*Author's Note.*)

said about me before; it is merely an ungrammatical attempt to designate a man as rudely as possible) 'Herzen, Alexandre, age 40'(they put me on two years), 'a Russian subject, living in such a place, is to leave Paris at once on receiving this announcement, and to depart from the frontiers of France within the shortest possible time.

'It is forbidden for him to return in future under pain of the penalties laid down by the eighth paragraph of the same law (imprisonment from one to six months and a money fine).

'All necessary measures will be taken to secure the execution of these orders.

'*Fait* in Paris, April 16, 1850.

'Prefect of Police,

'A. CARLIER.

'Confirmed by the general secretary of the Prefecture.

'CLÉMENT REYRE.'

On the margin:

'Read and approved April 19, 1850,

'Minister of Home Affairs,

'G. BAROCHE.

'In the year eighteen hundred and fifty, April the twenty-fourth.

'We, Emile Boulay, Commissaire of Police of the City of Paris and in particular of the Tuileries Arrondissement, in execution of the orders of M. le Prefect of Police of April 23 rd:

'Have notified the Sieur Alexandre Herzen, telling him in words as written herewith.' Here follows the whole text over again. It is just as children tell the story of the White Bull, prefacing every fresh incident with the same phrase: 'Shall I tell you the tale of the white bull?'

Then: 'We have summoned *le dit Herzen* to present himself in the course of the next twenty-four hours at the Prefecture for the reception of a passport and the assignment of a frontier through which he will leave France.

'*And that le dit Sieur Herzen n'en prétende cause d'ignorance* (what a jargon!) *nous lui avons laissé cette copie tant du dit arrêté en téte de cette présente de notre procès-verbal de notification.*'

Oh, my Vyatka colleagues in the secretariat of Tyufyaev; oh, Ardashov, who would write a dozen sheets at one sitting; Veprev, Shtin, and my drunken head clerk! Would not their hearts rejoice to know that after the days of Voltaire, of Beaumarchais, of George Sand, and of Hugo, documents are written like this in Paris?

And, indeed, not only they would be delighted, but also my father's village foreman, Vassily Epifanov, who from the deepest sentiments of politeness would write to his master: 'Your commandment by this present preceding post received, and by the same I have the honour to announce . . .' This stupid and vulgar temple *des us et coutumes*, only fitting for a blind and doting old goddess like Themis, ought surely to be razed to the ground.

The reading of this document did not produce the result expected; a Parisian imagines that exile from Paris is as bad as the expulsion of Adam from Paradise, and without Eve into the bargain. To me, on the contrary, it was a matter of indifference, since I had already begun to be sick of Parisian life.

'When am I to present myself before the Prefecture?' I asked, assuming a polite air in spite of the wrath which was filling me.

'I advise ten o'clock to-morrow morning.'

'With pleasure.'

'How early the spring is beginning this year!' observed the *commissaire* of the city of Paris and in particular of the Tuileries arrondissement.

'Exceedingly.'

'This is an old-fashioned hotel. Mirabeau used to dine here; that is why it bears his name. You have no doubt been well satisfied with it?'

'Very well satisfied. Only fancy what it must be to leave it so abruptly!'

'It's certainly unpleasant. . . . The hostess is an intelligent and excellent woman—Mlle. Cousin; she was a great friend of the celebrated Le Normand.'[1]

'Imagine that! What a pity I did not know it! Perhaps she has inherited her art of fortune-telling and might have predicted my *billet doux* from Carlier.'

'Ha, ha! . . . It is my duty, you know. Allow me to wish you good-day.'

'To be sure, anything may happen. I have the honour to wish you good-bye.'

Next day I presented myself in the Rue Jérusalem, more celebrated than Le Normand herself. First, I was received by some sort of a youthful spy, with a little beard, a little moustache, and all the manners of an abortive journalist and an unsuccessful democrat. His face, the look in his eyes, all wore the stamp of that refined corruption of soul, that envious hunger for enjoyment, power, acquisition, which I have learned to read so well on Western European faces, though it is completely absent from that of the English. He had probably only recently received his post; he still took pleasure in it, and therefore spoke a little condescendingly. He informed me that I must leave within three days, and except for particularly important reasons it was impossible to defer the date. His impudent face, his accent and his gestures, were such that without entering into further discussion with him I bowed and then asked, first putting on my hat, when I could see the Prefect.

---

[1] Mlle. Le Normand (1772-1843) was a well-known fortune-teller of the period.—(*Translator's Note.*)

'The Prefect only receives persons who have asked him for an audience in writing.'

'Allow me to write to him at once.'

He rang the bell; an old *huissier* with a chain on his breast walked in; saying to him with a dignified air, 'Pen and paper for this gentleman,' the youth nodded to me.

The *huissier* led me into another room. There I wrote to Carlier that I wished to see him in order to explain to him why I had to defer my departure.

On the evening of the same day I received from the Prefecture the laconic answer: 'M. le Préfet is ready to receive So-and-so to-morrow at two o'clock.'

The same disgusting youth met me next day: he had his own room, from which I concluded that he was something in the nature of a head clerk. Beginning his career so early and with such success, he will go far, if God grants him long life.

On this occasion he led me into a big office. There a stout, tall, rosy-cheeked gentleman was sitting in a big easy-chair at an immense table. He was one of those persons who are always hot, with sleek, white, but flabby flesh, with fat but carefully groomed hands, with a necktie reduced to a minimum, with colourless eyes, with that jovial expression which is usually found in men who are completely drowned in love for their comfort, and who can rise coldly and without great effort to the utmost infamies.

'You wish to see the Prefect,' he said to me; 'but he asks you to excuse him; he has been obliged to go out on very important business. If I can do anything for your benefit I ask nothing better. Here is an easy-chair: will you sit down?'

All this he brought out smoothly, very politely, screwing up his eyes a little and smiling with the little cushions of flesh which adorned his cheek-bones. 'Well, this fellow has been for years in the service,' I thought.

'You probably know what I've come about.' He made that gentle movement of the head which every one makes on beginning to swim, and did not answer.

'I have received an order to leave within three days. As I know that your minister has the right of expulsion without giving reasons or making investigations, I am not going to inquire why I am being expelled, nor to defend myself; but I have, besides my own house . . . '

'Where is your house?'

'Fourteen, Rue Amsterdam . . . very important business in Paris, and it is difficult for me to leave at once.'

'Allow me to ask, what is your business? Is it to do with the house or . . . ?'

'My business is with Rothschild. I have to receive four hundred thousand francs.'

'What?'

'A little over a hundred thousand silver roubles.'

'That's a very large sum!'

'*C'est une somme ronde.*'

'How much time do you need for completing your business?' he asked, looking at me more tenderly, as people look at pheasants stuffed with truffles in the shop windows.

'From a month to six weeks.'

'That is a terribly long time.'

'My business is being settled in Russia. I should not wonder if it is on that account I am leaving France, indeed.'

'How so?'

'A week ago Rothschild told me that Kisselyov spoke ill of me. Probably the Petersburg Government wishes to hush up the business; I dare say the ambassador has asked for my expulsion as a favour.'

'*D'abord,*' observed the offended patriot of the Prefecture, assuming an air of dignity and profound conviction, 'France permits no other Government to interfere in her domestic affairs. I am surprised that such an idea could enter your head. Moreover, what can be more natural than that the Government, which is doing its utmost to restore order to the suffering people, should exercise its right to expel from the country in which there is so much inflammatory material, foreigners who abuse the hospitality she has shown them?'

I determined to get at him by money. This was as sure a method of attack as the use of texts from the Gospel in discussion with a Catholic, and so I answered with a smile: 'I have paid a hundred thousand francs for the hospitality of Paris, and so consider I have almost settled my account.'

This was even more successful than my *somme ronde*. He was embarrassed, and saying after a brief pause, 'We cannot help it, we are obliged to do our duty,' he took from the table my *dossier*. This was the second volume of the novel, the first part of which I had once seen in the hands of Dubbelt. Stroking the pages, as though they were good horses, with his plump hand: 'You see,' he observed, 'your connections, your association with seditious journals' (almost word for word what Sahtynsky had said to me in 1840), 'and the considerable subventions which you have given to the most pernicious enterprises, have compelled us to resort to a very unpleasant but necessary step. That step can be no surprise to you. Even in your own country you brought political punishment upon yourself. Like causes lead to like results.'

'I am certain,' I said, 'that the Emperor Nicholas himself does not suspect this solidarity; you cannot really approve of his Government.'

'*Un bon citoyen* respects the laws of his country, whatever they may be. . . .'[1]

'Probably on the celebrated principle that it is in any

[1] Later on Professor Tchitcherin preached a doctrine somewhat similar in the Moscow University.—(*Author's Note*.)

case better there should be bad weather than no weather at all.'

'To prove to you that the Russian Government has absolutely nothing to do with it, I promise to obtain from the Prefect a postponement for one month. You will certainly not think it strange if we make inquiries of Rothschild concerning your business; it is not so much a question of doubting. . . .'

'Do by all means make inquiries. We are at war, and if it had been of any use for me to have resorted to stratagem in order to remain, do you suppose I should not have employed it?'

But the worldly and amiable *alter ego* of the Prefect would not be outdone.

'People who talk like that never say what is untrue,' he replied.

A month later my business was still unfinished. We were visited by an old doctor, Palmier, whose agreeable duty it is to make a weekly examination of an interesting class of Parisian women at the Prefecture. Since he gave such a number of certificates of health to the fair sex, I imagined he would not refuse to give me a certificate of illness. Palmier was acquainted, of course, with every one in the Prefecture: he promised me to give X. personally the history of my indisposition. To my great surprise Palmier came back without a satisfactory answer. This incident is worth noting because it shows a brotherly resemblance between the Russian and the French bureaucracies. X. had given no answer, but had replied evasively, offended at my not having come in person to inform him that I was ill, in bed, and could not get up. There was no help for it: I went next day to the Prefecture, glowing with health.

X. asked me with the greatest sympathy about my illness. As I had not had the curiosity to read what the doctor had written, I had to invent an illness. Luckily

I remembered Sazonov, who, with his bulky figure and inexhaustible appetite, complained of aneurism—I told X. I had heart disease and that travelling might be very bad for me.

X. was sorry for me, and advised me to be very careful; then he went into the next room, and returned a minute later, saying: 'You may remain another month. The Prefect has commissioned me at the same time to tell you that he hopes and desires that your health may be restored during that period; if this were not the case, he would greatly regret it, for he will not be able to postpone your departure a third time.'

I understood that, and made ready to leave Paris about the 20th of June.

I came across the name of X. once more a year later. This patriot and *bon citoyen* quietly withdrew from France, forgetting to account for some thousands of francs belonging to people of the poor or lower-middle class who had taken tickets in a Californian lottery run under the patronage of the Prefecture!

When the worthy citizen saw that in spite of all his respect for the laws of his country he might get into the galleys for swindling, then he preferred to take a steamer to Genoa. He was a consistent person, who did not lose his head with failure. He took advantage of the notoriety he gained by the scandal of the Californian lottery to proffer his services to a society of speculators which had been formed at that time at Turin for building railways; the society hastened to accept the services of so reliable a gentleman.

The last two months I spent in Paris were insufferable. I was literally *gardé à vue*; my letters arrived a day late and insolently unsealed; wherever I went I was followed in the distance by a loathsome individual, who at the corners passed me on with a wink to another.

It must not be forgotten that this was the time of the

most feverish activity of the police. The stupid conservatives and revolutionists of the Algiers-Lamartine persuasion helped the rogues and knaves surrounding Napoleon himself to prepare a network of espionage and supervision, so that, stretching them over the whole of France, they might at any given minute catch by telegraph, by the Ministry of Home Affairs and the Élysée, all the active forces of the country and strangle them. Napoleon III. cleverly turned the weapon entrusted to him against these men themselves. The 2nd of December meant the promotion of the police to the position of the executive power.

There has never anywhere, even in Austria or in Russia, been such a political police as existed in France from the time of the Convention. There are many causes for this, apart from the peculiar *national* propensity for police activity. Except in England, where the police have nothing in common with Continental espionage, the police are everywhere surrounded by hostile elements and consequently thrown on their own resources. In France, on the contrary, the police is the most popular institution. Whatever government seizes power, its police is *ready*; a part of the people will help it with a zest and a fanaticism which have to be restrained and not intensified, and will help, too, with all those terrible means at the disposal of private persons which are impossible for the police. Where can a man hide from his shopkeeper, his house-porter, his tailor, his washerwoman, his butcher, his sister's husband, his brother' wife, especially in Paris, where people do not live in separate houses as they do in London, but in something like coral reefs or hives with a common staircase, a common courtyard, and a common porter.

Condorcet escapes from the Jacobin police and successfully makes his way to some village near the frontier; tired and harassed, he goes into a little inn, sits down before the fire, warms his hands, and asks for a piece of chicken. The good-natured old woman who keeps the inn, and who is a great patriot, reasons like this: 'He is covered with dust, so he must have come a *long way*; he asks for chicken, so he must have *money*; his hands are white, so he must be an *aristocrat*.' Leaving the chicken on the stove, she goes to the next inn; there patriots are sitting—a Mucius Scaevola, the innkeeper—some *citoyen*, a Brutus—a Timoleon, the tailor. They ask for nothing better, and ten minutes later one of the wisest leaders of the French Revolution is in prison and handed over to one of the police of Liberty, Fraternity, and Equality!

Napoleon, who had the police talent highly developed, turned his generals into spies and informers. The butcher of Lyons, Fouché, founded a complete theory, system, science of espionage—through the prefects, behind the prefects, through prostitutes and virtuous shopkeepers, through servants and coachmen, through doctors and barbers. Napoleon fell, but his tool remained, and not only his tool but the man who wielded it. Fouché passed over to the Bourbons; the strength of the spies lost nothing—on the contrary, they were reinforced by monks and priests. Under Louis-Philippe, in whose reign bribery and corruption became one of the moral forces of government, half the petty-bourgeois became his spies, his police chorus, a result to which service in the National Guard—in itself a police duty—greatly contributed.

During the February republic three or four branches of genuinely secret police and several of professedly secret ones were formed. There was the police of Ledru-Rollin and the police of Caussidière, there was the police of Marrast and the police of the provisional government, there was the police of order and the police of disorder, the police of Napoleon and the police of the Due d'Orléans. All were on the look-out, all were watching each other and reporting on each other; assuming that these secret reports were made with conviction, with the best of motives, for no money gain, yet they were still secret reports. . . . This fatal habit, meeting on the one hand with mournful failures, and on the other morbid, unbridled lust of gold or pleasure, corrupted a whole generation.

We must not forget, too, the moral indifference, the instability of opinion, which was left like a sediment by successive revolutions and restorations. Men had grown used to regarding as heroism and virtue on one day what would on the morrow be a crime punished with penal servitude; the laurel wreath and the brand of the convict alternated several times on the same head. By the time they had become accustomed to this a nation of spies was created.

All the latest discoveries of secret societies and plots, all the latest denunciations of refugees were made by false members of societies, bribed friends, men who had won confidence with the object of treachery.

There were examples on all hands of cowards who, through fear of prison and exile, revealed secrets and ruined their friends—as a faint-hearted comrade ruined Konarski. But neither among us nor in Austria was there a legion of young men, cultured, speaking *our* language, making inspired speeches in clubs, writing revolutionary articles and serving as spies.

Moreover, the government of Napoleon was excellently placed for making use of informers of all parties. It represents the revolution and the reaction, war and peace, the year 1789 and Catholicism, the fall of the Bourbons and the 4½ per cents. It is served both by Falloux the Jesuit, and Billault the socialist, and La Rochejacquelein the legitimist, and the mass of the people to whom Louis-Philippe had been a benefactor. The refuse of all parties and shades of opinion naturally flows together and ferments in the Palace of the Tuileries.

Chapter 40

THE EUROPEAN COMMITTEE—THE RUSSIAN CONSUL AT
NICE—LETTER TO A. F. ORLOV—PERSECUTION OF A CHILD
—THE VOGTS—TRANSFERENCE FROM THE GRADE OF UPPER
COURT COUNCILLOR TO THAT OF SIMPLE PEASANT—
RECEPTION AT CHÂTEL
(1850-1851)

A YEAR after our arrival in Nice from Paris I wrote:
'In vain I rejoiced at my quiet seclusion, in vain I drew the pentagram on my doors: I have not found a quiet haven nor the peace I desired. Pentagrams protect us from unclean spirits—no polygons protect us from unclean men, unless perhaps the square of the prison-cell window.

'A tedious, wearisome, and extremely empty period, the exhausting journey between the halting place of 1848 and the halting place of 1852,—there is nothing new except perhaps some personal misfortune breaking the heart, another vital spring snapped.'—('Letters from France and Italy,' June 1, 1851.)

Indeed, going over that time makes my heart ache as it does at the memory of funerals, operations, agonising illnesses. Without touching here upon my inner life, which was more and more overcast by dark stormclouds, public events and the news in the papers were enough to make any one flee into the desert. France was dropping with the swiftness of a falling star to the 2nd of December. Germany lay at the feet of Nicholas, to which Hungary, sold and unhappy, had dragged her. The *condottieri* of the police met at their œcumenical councils, and secretly consulted together concerning common measures of international espionage. The revolutionaries maintained their empty agitation. The men at the head of the movement, disappointed in their hopes, lost their heads. Kossuth returned from America somewhat less nationalistic, Mazzini together with Ledru-Rollin and Ruge was founding in London the Central European Committee . . . while the reaction was growing more and more ferocious.

After our meeting in Geneva, and then again in Lausanne, I saw Mazzini in 1850; he was secretly in France, staying in some aristocratic family, and sent one of his intimate associates to fetch me. Then he told me of his project of an international league in London, and asked whether I would like to take part in it *as a Russian*; I made no definite answer. A year later Orsini came to me in Nice, handed me the programme, various manifestoes of the European Central Committee, and a letter from Mazzini renewing his proposition. I did not dream of joining the Committee; what element of Russian life could I have represented at that time, completely cut off from everything Russian as I was? But this was not the only reason why the European Committee did not attract me. It seemed to me that its basis lacked depth of thought and unity, that there had been no necessity for its foundation, and that its form was simply a mistake.

The side of the movement which the Committee represented—that is, the revolt of the oppressed nationalities—was not strong enough in 1851 to be openly represented by a league. The existence of such a Committee showed nothing but the tolerance of the English constitution, and partly too that the English Government did not believe in its power or they would have suppressed it, either by an alien bill or by a motion for the suspension of *habeas corpus*.

The European Committee, though it scared all the governments, did nothing, without perceiving that fact. Even the most earnest people are terribly easily led away by formalism, and persuade themselves that they are doing something by having periodical meetings, issuing masses of papers, minutes, motions, voting, accepting resolutions, printing manifestoes, *professions de foi*, and so on. The revolutionary bureaucracy dissolves things into words and forms just as our official bureaucracy does. In England there are masses of all sorts of associations which hold impressive meetings attended by dukes and lords, clergymen and secretaries. Treasurers collect funds, literary men write articles, and all of them together do absolutely nothing. These meetings, for the most part philanthropic and religious, on the one hand serve as an entertainment, on the other soothe the Christian conscience of people who are given up to worldly interests. But a revolutionary senate in London could not *en permanence* maintain this meek-and-mild character. It was a public conspiracy, a conspiracy with open doors—that is, an impossible one.

A conspiracy is bound to be secret. The period of secret societies is over only in England and America. Everywhere where there is a minority, in advance of the understanding of the masses and hoping to realise an idea they have grasped, secret societies will be formed, if there is no freedom of speech or right of free assembly. I speak of this quite impartially; after my youthful attempts, ending in my exile in 1835, I have *never been a member of any secret society*, but not at all because I consider the spending of energy on individual effort more worth while. I have not been a member of such societies because I have not happened to come upon a society which was in harmony with my own aims, and in which I could have achieved anything. If it had been my lot to be in touch with Pestel's or Ryleyev's society,[1] I should have flung myself into it heart and soul.

[1] Pestel was the leader of the Union of the South, and Ryleyev of the Union of the North, which combined in the attempt to overthrow the autocracy and establish constitutional government in Russia on December 14, 1825.—(*Translator's Note*.)

Another error or another misfortune of the Committee lay in its lack of unity. This focussing together of heterogeneous ideals could only have developed the power of its component parts by common action. If each member of the Committee had brought nothing but his exclusive nationality, that would not have mattered; they would have had a unity in their hatred for the chief enemy they had in common, the Holy Alliance. But their views, agreed on two negative principles, opposition to monarchy and to socialism, differed on every other subject. To act in unison they must have made compromises, and compromises of that kind are destructive of the one-sided force of each, for the sake of common accord, tying just the strings which sound most sharply, and so making the combined effect colourless, blurred, and hesitating.

After reading the papers which Orsini had brought me, I wrote the following letter to Mazzini:—

'DEAR MAZZINI,—I have a sincere respect for you, and so I am not afraid to tell you my opinion frankly. In any case you will give me a patient and indulgent hearing.

'You are perhaps one of the chief political leaders of recent times whose name has remained surrounded by sympathy and respect. One may differ from you in opinion, in method, but cannot fail to respect you personally. Your past, the Rome of 1848 and 1849, compel you to bear proudly your great bereavement until events call back their champion who is in advance of them. That is why it is painful to me to see your name coupled with the names of men of no ability who have ruined the cause, with names which only recall the calamities they have brought upon us.

'Is an organisation with these elements possible? It can lead to nothing but confusion.

'These men are of no use to you nor to history; all that one can do for them is to forgive them their transgressions. You want to cover them with your name, you want to share with them your influence and your past; they will share with you their unpopularity and their past.

'What is there new in the manifestoes, what is there new in the *Proscrit*? Where are the signs of the terrible lessons that should have been learnt from the twenty-fourth of February? This is the continuation of the old liberalism and not the beginning of a new freedom—it is an epilogue and not a prologue. Why is there not in London the organisation you desire? Because it cannot be formed on the basis of indefinite ideals, but only on a great idea held in common: and where is that?

'The first publication made under such conditions as the manifesto you have sent ought to have been full of sincerity, but who can read without a smile the signature of Arnold Ruge on a manifesto which speaks in the name of Divine Providence? From 1838 Ruge has been preaching philosophic atheism; for him (if his brain is constructed logically) the idea of Providence ought to present itself as everything reactionary in embryo. It is a compromise, a bit of diplomacy, of policy, a weapon in the hands of our enemies. Moreover, all that is unnecessary. The theological part of the manifesto is a pure luxury; it adds neither to its meaning nor to its popularity. The common people have a positive religion and church. Deism is the religion of the rationalists, the representative system applied to faith, religion surrounded by atheistic institutions.

'For my part, I advocate a complete rupture with incomplete revolutionaries. One scents the reaction a hundred yards from them. Having taken the burden of a thousand blunders on their shoulders, they go on justifying them to this day—the surest proof that they will repeat them.

'In the *Nouveau Monde* there is the same *vacuum horrendum*; the same melancholy chewing over of the cud, at once green and dry, which still is not digested.

'Please do not imagine that I am saying this in order to get out of doing anything. No, I am not sitting with my arms folded. I have too much blood in my veins and energy in my character to be satisfied with tie part of a passive spectator. From my thirteenth year I have served the same idea and the same standard—of war against every oppressive power, against every form of slavery in the name of absolute personal freedom. I should like to continue my little guerilla warfare—like a true Cossack . . . *auf eigene Faust*, as the Germans say, beside the great revolutionary army—not entering into its regular ranks until they are completely formed.

'In the interval of waiting, I am writing. Perhaps that interval of waiting will last long—it is not in my power to change the fitful development of men; but to speak, to appeal, to persuade is in my power—and I am doing this with all my heart and with all my mind.

'Forgive me, dear Mazzini, both the candour and the length of my letter, and do not cease to love me a little and to reckon me a man devoted to your cause—but also devoted to his own convictions.'

'Nice, *September* 13, 1850.'

To this letter Mazzini answered with a few friendly lines in which, without touching on the essential point, he spoke of the necessity of uniting all forces in one activity, deplored the difference of men's views, and so on.

In the same autumn in which Mazzini and the European Committee remembered me, the anti-European Committee of Nicholas remembered me too, at last.

One morning our maid, with a somewhat anxious look,

told me that the Russian consul was downstairs and asking whether I could see him. I looked upon my relations with the Russian Government as so completely at an end that I was surprised at this honour, and could not imagine what he wanted of me.

A German-looking official of the second order walked in.

'I have the honour to make a communication to you.'

'Although,' I replied, 'I do not know of what nature, I am almost certain that it will be unpleasant. I beg you to be seated.'

The consul flushed, was a little disconcerted; then sat down on the sofa, took a document out of his pocket, and after reading, 'Adjutant-General Count Orlov has notified to Count Nesselrode and His Im. . . ,' rose to his feet again.

At that point I fortunately remembered that the secretary in our Embassy in Paris had risen from his chair on announcing to Sazonov the Tsar's command that he should return to Russia, and Sazonov suspecting nothing had also got up from his chair, though the secretary had done this from a deep sense of duty which required that a loyal subject should be on his legs with his head a little bowed when conveying the sovereign's will; and therefore, the more stiffly erect the consul stood, the more comfortably I buried myself in my armchair, and, wishing him to observe the fact, said with a nod: 'Pray go on; I am listening.'

' . . . perial Majesty,' he went on, resuming his seat, 'has been graciously pleased to command that So-and-so shall promptly return to Russia and should be informed thereof, accepting from him no reasons for delaying his departure and granting him no postponement under any circumstances.'

He paused. I continued sitting without saying a word.

'What am I to answer?' he asked, folding up the paper.

'That I am not going.'

'How do you mean "not going"?'

'What I say: simply I'm not going.'

'Have you considered that such a step . . . ?'

'I have considered.'

'But this is beyond anything. . . . Kindly tell me what I am to write. For what reason . . . ?'

'You have been commanded not to accept any reasons.'

'What am I to say, then? Why, this is disobedience to the will of His Imperial Majesty!'

'Say so, then.'

'This is impossible. I should never venture to write that . . .' and he crimsoned more than ever. 'Really, you had better change your mind while it is all still within four walls.' (The consul evidently thought the Third Section was a monastery.)

Philanthropic as I am, I was not willing, for the sake of facilitating the correspondence of the consul at Nice, to go into one of Father Leonty's cells of the Peter-Paul Fortress or to Nertchinsk, especially as there seemed no prospect that Nicholas would sink into a decline.

'Surely,' I said to him, 'when you were coming here you could not for one second have imagined that I should go? Forget that you are a consul and consider the position yourself. My estate has been sequestrated, my mother's fortune was detained, and all that without asking me whether I wished to return. Can I go back after that without taking leave of my senses?'

He hesitated, continually flushing, and at last hit on a clever, adroit, and above all new idea.

'I cannot,' he said, 'enter into . . . I understand the difficulty of your position; on the other hand, the gracious mercy of the Sovereign!. . . '

I looked at him; he blushed again. ' . . . Besides, why cut off all way of retreat. Write to me you are very ill; I'll send that to the Count.'

'That's too stale; besides, what is the object of telling a lie for nothing?'

'Well, then, will you be so kind as to give me your answer in writing.'

'Certainly. Can you leave me a copy of the notice you read to me?'

'That is not usual.'

'What a pity! I am making a collection of them.'

Simple as my written answer was, the consul was alarmed by it. He seemed to think that he might be transferred on account of it to Beyrout or Tripoli, or I do not know where; he positively declined to venture either to accept or to forward it. In spite of my assurances that no responsibility could fall on him, he refused, and begged me to write another letter.

'That's impossible,' I answered. 'I am not taking this step as a joke, and I am not going to write nonsensical reasons: here is the letter for you, and you can do what you like with it.'

'Excuse me,' said the mildest consul since the days of Junius Brutus and Calpurnius Bestia: 'you write the letter, not to me but to Count Orlov, and I'll simply forward it.'

'That's an easy matter; I've only to put *M. le Comte* instead of *M. le Consul*. I agree to that.'

As I was copying my letter it struck me that there was no need for me to write to Orlov in French. If it were in Russian some cantonist in his office or in the office of the Third Section might read it; it might be sent to the Senate, and a young head secretary might show it to his clerks: why deprive them of this satisfaction? And so I translated the letter, and here it is:—

'DEAR SIR, COUNT ALEXEY FYODOROVITCH,—The Imperial Consul at Nice has notified me of the will of the Most High concerning my return to Russia. With every inclination to do so, I find it impossible to comply with it without making my position clear.

'Before any summons to return, more than a year ago, an injunction was placed on my estate, my business papers in private hands were confiscated, and, finally, money, a sum of ten thousand francs sent to me from Moscow, was seized. Such severe and extreme measures against me prove that I am not merely accused of some crime, but, before any inquiry, any trial has been held, am found guilty and punished by the deprivation of part of my property.

'I cannot hope that my mere return can save me from the melancholy consequences of a political trial. It is easy for me to explain every one of my actions, but in cases of that kind it is opinions and theories that are on trial. It is upon them that verdicts are based. Can I, should I, expose myself and all my family to such a trial? . . . Your Excellency will appreciate the simplicity and candour of my answer, and will bring to the consideration of the Most High the reasons that compel me to remain in foreign parts in spite of my deep and genuine desire to return to my country.'

'NICE, *September* 23, 1850.'

I really do not know whether it was possible to answer more simply and discreetly; but the habit of slavish silence is so deeply rooted among us that the consul at Nice thought even this letter monstrously audacious, and probably Orlov himself thought the same.

To be silent, not to laugh and not to cry, and to answer on a set pattern, without praise or criticism, without signs of pleasure or grief, is the ideal to which despotism tries to reduce its subjects and has reduced the soldiers; but by what means? Well, I will tell you.

On one occasion, Nicholas, seeing a fine young soldier

wearing a cross at a review, asked him: 'Where did you receive your cross?' Unluckily this soldier was a seminarist sent for a soldier in punishment for some prank, and, wishing to take advantage of the opportunity to display his eloquence, he answered: 'Under the victorious eagles of Your Majesty.' Nicholas looked sternly at him and at the general, pouted, and went on. When the general following him reached the soldier, white with rage he shook his fist in his face and said: 'I'll beat you into your coffin, you Demosthenes!'

Is it strange that eloquence does not flourish with such encouragement?

Having got rid of the emperor and the consul, I wanted to get out of the class of persons living without a passport.

The future was dark and gloomy. . . . I might die, and the thought that that same blushing consul would arrive to dispose of everything in my house, and to seize my papers, compelled me to think of obtaining the rights of citizenship somewhere. I need hardly say that I fixed upon Switzerland, in spite of the fact that just about that time the Swiss police had been playing pranks with me.

Within a year after the birth of my second son we noticed with horror that he was completely deaf. Various consultations and experiments soon proved that it was impossible to cure the deafness. But then the question arose whether we ought to leave him to become dumb, as is usually done. The schools I had seen in Moscow had seemed to me far from satisfactory. Talking on one's fingers and by signs is not conversation; talking must be by the mouth and the lips. I knew by what I had read that attempts had been made in Germany and Switzerland to teach deaf mutes to speak as we speak, and to listen by watching the lips. In Berlin I saw for the first time an oral lecture given to deaf mutes and heard them recite verses. This was an immense step in advance of the method of the Abbé de l'Epée.

This teaching was carried to great perfection in Zurich. My mother, who was passionately fond of Kolya, determined to settle with him for a few years in Zurich in order to send him to the school.

The child was gifted with exceptional abilities: the everlasting stillness about him, by concentrating his lively, impulsive character, assisted his development in a wonderful way, and at the same time encouraged an exceptional power of plastic observation. His eyes glowed with intelligence and interest; at five years old he could imitate every one who came to see us with intentional caricature, and with such comic mimicry that no one could help laughing.

In six months he had made great progress at the school. His voice was *voilée*; he scarcely marked the accent, but already spoke German very fairly and understood everything said to him slowly; nothing could have been better. On my way through Zurich I thanked the director and council of the school and paid them various civilities, and they did the same to me.

But after I had gone away the elders of the town of Zurich learnt that I was not a Russian count but a Russian *émigré*, and, moreover, friendly with the radical party, which they could not endure; and, what is more, with socialists, whom they hated; and, what was worse than all that put together, that I was not a religious man and openly admitted the fact. This last they learned from an awful little book, *Vom andern Ufer*, which had, as though to mock them, come out under their very noses with the imprint of the best Zurich firm of publishers. On learning this their conscience troubled them at the thought that they were giving an education to the son of a man who believed neither in Luther nor in Loyola, and they set to work to find means to get rid of him. Since Providence was particularly interested in the question, it at once showed them the way. The town police suddenly demanded the *child's passport;* I answered from Paris, supposing that it was a simple formality, that Kolya certainly was my son, that his name was on my passport, but that I could not obtain a separate one for him from the Russian Embassy, because I was not on the best of terms with them. The police were not satisfied, and threatened to turn the child out of the school and out of the town. I spoke of this in Paris; one of my acquaintances published a paragraph about it in the *National,* Put to shame by publicity, the police said that they did not insist on turning the child out, but only on the payment of an insignificant sum of money as a guarantee that the child was himself and not somebody else. What guarantee is there in a few hundred francs? On the other hand, if my mother and I had not had the money, the child would have been turned out. (I asked them about that through the *National.*) And this could happen in the nineteenth century in free Switzerland! After what had taken place I disliked the idea of leaving the child in this den of asses.

But what was to be done? The best teacher in the institution, a young man who devoted himself enthusiastically to the training of deaf mutes, a man of a thorough university education, luckily did not share the views of the police Sanhedrin, and was a great admirer of the very book which had so stirred the wrath of the pious police-constables of the canton of Zurich. We suggested to him that he should leave the school, enter my mother's household as tutor, and go with her to Italy. He of course consented. The authorities of the school were furious, but could do nothing. My mother prepared to go with Kolya and with this young man, Spielmann, to Nice. Before leaving she sent for her deposit; it was not given to her, on the pretext that Kolya was still in

Switzerland. I wrote from Nice. The Zurich police demanded proofs that Kolya had the legal right to live in Piedmont.

This was too much, and I wrote the following letter to the president of the Zurich canton:—

'M. LE PRÉSIDENT,—In 1849, I Placed My Son, aged five years, in the Zurich School for the Deaf and Dumb. A few months later the Zurich police asked my mother for his passport. Since among us passports are not required for newborn babies or for children going to school, my son had not a separate one but was entered upon mine. This explanation did not satisfy the Zurich police. They demanded a deposit. My mother, fearing that the child who had brought down upon himself such dangerous suspicions on the part of the Zurich police would be expelled, paid it.

'In August 1850, my mother, wishing to leave Switzerland, asked for the deposit, but the Zurich police did not return it; they wished to ascertain first that the child had actually left the canton. On reaching Nice my mother asked Messieurs Avigdor and Schultgess to receive the money, giving them a proof that we, and above all my suspicious six-year- old son, were in Nice and not in Zurich. The Zurich police, keeping a tight hold on the deposit money, then demanded another certificate, to be witnessed by the police here, "that my son is officially permitted to live in Piedmont" (*que l'enfant est officiellement toléré*). M. Schultgess communicated this to M. Avigdor.

'Seeing this eccentric curiosity on the part of the Zurich police I refused M. Avigdor's proposal to send a new certificate, which he very graciously offered to take for me himself. I did not want to afford the Zurich police this satisfaction, since, for all the dignity of its position, it has no right to constitute itself an international police, and because its demand is insulting not only to me but to Piedmont.

'The Sardinian Government, M. le Président, is a free and civilised one; how is it possible that it should not permit (*ne tolérera pas*) an invalid child of six years old to live in Piedmont? I am really at a loss as to how I am to regard this demand of the Zurich police, whether as a strange joke or as the result of a partiality for deposits in general.

'Presenting this affair for your scrutiny, M. le Président, I beg you as a special favour, in case of another refusal, to explain the proceeding, which is so curious and interesting that I do not think I shall be justified in concealing it from the knowledge of the public.

'I have written again to M. Schultgess to receive the money, and I can confidently assure you that neither my mother nor myself nor the child who is the object of suspicion have the smallest inclination to return to Zurich after these unpleasant attentions from the police. There is not the faintest risk of it.'

'NICE, *September 9, 1850.*'

I need hardly say that after that the police of the town of Zurich, in spite of their œcumenical pretensions, paid the deposit.

Except my Swiss naturalisation, I would not have accepted citizenship in any European country, not even England; I disliked the idea of voluntarily becoming anybody's subject. I did not want to change a bad master for a good one, but to escape from serfdom into being a free tiller of the soil. This was only possible in two countries: America and Switzerland.

America—I greatly respect. I believe that she is destined to a great future, I know that she is now twice as near to Europe as she was; but American life is distasteful to me. It is very likely that her angular, coarse, dry elements will be welded together into something different. America has not yet settled down, she is an unfinished edifice. Labourers and workmen in their workaday clothes are dragging about beams and stones, sawing, hewing, hammering. Why should outsiders settle in it before it is dry and warm?

Moreover, America, as Garibaldi said, is the 'land for forgetting home'; let those who have no faith in their fatherland go there—they ought to get away from their graveyards. It was quite the contrary with me: the more I lost all hope of a Latin-German Europe, the more my belief in Russia revived again; but to dream of returning there while Nicholas was Tsar would have been madness.

And so there was nothing left for it but to ally myself with the free men of the Helvetian Confederation.

As early as 1849, Fazy had promised to naturalise me in Geneva, but kept putting it off; perhaps he simply did not want to add to the number of socialists in his canton. I got sick of this. I was passing through a black period, the very walls were tottering and might crumble about my head, misfortune is never far off. . . . Karl Vogt offered to write about my naturalisation to J. Schaller, who was at that time president of the Freiburg canton and leader of the radical party. But, having mentioned Vogt, I must say something about him first.

In the monotony of the shallow and slow-moving life of Germany one meets at times, as though to redeem it, sturdy, healthy families full of strength, persistence, and talent. One generation of gifted persons is followed by another more numerous, still preserving the same sturdiness of mind and body. Looking at some dingy, old-fashioned house, in a dark, narrow side-street, it is hard to believe how many have been the young lads, in a hundred years, who have come down the worn stone steps of its staircase with a wallet on their shoulder and all manner of souvenirs, made of hair or of flowers in it, followed by the blessings and tears of their mother and sisters . . . and have gone out into the world with nothing but their own strength to look to, and have become distinguished men of science, celebrated doctors, naturalists, and literary men. And the little house, covered with tiles, is filled up again in their absence by a new generation of students, eagerly pressing forward into the unknown future.

In the lack of any other there is the inheritance of example, the inheritance of the family fibre. Each one begins for himself, and knows that the time will come when his old grandmother will lead him down the worn stone staircase: the grandmother who has seen three generations into the world, washed them in the little bath, and seen them off with full confidence in them. He knows that the proud old woman is sure of him, too, sure that he will do something . . . and he invariably does do something.

Dann und wann after many years all this scattered population is in the little old home again, all the originals —grown older—of the portraits hanging in the little drawing-room, in which they are wearing students' *bérets* and are wrapped in cloaks with a Rembrandt intention on the part of the artist: then there is bustle again in the little house, the two generations get to know each other, become intimate . . . and then all go back to work again. Of course, with all this some one is bound to be in love with somebody; of course, sentimentality, tears, surprises, and sweet tarts are the inevitable accompaniment; but all that is effaced by the real, purely living poetry, full of strength and muscle such as I have rarely met with in the degenerate, rickety children of the aristocracy, and still less among the petty-bourgeois, who strictly check the number of their children in accordance with their account-book.

The ancestral home of Vogt belonged to this class of blessed ancient German families.

Vogt's father was an extremely gifted professor of medicine in Berne; his mother was one of the Vollens, that eccentric Swiss-German family which was so much talked of at one time. The Vollens were leaders of Young Germany at the period of *Tugendbunds* and *Burschenschafts*, of Karl Sand and of the political *Schwärmerei* of 1817 and 1818. One Vollen was thrown into prison for the Wartburg celebration in memory of Luther: he certainly did deliver an incendiary speech, after which he made a bonfire of Jesuitical and reactionary books and various symbols of autocracy and the Papal power. The students dreamed of making him emperor of a one and undivided Germany. His grandson, Karl Vogt, actually was one of the *vicars of the empire* in 1849. Healthy blood must have flowed in the veins of the son of the Berne professor, in the grandson of the Vollens— *au bout du compte*, everything depends on the chemical combination and the quality of the elements. Karl Vogt is not the man to dispute that with me.

In 1851 I was passing through Berne. Straight from the posting-chaise, I went to Vogt's father with a letter from his son. The elder Vogt was at the university. His wife, a hospitable, lively, and extremely intelligent old woman, met me; she received me as her son's friend, and at once took me to see his portrait. She did not expect her husband home before six o'clock; I very much wanted to see him, and came back at that time, but he had already gone to some patients for a consultation. The old lady greeted me the second time like an old friend, and led me into the dining-room, wishing me to take a glass of wine. One part of the room was filled by a large round table fixed immovably into the floor; I had heard of this table long ago from Vogt, and so was delighted to make its personal acquaintance. Its inner part moved on an axle: various dishes were placed upon it; coffee, wine, and everything wanted, such as plates, mustard, salt, so that any one could turn what he wanted to himself, ham or preserves, without troubling any one and without the aid of servants. The only thing was that it would not do to be too dreamy or to talk too much, or one might put a spoon into the sugar-basin instead of into the mustard-pot . . . if any one had turned the disc. In this large population of brothers and sisters, intimate friends and relations, in which every one was differently engaged, and had to keep to fixed hours, a common dinner in the evening was difficult to arrange. Any one who came in, and wanted something to eat, sat down to the table, twirled it to the right or twirled it to the left and managed capitally. The mother and sisters superintended, and ordered this or that to be brought in.

I could not stay with them; Fazy and Schaller, who were in Berne at the time, wanted to come and see me in the evening. I promised to visit the Vogts again if I should stay another half-day, and, after inviting the younger brother, the law student, to supper with me, went home. I felt it was out of the question to invite the old father so late, and after such a day. But about twelve o'clock the waiter, respectfully opening the door to usher him in, announced: 'Der Herr Professor Vogt.' I got up from the table and went to meet him. A rather tall old man, extremely well preserved, with a clever, expressive face, walked into the room.

'Your visit,' I said, 'is doubly welcome; I had not dared to ask you so late after your labours.'

'I did not want to let you pass through Berne without seeing you. Hearing that you had been to us twice, and that you had invited Gustav, I invited myself. I am very, very glad to see you, both from what Karl writes of you, and, flattery apart, I wanted to make the acquaintance of the author of *From the Other Shore*.'

'I thank you most truly: here is a place, please sit down with us; we are in the middle of supper: what will you take?'

'I want nothing to eat, but I will drink a glass of wine with pleasure.'

There was so much ease and freedom in his appearance, words, and movements, together with not that good-heartedness characteristic of flabby, mawkish, and sentimental people, but with that special good-heartedness we see in strong natures confident in themselves. His appearance was not the least constraint to us; on the contrary, it made everything livelier.

The conversation passed from subject to subject; everywhere and in everything he was at home, intelligent, *éveillé*, original. The talk touched on the Federal concert which had been given in the morning in the Berne Cathedral, at which all had been present except Vogt. The concert was on an immense scale; musicians and singers had come from all parts of Switzerland to take part in it. It had, of course, been a concert of sacred music. Haydn's celebrated composition had been performed with talent and understanding. The audience was attentive but cold; it walked out of the cathedral as people walk out of the morning service; I do not know how much reverence there was, but there was no enthusiasm. I experienced the same thing myself. In a moment of candour I said so to the friends with whom I had gone. Unluckily, they were orthodox, learned, ardent musicians; they fell upon me, declared I was a profane outsider who did not know how to listen to deep and serious music.

'You care for nothing but Chopin's mazurkas,' they said.

'There is no great harm in that,' I thought, but,

considering myself not a very competent judge, I held my peace.

One needs considerable courage to acknowledge impressions which run counter to the generally accepted prejudice or opinion. It was a long while before I could bring myself to say, in the presence of outsiders, that *Jerusalem Delivered* was dull, that I could not finish reading the *New Héloïse*, that *Hermann and Dorothea* was a masterly production but disgustingly tedious. I said something of the sort to Vogt, telling him what I had observed about the concert.

'Well,' he asked, 'do you like Mozart?'

'Extremely! without reservation.'

'I knew as much, for I am in complete sympathy with you. How is it possible for an awakened modern man to force himself artificially into the religious mood which would make his enjoyment of it natural and complete? There is no sacred music for us, just as there is no religious literature; for us it has only an historical interest. In Mozart, on the other hand, we hear the note of the life familiar to us, he is singing out of the fulness of feeling and passion, not praying. I remember when *Don Giovanni* and the *Nozze di Figaro* were new, what a delight they were, what a revelation of a new source of enjoyment! Mozart's music created an epoch, a revolution in men's minds, like Goethe's *Faust*, like the year 1789. We saw in his compositions the enlightened thought of the eighteenth century with its secularisation of life invading music; with Mozart the revolution and the new age have entered into art. How can we read Klopstock after *Faust*, or listen to these musical liturgies without faith?'

The old man talked at length and extraordinarily interestingly. He grew animated; twice I filled his glass, he did not refuse it, and was in no haste to drink. At last he looked at his watch: 'Bah! it's two o'clock; good-bye, I have to be with a patient at nine!'

With real affection I escorted him home.

Two years later he showed how much vigour was left in his grey head and how *real* his theories were—that is, how close to practice. A Viennese refugee, Dr. Kudlich, courted one of Vogt's daughters: the father consented to the marriage; but, all at once, the Protestant Consistory demanded the bridegroom's certificate of baptism. Of course, as an exile, he could get nothing from Austria, and he presented the sentence which had been passed upon him in his absence. The mere testimony and permission of Vogt would have been sufficient for the Consistory, but the Berne pietists, instinctively hating Vogt and all exiles, persisted. Then Vogt gathered together all his friends, the professors and various leading personages of Berne, told them the position, then called his daughter and Kudlich, took their hands, made them clasp hands, and said to those present: 'I call you, friends, to witness that I as father bless this marriage and give my daughter at her desire to this man.'

This action petrified the pious society of Switzerland; it looked with indignation and horror at the precedent created not by a hot-headed youth, nor a homeless refugee, but by an old man of irreproachable character, respected by every one.

Now let us pass from the father to the elder son.

I made his acquaintance in 1847, at Bakunin's, but we became particularly intimate during the two years of our life at Nice. He had not only a serene intelligence, but one of the serenest characters of all the men I have seen. I should reckon him a very happy man if I knew that he would not live long; but there is no counting upon fate, though she has spared him hitherto, letting him off with nothing worse than a few migraines. His realistic temperament, full of life and open to everything, has much to ensure enjoyment, everything to make dullness impossible, and almost nothing to cause inner torment, the fretting of intellectual discontent, the suffering from theoretical doubt, and disappointment in practical life over dreams that cannot be fulfilled. A passionate worshipper of the beauties of nature, an indefatigable worker in science, he did everything with extraordinary ease and success; he was not in the least a dry pedant, but an artist in his own work, he enjoyed it; a radical by temperament, a realist by constitution, and a humane man through his clear and good-heartedly ironical outlook, he lived precisely in that sphere of life to which alone Dante's words—*Qui è l' uomo felice*—apply.

He spent his life actively and carelessly, never lagging behind, but everywhere in the foremost rank. He had no fear of bitter truths, and looked as steadily at men as at polypi and medusæ, expecting nothing from either but what they could give. His researches were not superficial, but he felt no impulse to pass beyond a certain depth below which everything clear ends, and which is in truth, after a fashion, an escape from reality. He was not lured into those sloughs of despond in which men revel in their neurotic sufferings. His clear and simple attitude to life excluded from his healthy outlook the poetry of melancholy, the ecstasies and morbid humours, which we love as we do everything thrilling and pungent. His irony, as I observed, was good-natured, his mockery was light-hearted; he was the first to laugh, and from his heart, at his own jokes, with which he poisoned the ink and the beer of the pedantic professors and his parliamentary colleagues *in der Paul's Kirche*.

This living realism was the common bond of sympathy between us, though our lives and development had been so different that we disagreed about many things.

I had not and could not have the harmony and unity

that Vogt had. His education had been as regular as mine had been unsystematic; neither family continuity nor theoretical growth had ever been interrupted in him; he was carrying on the tradition of his family. His father stood beside him an example and a helper; following him, he took up the study of natural science. Among us each generation is usually at variance with the one before; there is no common moral tie between us. From my earliest years I was inevitably struggling against the outlook of every one surrounding me; I was in opposition in the nursery, because our elders, our grandfathers, were not Vollens but serf-owners and senators. When I left it, I flung myself with the same impetuosity into another struggle, and, as soon as I had finished at the university, was in prison and then in exile. My continuity of learning was destroyed by this, but it gave me another kind of training, experience of a world on the one hand wretched, and on the other hand dirty.

When I was sick of the study of this pathology, I flung myself greedily upon philosophy, for which Vogt felt an invincible aversion. When he had completed the medical course and had received his doctor's diploma, he could not bring himself to practise, saying that he had not sufficient faith in the medical hocus-pocus, and devoted himself entirely to physiology again. His work very soon attracted the attention not only of German scientists but also of the Parisian Academy of Science. He was already Professor of Comparative Anatomy in Giessen and the colleague of Liebig (with whom he afterwards carried on a furious chemico-theological controversy), when the revolutionary hurricane of 1848 tore him from his microscope and flung him into the Frankfort Parliament.

I need hardly say that he was in the most radical section, that he made speeches full of wit and daring, and exhausted the patience of the most moderate progressives, and sometimes even of the immoderate Prussian King. Being by no means a politician, he became, through his atomic weight, one of the leaders of the opposition; and when Archduke Johann, who had been a vicar of the Empire, finally threw off the mask of good-nature and popularity won by marrying the daughter of a station-master and sometimes wearing a frock-coat, Vogt and four others were elected in his place. Then the fortunes of the German revolution went rapidly downhill: the governments had attained their object, had gained time (as Metternich advised), and had no longer need to spare the parliament. Banished from Frankfort, the parliament had a brief, shadowy existence at Stuttgart under the melancholy title of *Nach-parlament*. And there the reactionaries made an end of it. There was nothing left for the vicars of the Empire but to get away as best they could from certain prison and penal servitude. . . . When he crossed the Swiss mountains Vogt shook the dust of the Frankfort assembly from off his feet, and inscribing himself in the traveller's book as 'K. Vogt, runaway vicar of the German Empire,' set to work again upon natural science with the same untroubled serenity, light-hearted temper, and unwearying industry. He came to Nice in 1850, with the object of studying marine zoophytes.

Although we started from different directions and came by different paths, we met in sober maturity in science.

Was I as consistent as Vogt—and in life, did I look at it as soberly? Now I fancy not. Though indeed I do not know whether it is good to begin with being sober; it wards off not only many calamities, but also the best moments of life. It is a difficult question which luckily is settled for each man, not by choice nor by considerations of what is best, but by constitution and circumstance. It was not that I tried to retain all sorts of inconsistent convictions, but *they remained of them-*

selves, though I was theoretically emancipated. I outlived the romanticism of revolution, the mystic belief in progress and in humanity lasted longer than other theological dogmas; but when I had outlived them, I still had left a religious belief in individuals, a faith in two or three men, a confidence in myself, in the human will. There were, of course, contradictions in this; inner contradictions lead to misfortunes, the more painful and mortifying because they are deprived of the last comfort of man, justification in his own eyes. . . .

In Nice, Vogt set to work with extraordinary zeal. . . . The calm, warm bays of the Mediterranean Sea is a rich breeding-ground for all *frutti di mare*, the water is simply full of them. At night the streaks of their phosphorescent light trail gleaming after a boat and drip from the oar, the *salpi* can be picked up with the hand or with any cup or dish. So he had no lack of material. From early morning Vogt would sit at the microscope, would watch, would draw, write, or read, and at five o'clock rush, sometimes with me, into the sea (he swam like a fish); then he would come to us to dine, and, everlastingly good-humoured, was ready for a learned discussion or for any sort of nonsense, sang killing songs, accompanying them on the piano, or told the children stones with such masterly art that they listened to him for hours without moving.

Vogt possessed an immense talent for exposition. Half in joke he delivered several lectures on 'physiology for ladies' in our house. Everything came out so living, so simple, and so artistically expressed, that all the ground he had covered before attaining this clarity was not suspected. That is the whole problem in teaching — to render science so intelligible and well assimilated as to make it speak a simple, everyday language.

There are no difficult sciences; the difficulty lies in the exposition which is not fully digested. The language of learning, a technical language with coined words, a shorthand, temporary language, is of use for students; the meaning is concealed in its algebraic formulae in order that in explaining the law the same thing may not be repeated a hundred times over. Passing through a series of scholastic methods, science has been overgrown by all this rubbish of the schools, where pedants have grown so accustomed to the monstrous jargon that they use no other, and it seems intelligible to them: in former years they even prized it as something won by hard labour and distinguished from the vulgar tongue. As we pass from students to real knowledge, props and scaffoldings become distasteful, and we look for simplicity. Who has not observed that beginners as a rule make use of many more abstruse words than those who have mastered the subject?

A second cause of obscurity in science arises from the unconscientiousness of those who teach it, shown in trying to conceal part of the truth and to avoid risky questions. Science which has any object except the knowledge of the truth is not science. It ought to have the courage of direct, open speech. No one could charge Vogt with lack of candour, with timid compromise. 'Sensitive souls' more readily reproach him with telling too directly and too simply what he holds for the truth, in direct contradiction with the generally received deception. The Christian attitude has trained us to dualism, to ideal imagery, so thoroughly that everything naturally healthy strikes us unpleasantly. Our intelligence, warped through ages, is disgusted by naked beauty, by daylight, and craves for twilight and a veil.

Many when reading Vogt are offended at his accepting the most startling consequences so readily, at his finding it so easy to sacrifice things, at his having to make no effort, at his not worrying to try to reconcile theology with biology; it is as though he had nothing to do with the former.

As a matter of fact, Vogt's temperament was such that he never had thought differently and was incapable of thinking differently; that was just where his direct realism came in. Theological objections could have for him only an historical interest; the absurdity of dualism was so clear to his simple outlook that he could not enter into serious controversy with it, just as his opponents—the theologians of chemistry and the holy fathers of physiology—cannot seriously discuss magic or astrology. Vogt brushed aside their attacks with a jest—and, unluckily, that is not enough.

The nonsense with which they answered him is the nonsense believed all the world over, and for that reason very important. The childishness of the human brain is such that it will not accept the simple truth; for vague, muddled, and incoherent minds nothing is intelligible but what is incomprehensible, what is impossible or absurd.

There is no need to go to the common herd for examples; literary and cultivated circles, legal and learned institutions, governments and revolutionaries, vie with each other in maintaining the innate senselessness of mankind. And just as seventy years ago the frigid deist Robespierre executed Anacharsis Cloots,[1] so the Wagners and their like would to-day hand Vogt over to the hangman.

The struggle is impossible; all the strength is on their side. Against a handful of scientists, naturalists, doctors, two or three thinkers and poets, stands the whole world, from Pius ix. with the Immaculate Conception to Mazzini with the Republican Iddio; from the Moscow orthodox hysterics of Slavophilism to Lieutenant-General Radowitz,

[1] A French revolutionist, one of the founders of the *culte de la raison*, beheaded in 1794.—(*Translator's Note*.)

SWISS NATURALISATION

who when he was dying bequeathed to Wagner, the professor of physiology, what it had never occurred to any one to bequeath before—the immortality of the soul, and its defence; from American spiritualists who call up the dead, to English missionary colonels who preach the Word of God to Indians on horseback at the head of their soldiers. There is nothing left for free men but the consciousness of being right, and hope in future generations.

And suppose it is proved that this senselessness, this religious mania, is the essential condition of organised society, that for men to live quietly side by side they must be driven out of their wits and terrified, that this mania is the one dodge by which history is created?

I remember a French caricature aimed at some time or other against the Fourierists with their *attraction passionnée*; it represents an ass with a stick fixed upon its back, and a wisp of hay hung on the stick so that he can see it. The donkey, thinking to reach the hay, is obliged to move forward—the hay, of course, moves too, and he follows it. Perhaps the worthy animal might progress in that way, but all the same he would be made a fool of!

I will pass now to an account of how hospitably I was received by one country when another had just turned me out for no reason whatever. Schaller promised Vogt to take steps about my naturalisation—that is, to find a commune which would consent to receive me and then to support the case in the Great Council. For naturalisation in Switzerland it is essential that some town or village commune should previously agree to accept the new citizen, a regulation quite in keeping with the self-government of each canton and each little district. The village of Châtel near Morat (Murten) agreed to receive my family into the number of its peasant families for a small money contribution to the village society. This village is not far from the lake of Murten, the neighbourhood of which was the scene of the defeat and slaying of Charles the Bold, whose unhappy death and name were so adroitly used by the Austrian censorship (and afterwards the Petersburg one) to replace the name of William Tell in Rossini's opera.

When the case came before the Great Council, two Jesuitical deputies raised their voices against me, but did nothing. One of them said that it ought to be ascertained why I was in exile, and how I had provoked the anger of Nicholas. 'Why, but that's a recommendation in itself!' somebody answered, and they all laughed. Another, from far-sighted prudence, asked for fresh guarantees that in case of my death the education and maintenance of my children would not fall on the poor commune. This son in Jesus too was satisfied by Schaller's answer. My rights of citizenship were accepted by a vast majority, and I was transformed from an upper court councillor to a peasant of the village of Châtel near Murten, *originaire de Châtel près Moral*, as the Freiburg clerk wrote on my passport.

Naturalisation, however, is no hindrance to a career in Russia. I have two illustrious examples before my eyes: Louis-Napoleon became a citizen of Thurgovie, and Alexander the Second a burgher of Darmstadt; both became emperors after their naturalisation. I am not going so far as that.

On receiving the news of the ratification of my rights, it was almost necessary for me to go and thank my new fellow-citizens and to make their acquaintance. Moreover, just at that time I had an intense craving to be alone, to look into myself, to revise the past, to discern something in the mist of the future, and I was glad of this external reason.

On the eve of my departure from Nice, I received a summons from the head of the police *di la Sicurezza publica.* He informed me that I was ordered by the Minister of the Interior to leave immediately the domains of Sardinia. This strange step on the part of the tame and evasive Sardinian Government surprised me far more than my banishment from Paris in 1850; besides, there was no sort of occasion for it.

I am told that I was indebted for it to the zeal of two or three faithful Russian subjects living in Nice, and among them it is pleasant for me to name the Minister of Justice, Panin; it was more than he could tolerate that a man who had brought upon himself the Imperial wrath of Nicholas was not only living in peace and in the same town as himself, but was actually writing articles, though aware that the Most High did not look upon this with favour. When he went to Turin, this Minister of Justice, I am told, asked the minister Azeglio, as a friend, to banish me. Azeglio's heart, probably, had some intuition that when I was learning Italian in the Krutitsky Barracks I had read his *La Disfida di Barletta*—a novel neither 'classical nor old-fashioned,' though nevertheless tedious; and so he did nothing, or perhaps he hesitated to send me out because such friendly attentions should have been preceded by the sending of a Russian ambassador, and Nicholas was still sulking over the revolutionary ideas of Charles Albert.

On the other hand, the chief of police in Nice and the ministers in Turin took advantage of the suggestion at the first opportunity. Some days before I was turned out, there was a popular demonstration in Nice, in which the boatmen and shopkeepers, carried away by the eloquence of the banker Avigdor, protested, and rather audaciously too, against the suppression of the free port, talking of the independence of the duchy of Nice, and its inalienable rights. The imposition of a light customs-duty on the whole kingdom diminished their privileges, regardless of the 'independence of the duchy of Nice,' and its rights 'inscribed on the scrolls of history.'

Avigdor, that O'Connell of the Paillon (that is the name of the dry river that runs through Nice), was thrown into prison, patrols paraded the streets at night, and so did the people, and both sang songs, the same songs too; and that was all. Need I say that neither I nor any other foreigner took any part in this domestic quarrel over tariffs and customs-duties? Nevertheless, the *Intendant* pitched upon several of the refugees as ringleaders, and among them, upon me. The ministry, wishing to set an example of salutary severity, ordered me to be turned out together with the rest.

I went to the *Intendant* (a Jesuit), and, observing to him that it was a superfluous luxury to turn a man out when he was going of himself and had his passport already viséd in his pocket, asked him what was wrong. He declared that he was as surprised as I was, and that the measure had been taken by the Ministry of the Interior without any preliminary reference to himself. At the same time, he was so extremely polite that I had no doubt in my mind that he was responsible for the whole nasty business. I reported my conversation with him to the well-known deputy in the opposition, Lorenzo Valerio, and went off to Paris.

Valerio made a savage attack upon the minister in his interpellation, and demanded the reasons for my deportation. The minister was disconcerted, denied any influence of the Russian diplomacy, threw everything upon the report of the *Intendant*, and meekly concluded by saying that if the ministry had acted too hastily and imprudently it would with pleasure alter its decision.

The opposition applauded; consequently, *de facto*, the prohibition was withdrawn, but though I wrote to the minister he made no answer. I read Valerio's speech and the answer to it in the newspapers, and resolved to go simply to Turin on the return journey from Freiburg. That I might not be refused a visa, I went without a visa; on the Swiss border of Piedmont, passports are not examined with the savage zeal of French gendarmes. In Turin I went to the Minister of the Interior: I was received by his deputy, who superintended the superior police, Count Pons de la Martino, a man well known in those parts, clever, crafty, and devoted to the Catholic party.

His reception surprised me. He said to me everything I had meant to say to him; something similar had happened to me in one of my interviews with Dubbelt, but Count PONS far outdid that.

He was a very elderly, thin, sickly-looking man of most unprepossessing appearance, with malicious, sly-looking features, rough grey hair, and a rather clerical aspect. Before I had time to say a dozen words in regard to the reason of my asking for an interview with the minister, he interrupted me with the words:—

'Why, upon my word, what doubt can there be about it?. . . Go to Nice, go to Genoa, stay here—only without the slightest *rancune* . . . it was all the doing of the *Intendant* . . . you see, we are still learning our business, we are not accustomed to legality, to constitutional order. If you had done anything contrary to the law, there is a law-court for that; then you would have no cause to complain of injustice, would you?'

'I quite agree with you, I should not.'

'Instead of that *they take* steps which cause irritation . . . and excite an uproar—and without any need whatever!'

After this speech against *himself*, he hastily snatched up a piece of paper with the ministerial imprint, and wrote: *Si permette al Sig. A. H. di ritornare a Nizza e di restarvi quanto tempo credera conviniente. Per il ministro S. Martino*—12 *Giulio* 1851. 'Here, take this to provide for all possibilities, though you may rest assured that you will never need it. I am very glad, very glad indeed, that we have settled this business with you.'

As this was equivalent, in the vulgar tongue, to 'Go, and God bless you,' I left my Pons, smiling at the thought of the face of the *Intendant* at Nice; but Providence did not favour me with the sight of it—he had been transferred.

But to return to Freiburg and its canton: when, like all mortals who have been in Freiburg, we had listened to the celebrated organ and driven over the celebrated bridge, we set off for Châtel, accompanied by a good-natured old man, the treasurer of the Freiburg canton. At Murten the prefect of police, a vigorous man and a radical, asked us to stay with him, telling us that the village elder had charged him to send word beforehand of our arrival, as he and the other householders would be very much disappointed if I came without letting them know; and they were all in the fields at work when I arrived. After walking about Morat or Murten for a couple of hours, we set off, and the prefect with us.

Near the elder's house several old peasants were awaiting us, headed by the elder himself, a tall, venerable, grey-headed, and rather bent but muscular old man. He stepped forward, took off his hat, held out his broad, strong hand to me, and saying, *'Lieber Mitbürger . . . ,'* delivered a speech of welcome in such Swiss-German that I did not understand a word of it. It was possible to make a rough guess at what he could say to me, and therefore, reflecting that if I concealed that I did not understand him, he would conceal that he did not understand me, I boldly answered him:—

'Dear Citizen Elder, and dear fellow-citizens of Châtel! I am come to thank you for giving a refuge to me and my children in your commune, and putting an end to my homeless wandering. I, dear citizens, did not leave my native land to seek another; I loved the Russian people with my whole heart, but I left Russia because I could not be a dumb, inactive witness of oppression. I left it after exile pursued by the ferocious despotism of Nicholas. His powerful arm, which has reached me everywhere where there is a king or a lord, is not long enough to reach me in your commune! Without fear I put myself under your protection, as in a haven where I can always find peace. You, citizens of Châtel, you a handful of men, you taking me amongst you, have been able to arrest the lifted hand of the Russian Emperor armed with a million bayonets. You are stronger than he! But you are strong only through the free republican institutions that have been yours for ages! With pride I enter into your commune, and hurrah for the Helvetian Republic!'

'*Dem neuen Bürger hoch*! *Es lebe der neue Bürger*!' answered the old men, and warmly pressed my hand; I myself was somewhat agitated!

The village elder invited us into his house.

We went in, and sat down on benches at a long table on which there was bread and cheese. Two peasants dragged in a bottle of terrific size, larger than those famous bottles which are snugly stored away for whole winters in our old-fashioned houses in some corner by the stove, filled with home-made liqueurs and cordials. This bottle was covered with basket-work, and full of white wine. The village elder told us that this was the local wine, but that it was very old, that he remembered the bottle for over thirty years, and that this wine was only drunk on very special occasions. All the peasants sat down with us to the table except two, who were busy with the cathedral-like bottle. They poured wine from it into a large jug, and the village elder poured it from the jug into the glasses; there was a glass before every peasant, but he brought me a grand crystal goblet, observing as he did so to the treasurer and the prefect: 'You must excuse me on this occasion; to-day we offer the cup of honour to our fellow-citizen; you are old friends.'

While the elder was filling the glasses, I noticed that one of the company, dressed not quite like a peasant, was very restless, mopping his face, turning crimson, and seeming ill at ease; when the village elder proposed they should drink my health, he leaped on his feet with the courage of despair, and addressing me began a speech. 'That,' the elder whispered in my ear with a significant air, 'is the citizen teacher in our school. 'I stood up.

The teacher spoke not Swiss but German, and not simply but on the model of particularly famous orators and writers: he referred both to William Tell and to Charles the Bold (what would the Austrian and Russian stage censorship have done?—perhaps they would have called them William the Bold and Charles Tell), and at the same time did not forget the less new than expressive comparison of bondage with a gilded cage from which the bird will still strive to be free. Nicholas caught it hot from him; he ranked him with very disreputable persons from Roman history. I almost interrupted him at that point to say, 'Don't insult the dead,' but, as though from a presentiment that Nicholas would soon be among them, held my peace.

The peasants listened to him, craning their wrinkled sunburnt necks and putting up their hands to their ears like sunshades; the treasurer had a little nap, and to conceal the fact was the first to praise the orator.

Meanwhile the village elder was not sitting idle, but zealously filling up glasses and preparing toasts like the most practised master of the ceremonies—'To the

Confederation!' 'To Freiburg and its radical government!' 'To President Schaller!'

'To my kindly fellow-citizens of Châtel!' I proposed at last, feeling that the wine, though its taste was not strong, was far from weak in its effects. All rose to their feet. . . . The elder said: 'No, no, *lieber Mitbürger*, a a full glass, as we drank a full glass to you.' My venerable friends were becoming expansive, the wine was warming them up. . . . 'Bring your children,' said one. 'Yes, yes, 'others chimed in; 'let them see how we live: we are simple people, they will learn no harm from us, and we shall have a look at them.'

'Certainly!' I answered, 'certainly!'

Then the village elder began apologising for the poorness of their reception, saying that it was all the treasurer's fault, that he ought to have let them know two days beforehand, that then it would have been very different, they might have provided a band, and that they would have welcomed and escorted me with gunshots. I very nearly said to him, *à la* Louis-Philippe: 'After all, what has happened? — only one peasant more in Châtel.'

We parted great friends. I was rather surprised that I had seen not one woman or girl, nor even one young man. It was a working day, however. It is noteworthy, too, that to a festivity so unusual for them the pastor had not been invited.

I felt greatly indebted to them for that. The pastor would certainly have spoilt it all; he would have delivered a stupid sermon, and with his decorous propriety would have been like a fly in a glass of wine which must be removed before you can drink with pleasure.

At last we were seated again in the treasurer's little carriage, or rather chaise; we took the prefect to Morat, and set off for Freiburg. The sky was covered with storm-clouds; I felt sleepy and giddy. I tried not to go to sleep: surely it cannot be their wine? I wondered with some contempt for myself. . . . The treasurer smiled slyly, and then himself began dozing; drops of rain began falling, I covered myself with my overcoat, must have fallen asleep . . . then woke up at the contact of cold water. . . . The rain was pouring in bucketsful, black storm-clouds seemed striking fire from craggy heights, far-away peals of thunder came rolling over the mountains. The treasurer was standing in the hall laughing loudly and talking with the host of the Zöringer Hof.

'Well,' the host asked me, 'it seems our simple peasant wine is very different from the French, eh?'

'Why, can we have arrived?' I asked, emerging drenched from the chaise.

'There's nothing strange in that,' observed the treasurer; 'what is strange is that you have slept through a storm such as we have not had for a long time. Did you really hear nothing?'

'Nothing!'

Afterwards I found out that the simple Swiss wines, which do not taste at all strong, acquire great strength with age and act powerfully on those unaccustomed to them. The treasurer avoided telling me this on purpose; besides, even if he had told me I could not have refused the peasants' good-natured hospitality and their toasts, still less could I have ceremoniously moistened my lips and made difficulties. That I did the right thing is proved by the fact that when a year later, on my way from Berne to Geneva, I met the prefect of Morat at the station, he said to me: 'Do you know how you acquired great popularity among our Châtel peasants?' 'No!' 'To this day they tell with proud self-satisfaction how their new fellow-citizen, after drinking their wine, slept through a storm and drove in a downpour of rain from Morat to Freiburg, knowing nothing about it.'

And so that is how I became a free citizen of the Swiss Confederation and got drunk on Châtel wine.[1]

[1] I cannot forbear adding that I had to correct this very page at Freiburg, and in the same Zöringer Hof. And the host was still the same, looking like a regular innkeeper, and the dining-room in which I sat with Sazonov in 1851 was the same, and the room in which a year later I wrote my will, making Karl Vogt my executor: and this page brings back to me so many details.

Fifteen years!

Unconsciously, unaccountably, one is seized with terror. . . .

14th October 1866.—(*Author's Note.*)

Chapter 41

P. J. Proudhon—Publication of the 'Voix du Peuple'
—Correspondence—The Significance of Proudhon

AFTER the June barricades had fallen the printing-presses fell too. The panic-stricken journalists held their peace. Only old Lamennais rose up like the gloomy shadow of a judge, cursed Cavaignac—the Duc d'Alba of the June days—and his companions, and gloomily told the people: 'And you be silent: you are too poor to have the right to speak!'

When the first alarm at this state of siege was over and the newspapers began coming to life again, they found themselves confronted, not with violence, but with a perfect arsenal of legal quibbles and judicial traps. The old baiting, *par force*, of editors, the process in which the ministers of Louis-Philippe so distinguished themselves, began again. Its method was to exhaust the guaranteed fund by a series of lawsuits invariably ending in prison and a money fine. The fine is paid out of the fund; until that is made up again, the paper cannot be published; as soon as it is made good, there is a new lawsuit. This game is always successful, for the legal authorities are always hand in glove with the government in all political prosecutions.

At first Ledru-Rollin, and afterwards Colonel Frappoli[1] as the representative of Mazzini's party, contributed large sums of money, but could not save *La Réforme*. All the more outspoken organs of socialism and republicanism were destroyed by this method. Among these, and at the very beginning, was Proudhon's *Le*

---

[1] Frappoli, Ludovico (1815-1878), an Italian politician who took part in the revolutionary movement of 1848, was a partisan of Garibaldi's, and always on the extreme left in the Italian Parliament. He reintroduced Freemasonry into Italy.—(*Translator's Note.*)

Représentant du Peuple, and later on *Le Peuple*. Before one prosecution was over, another began.

One of the editors—it was Duchesne, I remember—was three times brought out of prison into the law-courts on fresh charges; and every time was again sentenced to prison and a fine. When on the last occasion before the ruin of the paper the verdict was declared, he said to the prosecutor: *'L' addition, s'il vous plaît!'* As a matter of fact, it amounted to ten years of prison and fifty thousand francs fine.

Proudhon was on his trial when his newspaper was suppressed on the 13th of June. The National Guards burst into his printing-office on that day, broke the printing-press, dispersed the type, as though to assert, in the name of the armed bourgeois, that the period of the utmost violence and police tyranny had come in France.

The irrepressible gladiator, the stubborn Besançon peasant, would not lay down his arms, but at once contrived to publish a new journal, *La Voix du Peuple*. It was necessary to obtain twenty-four thousand francs for the guarantee fund. E. Girardin would have been ready to give it, but Proudhon did not want to be dependent on him, and Sazonov suggested that I should contribute the money. I owed a great deal to Proudhon in my intellectual development, and, after a little consideration, I consented, though I knew that the fund would soon be gone.

Reading Proudhon, like reading Hegel, cultivates a special faculty, sharpens the weapon, and furnishes not results but methods. Proudhon is pre-eminently the dialectician, the controversialist of social questions. The French seek experimental solutions in him, and, finding no plans of the phalanstery nor of the Icarian community, shrug their shoulders and lay the book aside.

It is Proudhon's own fault, of course, for having put as the motto on his *Contradictions*: '*Destruo et œdificabo*'; his strength lay not in construction but in criticism of the existing state of things. But this mistake has been made from time immemorial by all who have broken down what was old. Man dislikes mere destruction: when he sets to work to break things down, he is unconsciously haunted by some ideal of future construction, though sometimes this is like the song of a mason as he pulls down a wall.

In the greater number of sociological works the ideals advocated, which almost always are either unattainable at present or lead to some one-sided solution, are of little consequence; what is of importance is that, in working up to them, the *problem* is stated. Socialism has to deal not only with the solutions of the old empirically religious tradition, but also with the conclusions of one-sided science; not only with the juridical deductions resting on traditional legislation, but also with the deductions of political economy. It is confronted with the rational system of the epoch of guarantees and of the bourgeois economic regime, as its immediate predecessor, just as political economy is related to the theoretically feudal state.

It is in this denial, this destruction of the old social tradition, that the great power of Proudhon lies; he is as much the poet of dialectics as Hegel is, with the difference that the one rests on the calm heights of the philosophic movement, while the other is thrust into the turmoil of popular passions and the hand-to-hand struggle of parties.

Proudhon is the first of a new set of French thinkers. His works mark a transition period, not only in the history of socialism but also in the history of French logic. He has more strength and freedom in his argumentative tenacity than the most talented of his fellow-countrymen. Intelligent and single-minded men like Pierre Leroux[1] and Considérant[2] do not grasp either his point of departure or his method. They are accustomed to play with ideas as with marked cards, to walk in a certain attire along the beaten track to familiar spots. Proudhon often presses on without hesitating to crush anything on the way, without fearing to destroy or to go too far.

He has none of that sensitiveness, that rhetorical revolutionary chastity, which takes the place of Protestant pietism in the French . . . that is why he remains a solitary figure among his own people, rather alarming than convincing them.

People say that Proudhon has a German mind. That is not true; on the contrary, his mind is absolutely French: he has that racial Gallo-Frankish genius which appears in Rabelais, in Montaigne, in Voltaire, and in Diderot . . . even in Pascal. It is only that he has assimilated Hegel's dialectical method, as he has assimilated all the methods of Catholic controversy. But neither the Hegelian philosophy nor the Catholic theology furnished the content nor the character of his writings; for him these were only weapons with which he tested his subject, and these weapons he mastered and adapted to his own purposes just as he adapted the French language to his powerful and vigorous thought. Such men stand much too firmly on their own feet to be dominated by anything or to allow themselves to be caught in any net.

'I like your system very much,' an English tourist said to Proudhon.

'But I have no system,' Proudhon answered with annoyance, and he was right.

It is just that that puzzles his fellow-countrymen,

---

[1] Leroux, Pierre (1797-1871), a prominent follower of St. Simon.
[2] Considérant, Victor (1808-1893), a philosopher and political economist, advocate of Fourierism.—(*Translator's Notes*.)

accustomed to a moral at the end of the fable, to systematic formulas, to classification, to abstract binding precepts.

Proudhon sits by a sick man's bedside and tells him that he is in a very bad way for this reason and for that reason. You do not help a dying man by constructing an ideal theory of how he might be perfectly well if he were not ill, or by suggesting remedies, excellent in themselves, which he cannot take or which are not to be had.

The external signs and manifestations of the financial world serve him, just as the teeth of animals served Cuvier as a ladder by which he descends into the mysteries of social life; by means of them he studies the forces that are dragging the sick body on to decomposition. If after every such observation he proclaims a new victory for death, is that his fault? In this case there are no relatives whom one is afraid to alarm: we are ourselves dying this death. The crowd shouts with indignation: 'Remedies! Remedies! Or don't speak of the disease!' But why not speak of it? It is only under despotic governments that we are forbidden to speak of crops failing, of epidemic diseases, of the numbers slain in war. The remedy, it seems, is not easily to be found; they have made plenty of experiments on France since the days of the copious blood-letting of 1793; they have tried victories and violent exercise with her. Setting her marching to Egypt and to Russia, they have tried parliamentarianism and *agiotage,* a little republic and a little Napoleon—and has anything done any good? Proudhon himself once tested his pathology and came to grief over the People's Bank—though in itself his idea was good. Unluckily, he did not believe in magical formulas, or else he would have been singing out to everybody: 'League of Nations! League of Nations! Universal Republic! Brotherhood of all the World! *Grande Armée de la Démocratie!*' He did not use these phrases, he did not spare the Old Believers of the revolution, and for that reason the French look upon him as an egoist, as an individualist, almost as a renegade and a traitor.

I remember Proudhon's works, from his reflections *On Property* to his *Financial Guidance*; many of his ideas have changed—a man could hardly live through a period like ours and whistle the same duet in A minor like Platon Mihailovitch in *Woe from Wit*. What is so startling in the midst of these changes is the inner unity that holds them all together, from the essays written as a school task in the Besançon Academy to the *carmen horrendum* of Stock Exchange depravity, which has lately appeared; the same order of thought developing, changing in form, reflecting events, runs through the *Contradictions of Political Economy*, and through his *Confessions,* and through his *Journal*.

Inertia of thought is characteristic of religion and doctrinarianism; they presuppose a persistent narrowness, a finished limitedness, living apart or in its own narrow circle, rejecting everything new that life offers . . . or at any rate not troubling about it. The real truth must be found under the influence of events, must reflect them, while remaining true to itself, or it would not be the living *truth,* but an eternal truth, at rest from the agitations of this world in the deadly stillness of holy stagnation.[1] Where, and in what case, I have sometimes asked, was Proudhon false to the fundamental principles of his philosophy? I have always been answered that he was so in his political mistakes, his blunders in revolutionary diplomacy. For his political mistakes he was, of course, responsible as a journalist; but even in that case he was not false to himself: on the contrary, some of

[1] In Stuart Mill's new book *On Liberty*, he uses an excellent expression in regard to these truths settled once and for ever: 'the deep slumber of a decided opinion.'—(*Author's Note*.)

his mistakes were due to his believing more in his principles than in the party to which he, against his own will, belonged, with which he had nothing in common, and with which he was only associated by hatred for a common foe.

It was not in political activity that his real strength lay; it was not there that he found the basis of the thought which he clad in all the armour of his arguments. On the contrary, it is everywhere clearly evident that politics in the sense of the old liberalism and constitutional republicanism were, in his eyes, of secondary importance, as something half over, passing. He was not greatly concerned over political questions, and was ready to make compromises because he did not attach special significance to the forms, which in his view were not essential. All who have abandoned the Christian point of view take up a similar attitude to religious questions. I may recognise that the constitutional religion of Protestantism is somewhat freer than the autocracy of Catholicism, but I cannot take to heart any questions in regard to church and denomination; probably I should make mistakes, and concessions in consequence, which the most ordinary graduate in divinity or parish priest would avoid.

Doubtless, there was no place for Proudhon in the National Assembly as it was constituted, and his individuality was lost in that den of petty-bourgeois. In the *Confessions of a Revolutionary* Proudhon tells us that he was completely at a loss in the Assembly. And indeed, what could be done there by a man who said of Marrast's constitution, that sour fruit of seven months' work of seven hundred heads: 'I give my vote against your constitution, not only because it's bad, but because it's a constitution.'

The parliamentary dregs greeted one of his speeches: 'The speech to the *Moniteur*, the orator to the madhouse!' I do not think that in the memory of man there had ever been such parliamentary scenes from the days when the Archbishop of Alexandria brought to the Œcumenical Councils monks armed with clubs in the name of the Virgin, up to the days of the Washington senators who proved the benefits of slavery on each other with sticks.

But even there Proudhon succeeded in rising to his full height, and in the midst of the wrangling displayed a brilliance that will not be forgotten.

Thiers in rejecting Proudhon's financial scheme made some insinuations as to the moral depravity of the men who advocated such theories. Proudhon mounted the tribune, and with his stooping figure and his menacing air of a sturdy field-worker said to the smiling old creature: 'Speak of finance, but do not speak of morality: I may take that as personal, I have told you so in committee. If you will persist, I—I will not challenge you to a duel' (Thiers smiled); 'no, your death is not enough for me—that would prove nothing. I challenge you to another sort of contest. Here from this tribune I will tell the whole story of my life, fact by fact—any one can pull me up if I forget or omit anything; and then let my opponent tell the story of his!' The eyes of all were turned upon Thiers; he sat scowling, with no trace of a smile on his face, and made no answer either.

A hostile Chamber sank into silence while Proudhon, looking contemptuously at the champions of religion and the family, came down from the platform. That was where his strength lay. In his words one hears clearly the language of the new world with its new standards and its new penalties.

From the revolution of February Proudhon foretold what France had come to; to a thousand different tunes he kept repeating, 'Beware, do not trifle; "this is not Catiline at your gates, but death."' The French shrugged their shoulders. The skull, the scythe, the hour-glass—all the trappings of death—were not to be seen. How could it be death?—it 'was a momentary defeat, the after-dinner nap of a great people!' At last many people discerned that things were in a bad way. Proudhon was less downcast than others, less panic-stricken, because he had foreseen it; then he was accused of callousness and even of having invited disaster. They say the Chinese Emperor pulls the Court star-gazer's hair every year when the latter announces that the days are beginning to draw in.

The genius of Proudhon is really antipathetic to the rhetorical French, his language is offensive to them. The revolution developed its own special puritanism, narrow and intolerant, its own obligatory jargon; and patriots resent everything not written in the official form, just as the Russian judges do. Their criticism stops short' at their symbolic books, such as the *Contrat Social* and *Declaration of the Rights of Man*. Men of faith, they hate analysis and doubt; conspirators, they do everything in common and turn everything into a party question. An independent mind is hateful to them as a disturber of discipline, they dislike original ideas even in the past. Louis Blanc is almost vexed with the eccentric genius of Montaigne.[1] It is upon this Gallic feeling, which seeks to subject individuality to the herd, that their partiality for *equalising*, for the dead level of military discipline, for centralisation—that is, for despotism—is based.

The blasphemy of the French, their sweeping judgments, are more due to mischief, caprice, the pleasure of mockery, than the craving for analysis, than the scepticism that frets the soul. The Frenchman has an endless number of little prejudices, minute religions, and these he will defend with the persistence of a Don

[1] *Histoire de la Rèvolution Francaise.*

Quixote, the pertinacity of a *raskolnik*. That is why they cannot forgive Montaigne or Proudhon for their free-thinking and lack of reverence for generally accepted idols. Like the Petersburg censorship, they permit a jest at a titular councillor, but you must not touch a privy councillor. In 1850 E. Girardin printed in the *Presse* a bold and new idea, that the principles of law are not eternal but go on evolving in different forms with the development of history. What an uproar this article excited! The campaign of abuse, of cries of horror, of charges of immorality begun by the *Gazette* of France was kept up for months.

To assist in restoring such an organ as the *Peuple* was worth a sacrifice; I wrote to Sazonov and Hoetsky that I was ready to supply the guarantee fund.

Until then I had not seen much of Proudhon; I had met him twice at the lodgings of Bakunin, with whom he was very intimate. Bakunin was living at that time with A. Reihel in an extremely modest lodging at the other side of the Seine in the Rue de Bourgogne. Proudhon often went there to listen to Reihel's Beethoven and Bakunin's Hegel—the philosophical discussions lasted longer than the symphonies. They reminded me of the famous all-night arguments of Bakunin with Homyakov at Tchaadayev's and at Madame Yelagin's, also over Hegel. In 1847, Karl Vogt, who also lived in the Rue de Bourgogne, and often visited Reihel and Bakunin, was bored one evening with listening to the endless discussions on phenomenology, and went home to bed. Next morning he went round for Reihel, as they were to go to the Jardin des Plantes together; he was surprised to hear conversation in Bakunin's study at that early hour. He opened the door—Proudhon and Bakunin were sitting in the same places before the burnt-out embers in the fireplace, finishing their brief summing-up of the argument begun overnight.

At first, afraid of the humble rôle of our fellow-countrymen, of being patronised by great men, I did not try to become more intimate even with Proudhon himself, and I believe I was not altogether wrong there. Proudhon's letter in answer to mine was courteous, but cold and somewhat reserved.

I wanted to show him from the very first that he was not dealing with a mad *prince russe* who was giving the money from revolutionary dilettantism, and still more from ostentation, nor with an orthodox admirer of French journalists, deeply grateful for their accepting twenty-four thousand francs from him, nor with a dull-witted *bailleur de* fonds who imagines that providing the guarantee funds for such a paper as the *Voix du Peuple* is a serious business investment. I wanted to show him that I knew very well what I was doing, that I had my own definite aim in it, and so wanted to have a definite influence on the paper. While I accepted unconditionally all that he wrote about money, I demanded in the first place the right to insert articles, my own and other people's; secondly, the right to superintend all the foreign part, to recommend editors, correspondents, and so on for it, and to insist on payment for the latter for articles inserted. This last may seem strange, but I can confidently assert that the *National* and the *Réforme* would open their eyes with astonishment if any foreigner ventured to ask to be paid for an article. They would take it for impudence or madness, as though for a foreigner to see himself in print in a Parisian paper were not

'Lohn der reichlich lohnet.'

Proudhon agreed to my conditions, but still they made him wince. This is what he wrote to me in Geneva on the 29th of August 1849: 'And so the thing is settled: under my general direction you have a share in the editorship of the paper; your articles must be accepted with *no restriction*, except that to which the editors are bound by respect for their *own opinions* and fear of legal responsibility. Agreed in ideas, we can only differ in deductions; as regards the criticism of foreign events, we leave that entirely to you. You and we are missionaries of one idea. You will see our line in general discussion, and you will have to support it: I am sure I shall never have to *correct your views*; I should regard that as the greatest calamity. I tell you frankly, the whole success of the paper depends on our agreement. The democratic and social question must be raised to the level of an undertaking by a European League. To presuppose that we shall not agree means to assume that we have not the essential conditions for publishing the paper, and that *we had better be silent.*'

To this severe missive I replied by the despatch of twenty-four thousand francs and a long letter, quite friendly, but firm. I told him how completely I agreed with him theoretically, adding that, like a true Scythian, I saw with joy that the old world was falling into ruins, and believed that it was our mission to announce to it its speedy end. '*Your fellow-countrymen are far from sharing these ideas.* I know one free Frenchman —that is you. Your revolutionists are conservatives. They are Christians without recognising it, and monarchists fighting for a republic. You alone have raised the question of negation and revolution to a scientific level, and you have been the first to tell France that there is no salvation for the edifice that is crumbling from within, and that there is nothing worth saving from it; that its very conceptions of freedom and revolution are saturated with conservatism and reaction. As a matter of fact, the political republicans are but one of the variations on the constitutional tune of which Guizot, Odilon Barrot, and the rest play their several versions. This is the view that should be followed in the analysis of the latest European events, in attacking reaction, Catholicism, monarchism, not in the ranks of our enemies—that is extremely easy—but in our own camp. We must unmask the mutual guarantees existing between the democrats and the powers that be. Since we are not afraid to attack the victors, let us not from false sentimentality be afraid to attack the vanquished also.

'I am thoroughly convinced that if the inquisition of the republic does not kill our newspaper, it will be the best newspaper in Europe.'

I think that even now. But how Proudhon and I could imagine that Napoleon's government—they never stood on ceremony—would put up with a paper like that, it is difficult to explain.

Proudhon was pleased with my letter, and wrote to me on the 15th of December from the Conciergerie: 'I am very glad to have been associated with you in the same work. I, too, wrote something in the nature of a philosophy[1] under the title of the *Confessions of a Revolutionary*. You will not perhaps find in it the *verve barbare* to which you have been trained by German philosophy. Do not forget that I am writing for the French, who, for all their revolutionary ardour, are, it must be confessed, far inferior to their rôle. However limited my view may be, it is a hundred thousand times higher than the loftiest heights of our journalistic, academic, and literary world. I have enough in me to be a giant among them for another ten years.

'I completely share your opinion of the so-called republicans; of course, they are only one species of the genus doctrinaires. As regards these questions there is no need to convince each other; you will find in me and my colleagues men who go hand in hand with you. . . .

'I too think a peaceful methodical advance by imperceptible transitions, as the political economists and

[1] I had then published *Vom andern Ufer*.—(*Author's Note*.)

philosophical historians would have it, is no longer possible for the revolution; we must make terrible leaps. But as journalists foreseeing the coming catastrophe, it is not for us to present it as something inevitable and just, or we shall be hated and kicked out; and we have got to live. . . .'

The paper was a wonderful success. Proudhon from his prison cell conducted his orchestra in masterly fashion. His articles were full of originality, fire, and that irritability which prison inflames.

'What are you, *M. le President*?' he writes in one article, speaking of Napoleon; 'tell me—man, woman, hemaphrodite, beast, or fish?' And we still imagined that such a paper might be kept going!

The subscribers were not numerous, but the street sales were large; thirty-five thousand to forty thousand were sold per day. The circulation of particularly attractive numbers—for instance, of those in which Proudhon's articles appeared—was even larger; fifty thousand to sixty thousand were printed, and often on the following day copies were being sold for a franc instead of a sou.[1]

But for all that, by the 1st of March—that is, in six months' time—not only was there no cash in hand, but already part of the guarantee fund had gone in payment of fines. Ruin was inevitable; Proudhon hastened it considerably. This was how it happened. On one occasion at his rooms in Ste. Pélagie I found D'Alton-Shee and two of the editors. D'Alton-Shee, that peer of France who scandalised Pacquier and frightened all the peers by answering from the platform the question, 'Why, are you not a Catholic?' 'No! and what's more, I am not a Christian at all, and I don't know whether

[1] My answer to the speech of Donozo Cortes, of which fifty thousand copies were printed, was all sold out, and when two or three days later I asked for a few copies for myself, they had to be bought through the bookshops.—(*Author's Note*.)

I am a deist.' He was saying to Proudhon that the last numbers of the *Voix du Peuple* were feeble: Proudhon was looking through them and growing more and more morose; then, thoroughly incensed, he turned to the editors: 'What is the meaning of it? You take advantage of my being in prison, and go to sleep there in the office. No, gentlemen: if you go on like this I will refuse to have anything to do with the paper, and will publish the grounds for my refusal. I don't want my name to be dragged in the mud; you need some one to stand behind you and overlook every line. The public takes this for my newspaper: no, I must put a stop to this. To-morrow I will send an article to efface the ill effects of your scribbling, and I will show how I understand what ought to be the spirit of my paper.'

Seeing his irritation, it might well be anticipated that the article would not be the most moderate, but he surpassed our expectations: his *Vive l'Empereur!* was a rhapsody of irony—malignant, terrible irony.

In addition to a new action against the paper, the government revenged itself on Proudhon in its own way. He was transferred to a horrible room—that is, given a far worse one than before: the window was half boarded up so that nothing could be seen but the sky; no one was admitted to see him, and a special guard was put at the door. And these measures, unseemly for the correction of a naughty boy of sixteen, were taken seven years ago against one of the greatest thinkers of our age. Men have grown no wiser since the days of Socrates, no wiser since the days of Galileo; they have only become more petty. This disrespect for genius, however, is a new phenomenon that has reappeared during the last ten years. From the time of the Renaissance talent has to some extent become a protection; neither Spinoza nor Lessing was shut in a dark room or stood in a corner. Such men are sometimes persecuted and killed, but they are not humiliated in trivial ways; they are sent to the scaffold, but not to the workhouse.

Bourgeois imperial France is fond of equality.

Though persecuted, Proudhon still struggled in his chains; he still made an effort to bring out the *Voix du Peuple* in 1850; but that attempt was soon crushed. My guarantee money had been seized to the last farthing; the one man in France who still had something to say had no choice but to be silent.

The last time I saw Proudhon in Ste. Pélagie, I was being turned out of France, while he still had two years of prison. We parted gloomily; there was no trace of hope in the near future. Proudhon maintained a concentrated silence, whilst I was boiling with vexation; we both had many thoughts in our minds, but no desire to speak.

I had heard a great deal of his roughness, *rudesse,* and intolerance; I never had any experience of it in my own case. What soft people call his harshness was the tense muscle of the fighter; his scowling brow showed only the intense workings of his mind: in his anger he reminded me of a wrathful Luther or of Cromwell jeering at an opponent. He knew that I understood him, and, knowing, too, how few did understand him, appreciated it. He knew that he was considered an undemonstrative man; and hearing from Michelet of the unhappy death of my mother and Kolya, he wrote to me from Ste. Pelagie, among other things: 'Is it possible that fate should attack us on that side too? I cannot get over the shock of this terrible accident. I love you, and carry your image deep here in this heart which so many think is of stone.'

After that I did not see him:[1] in 1851, when, thanks to Léon Faucher, I visited Paris for a few days, he had been sent away to some central prison. A year later,

[1] After this was written I met him again in Brussels.—(*Author's Note.*)

when I was passing through Paris in secret, Proudhon was ill at Besançon.

Proudhon had his weak spot, and there he was incorrigible; there the limit of his character was reached, and, as is always the case, beyond it he was a conservative and a follower of tradition. I am speaking of his views of family life, and of the significance of woman in general. 'How lucky is our friend N.!' Proudhon would say jestingly; 'his wife is not so stupid that she can't make a good *pot-au-feu*, and not clever enough to discuss his articles. That's all that is wanted for domestic bliss.'

In this jest Proudhon expressed, laughing, what was the serious basis of his views on woman. His conceptions of family relations were coarse and reactionary, but they betrayed, not the bourgeois element of the townsman, but rather the stubborn feeling of the rustic paterfamilias, haughtily regarding woman as an inferior, and a servant, and himself as the autocratic head of the family.

A year and a half after this was written, Proudhon published his great work on *Justice in the Church and Revolution*.

This book, for which France, sunk into barbarism, condemned him again to three years' imprisonment, I read through attentively, and I closed the third volume weighed down by gloomy thoughts.

It is a terrible . . . terrible time! . . . The atmosphere of decomposition stupefies the strongest. . . .

This 'brilliant fighter,' too, could not resist it, and was broken: in his last work I see the same controversial power, the same mighty stroke; but it brings him now to preconceived results—it is no longer free in the very fullest sense. Towards the end of the book I watched over Proudhon as Kent watched over King Lear, expecting him to recover his reason, but he talked more and more wildly—there were the same fits of intolerance, of unbridled speech, as in Lear; and at the same time *'everyinch'* betrays talent, but . . . a talent that is *'touched'* . . . and he runs with the corpse, not of a daughter but of a mother, whom he takes to be living.[1]

Latin thought, religious in its very negation, superstitious in doubt, rejecting one set of authorities in the name of another, has rarely gone further, rarely plunged more deeply *in medias res* of reality, rarely freed itself from all tangles, with such dialectic boldness and certainty as in this book. In it, not only the crude dualism of religion but the more subtle dualism of philosophy is cast off; the mind is set free not only from heavenly phantoms but from those of the earth, it passes beyond the sentimental apotheosis of humanity and the fatalism of progress, has none of the everlasting litanies of brotherhood, democracy, and progress, which are so pitifully wearisome in the midst of rancour and violence. Proudhon sacrificed the idols and the language of revolution to the true understanding of it, and put morality on its only real basis—the heart of man, recognising no idols, nothing but reason, 'if it.'

And after all that, the great iconoclast was frightened of human nature being set free; for, having freed it abstractly, he fell back again into metaphysics, endowed it with *incredible will,* could not manage it, and led it to be immolated on the altar of the cold, inhuman God of *justice*—the God of equilibrium, of stillness and peace, the God of the Brahmins, who seek to lose all that is personal and to be dissolved, to come to rest in an infinite ocean of annihilation.

On the empty altar scales were set up. This would be a new Caudine Forks for humanity.

The 'justice' which is his goal is not even the artistic

[1] I have to some extent modified my opinion of this work of Proudhon (1866).—(*Author's Note.*)

harmony of Plato's Republic, the elegant equilibrium of passion and sacrifice; the Gallic tribune takes nothing from 'anarchic and frivolous Greece'; he stoically tramples personal feelings under foot, and does not seek to harmonise them with the demands of the family and the commune. His 'free man' is a sentry on guard, and a workman who can never rise; he must serve and stand on guard until he is relieved by death; he must stifle in himself all personal passion, everything outside duty, because he is not himself: his meaning, his essence, lies outside himself; he is the instrument of justice; he is predestined, like the Virgin Mary, to bear the idea in suffering and to bring it into the world for the salvation of the state.

The family, the first embryo of society, the first cradle of justice, is doomed to everlasting, hopeless toil; it is to serve as the means of purification of the personal; in it the passions are to be stamped out. The austere Roman family in the workshop of to-day is Proudhon's ideal. Christianity has softened family life too much for him: it preferred Mary to Martha, the dreamer to the housewife: it forgave the sinner and held out a hand to the penitent, because she loved much; but in Proudhon's family, just what is essential is to love little. And that is not all: Christianity puts the individual far higher than his family relations. It says to the son: 'Forsake father and mother and follow me'—to the son who in the name of Proudhon's *realisation of justice* must be put back into the fetters of absolute paternal power, who in his father's lifetime can have no freedom, least of all in the choice of a wife. He is to be inured to slavery, to become in his turn a tyrant over the children who are born without love through duty for the continuation of the family. In this family marriage will be indissoluble, but it will be cold as ice. Marriage is simply a victory over love; the less love there is between the cook-wife and the workman-husband the better. And to think that I should meet these old shabby bogeys from the Hegelianism of the right wing in the writings of Proudhon!

Feeling is banished, everything is frozen, the colours are gone, nothing is left but the dull, exhausting toil of the proletariat of to-day, the toil from which the aristocratic family of ancient Rome, based on slavery, was at least free: gone is the poetic beauty of the Church, the delirium of faith, the hopes of paradise; even poetry in those days 'will be written no more,' so Proudhon asserts. On the other hand, labour will become 'more severe.' For individual freedom, for the right of initiative, for independence, one may well sacrifice the lullabys of religion; but to sacrifice everything for the realisation of the idea of justice—what nonsense!

Man is doomed to toil, he must labour till his hand drops and the son takes from the cold fingers of the father the plane or the hammer and carries on the everlasting work. But what if among the sons there happens to be one with a little more sense who lays down the drill and asks: 'But what are we wearing ourselves out for?' 'For the triumph of justice,' Proudhon tells him. And the new Cain answers: 'But who made me the keeper of the triumph of justice?' 'Who?—why, is not your whole vocation, your whole life, the realisation of justice?' 'Who has set up that object?' Cain will answer. 'It is too stale; there is no God, but the Commandments remain. Justice is not my vocation; work is not a duty but a necessity; the family is not for me the fetters of life but the setting for my life, for my development. You want to keep me in slavery, but I rebel against you. I revolt against you, against your steelyard, just as you have been revolting all your life against bayonets, capital, and Church, just as all the French revolutionists rebelled against the feudal and Catholic tradition. Or do you imagine that after the taking of the Bastille, after the terror, after the war and the famine, after the bourgeois king and the bourgeois republic, I am going to believe you when you tell me that Romeo had no right to love Juliet because those old fools of Montagues and Capulets kept up an everlasting feud, and that, even at thirty or forty, I must not choose the companion of my life without my father's permission, that a woman who has been unfaithful must be punished and disgraced? Why, what do you take me for with your justice?'

And in support of Cain we would add, from the dialectical side, that Proudhon's whole conception of an *aim* is utterly inconsistent. This teleology is also theology; this is the republic of February—that is, the same as the monarchy of July, but without Louis-Philippe. What difference is there between predetermined teleology and providence?[1]

After emancipating human nature to the last limit, Proudhon took fright looking at his contemporaries, and, that these convicts, these *ticket-of-leave men*, might do no mischief, he catches them in the rat-trap of the Roman family.

The doors of the restored *atrium*, free from *Lares* and *Penates*, have been flung open; but not Anarchy, not the annihilation of authority and the state, is seen seated in the midst, but stern Order, with centralisation, with regulation of family relations, with inheritance and deprivation of it as a punishment; and with these things all the old Roman sins peep out of every crevice with the dead eyes of statues.

The family of antiquity naturally implies the ancient conception of the fatherland with its jealous patriotism, that ferocious virtue which has shed ten times more blood than all the vices put together.

Man bound in serfdom to the family becomes again

[1] Proudhon himself said: '*Rien ne ressemble plus a la préméditation que la logique des faits.*'

the bondslave of the soil. His movements are restricted, he puts down roots into his land; only upon it he is what he is: 'the Frenchman living in Russia,' says Proudhon, 'is a Russian, and not a Frenchman.' No more colonies, no more settlements abroad; every man must live where he is. . . .

'Holland will not perish,' said William of Orange in the years of terror; 'it will go aboard ships and will sail off to Asia, and here we will lift up the sluices.' It is people like that who are free.

The English are like that: as soon as they begin to be oppressed, they sail over the ocean and there found a younger, freer England. And yet nobody could say of the English that they do not love their country, or that they are lacking in national feeling. Emigrating in all directions, England has peopled half the world; while France, lacking in vitality, has lost one set of colonies and does not know what to do with the rest. She does not need them; France is pleased with herself and clings more and more to her centre, and the centre to its master. What independence can there be in such a country?

On the other hand, how can one abandon France, *la belle France*? 'Is not she even now the freest country in the world, is not her language the finest language, her literature the finest literature, is not her syllabic line more musical than the Greek hexameter!' Moreover, her universal genius absorbs the thought and the literature of all ages and all countries: 'has not France made Shakespeare and Kant, Goethe and Hegel her own?' And what is more: Proudhon forgot that they corrected them and dressed them up, as landowners dress up the peasants when they take them to Court.

Proudhon concludes his book with a Catholic prayer adapted to socialism; all he had to do was to secularise a few Church phrases and to put the Phrygian cap in the place of the mitre, for the prayer of the 'Byzantine' bishops to be the very thing for the bishop of socialism. What a chaos! Proudhon, emancipated from everything except reason, still wants to remain not only a husband after the style of Bluebeard, but also a French nationalist—with his literary chauvinism and his unlimited power of the father; and so behind the strong, vigorous words of a free thinker one seems to hear the voice of the savage old man, dictating his will, and trying now to preserve for his children the decrepit temple he has been undermining all his life.

The Latin world does not like freedom, it only likes to struggle for it; it sometimes finds the force for setting free, never for freedom. Is it not melancholy to see such men as Auguste Comte and Proudhon setting up as their last word, the one a sort of mandarin hierarchy, the other his domestic penal servitude and apotheosis of an inhuman *pereat mundus, fiat justitia!*

Appendix

(To Chapter 41)

I

. . . On the one hand we have the Proudhon family, irrevocably welded together and nailed down, indissoluble marriage, the absolute power of the father—a family in which for the sake of society all the persons except one are brought to misery, the savage marriage in which unchanging feeling, the magic power of a vow, are assumed; on the other hand, the theories that are coming into vogue, in which marriage and the family are no longer binding, the irresistible force of passion is assumed, the past is thought to lay no obligations, and the complete independence of the individual is asserted.

On the one hand we have woman almost stoned for faithlessness; on the other, jealousy itself put *hors la loi* as a morbid, abnormal feeling of egoism and ownership and the romantic distortion of healthy and natural ideas.

Where is the truth . . . where is the middle line? Twenty-three years ago I was already seeking a way out of this forest of contradictions.

We are bold in denial and always ready to fling any of our idols into the river, but the gods of home and family are somehow 'waterproof'—they always rise again. Perhaps there is no sense left in them, but there is still life in them; it seems as though the weapons used against them have simply glided over their snaky scales, felled them, stunned them . . . but have not killed them.

Jealousy . . . Fidelity . . . Infidelity . . . Chastity . . . Dark forces, menacing words, thanks to which rivers of tears, rivers of blood have flowed—words that set us shuddering like the memory of the Inquisition, of torture, of the plague . . . and yet they are the words under the shadow of which, as under the sword of Damocles, the family has lived and is living.

There is no turning them out of doors by abuse or by denial. They remain round the corner, slumbering, ready at the slightest call to ruin everything near and far, to ruin us ourselves. . . .

It seems as though we must abandon the excellent intention of extinguishing these smouldering embers and confine ourselves humbly to mitigating and humanely directing the destructive fire. You can no more bridle passions with logic than you can justify them in the lawcourts. Passions are facts and not dogmas.

Moreover, jealousy has always enjoyed special privileges. In itself a strong *absolutely natural* passion, it has hitherto only been encouraged instead of being restrained and softened. The Christian doctrine making, through hatred of the body, everything fleshly of extraordinary value, and the aristocratic worship of blood, of purity of race, have developed to the point of absurdity the conception of insulted honour, of a blot that cannot be effaced. Jealousy has received the *jus gladii*, the right of judgment and revenge. It has become a duty of *honour*, almost a virtue. All that will not stand a moment's criticism—but yet there still remains at the bottom of the heart a very real insurmountable feeling of pain, of unhappiness called jealousy, a feeling as elementary as the feeling of love itself, resisting every effort to deny it, an 'irreducible' feeling.

. . . Here again are the everlasting limits, the Caudine Forks into which history drives us. On both sides there is truth, on both there is falsehood. The bold asking for a clear alternative will lead you nowhere. At the moment of complete denial of one of the terms, it comes back—just as after the last quarter of the moon the first appears on the other side.

Hegel removed the boundary-posts of human reason, by rising to the *absolute spirit*; in it they did not vanish but were *transformed—fulfilled*, as the German theological philosophy expresses it: this is mysticism, philosophical theodicy, allegory, and reality purposely mixed up. All religious reconciliations of the irreconcilable are won by means of *redemption*—that is, by sacred transmutation, a sacred deception, a solution which solves nothing but rests on faith. Can anything be more opposite to free-will than necessity?—but by faith they are easily reconciled. Man will accept without a murmur the justice of punishment for an action which was pre-ordained.

Proudhon himself, in a different range of questions, was far more humane than German philosophy. From economic contradictions he escapes by the recognition of both sides under the restraint of a higher principle. Property as a right and property as a theft are set side by side in everlasting balance, everlastingly complementary, under the ever-growing dominance of *justice*. It is clear that the argument and the contradictions are transferred to another sphere, and that it is the conception of justice we have to criticise rather than the rights of property.

The simpler, the less mystic, and the less one-sided, the more real and practically applicable the higher principle is, the more completely it brings the contradictory terms to their lowest denomination.

The absolute, 'all-embracing' spirit of Hegel is replaced in Proudhon by the menacing idea of justice. But the problem of the passions is not likely to be solved by that either. Passion is intrinsically unjust; justice is remote from the personal, it is mpersonal—passion is only individual.

The solution here lies not in the law-courts but in the humane development of individual character, in its escape from lyrical self-centredness into the light of day, in the development of common human interests.

The radical elimination of jealousy implies eliminating love for the individual, replacing it by love for woman or for man, by love of the sex in general. But it is just the personal, the individual, that is attractive; it is just that which gives colour, tone, intensity to the whole of our life. Our emotion is personal, our happiness and unhappiness are personal happiness and unhappiness.

Rationalism with all its logic is as little comfort in personal sorrow as the consolations of the Romans with their rhetoric. Neither the tears of loss nor the tears of jealousy can be wiped away, nor should they be, but it is right and possible that they should flow humanely . . . and that they should be equally free from monastic poison, the ferocity of the beast, and the wail of the man robbed of his property.[1]

---

[1] As I was correcting the proofs of this, I came upon a French newspaper with an extremely characteristic incident in it. Near Paris a student had a liaison with a girl, which was discovered. The girl's father went to the student and on his knees besought him, with tears, to vindicate his daughter's honour and marry her; the student refused with contumely. The kneeling father gave him a slap in the face, the student challenged him, they shot at each other; during the duel the old man had a paralytic stroke. The student was disconcerted, and 'decided to marry,' and the girl was grieved, and also decided to marry. The newspaper adds that this happy *denouement* will no doubt do much to promote the old father's recovery. Can this have happened outside a madhouse? Can China or India, at whose grotesque absurdities we mock so much, furnish anything uglier or sillier than this story? I will not say more immoral. This Parisian romance is a hundredfold more wicked than the burning of a widow or the burying of a vestal virgin. In those cases there was religious faith, removing all personal responsibility, but in this case there is nothing but conventional, shadowy ideas of external honour, of external reputation. . . . Is it not clear from this story what the student was like? Why should the girl's life be bound to his *à perpétuité*? Why was she ruined to save her reputation? Oh, Bedlam! (1866.)—(*Author's Note*.)

II

To reduce the relations of man and woman to a casual sexual connection is just as impossible as to exalt and distort them into marriage indissoluble to the grave. The one and the other may be met at the extreme of sexual and marriage relations, as a special case, as an exception but not as a general rule. The casual relation will be broken off or will continually tend to a closer and firmer union, just as the indissoluble marriage will tend to grow more and more free from external bonds.

People have continually protested against both extremes. Indissoluble marriage has been accepted by them hypocritically, or in the heat of the moment. Casual relations never have had complete recognition; they have always been concealed, just as marriage has been a subject of boasting. All attempts at the official regulation of brothels, although aiming at their restriction, are offensive to the moral sense of society, which sees in organisation, recognition. The scheme elaborated by a gentleman in Paris, in the days of the Directorate, of establishing privileged brothels with their own hierarchy and so on, was even in those days received with hisses and overwhelmed by a storm of laughter and contempt.

The normal life of man is as remote from the monastery as from the cattle-yard; from the sexlessness of the monk, which the Church esteems above marriage, as from the childless gratification of passion....

Marriage is for Christianity a concession, an inconsistency, a weakness. Christianity regards marriage as society regards concubinage. The monk and the Catholic priest are condemned to perpetual celibacy by way of reward for their foolish triumph over human nature.

Christian marriage in general is gloomy and unjust; it establishes inequality against the teaching of the

Gospel, and delivers the wife into slavery to the husband. The wife is sacrificed, love (hateful to the Church) is sacrificed; after the Church ceremony it becomes a superfluity, and is replaced by duty and obligation. Of the brightest and most joyous of feelings Christianity has made a pain, a weariness, and a sin. The human race had either to die out or be inconsistent. Outraged nature protested.

It protested not only by acts followed by penitence and stings of conscience, but by sympathy, by rehabilitation. The protest began in the very heyday of Catholicism and chivalry. The terrible husband, the Bluebeard in armour with the sword, tyrannical, jealous, and merciless; the barefoot monk, sullen, senseless, superstitious, ready to avenge himself for his privations, for his useless struggle; jailers, torturers, spies, . . . and in some cellar or turret a sobbing woman, a page in chains, for whom no one intercedes. All is darkness, savagery, blood, bigotry, violence, and Latin prayers chanted through the nose.

But behind the monk, the confessor, and the jailer, who, with the terrible husband, the father, and the brother, guard the sanctity of marriage, the folk-legend is forming in the stillness, the ballad is heard carried from place to place, from castle to castle, by troubadour and minnesinger—it champions the unhappy woman. The judge condemns, and the song absolves. The Church hurls its anathema at love outside marriage, the ballad curses marriage without love. It champions the love-sick page, the fallen wife, the oppressed daughter, not by argument but by sympathy, by pity, by lamentation. The song is for the people its secular prayer, its other escape from the cold and hunger of life, from spiritual misery and heavy toil.

On holidays the litanies to the Madonna were replaced by the mournful strains *des complaintes*, which did not heap shame on the unhappy woman, but wept for her, and set above all the Virgin of Sorrows, beseeching Her intervention and forgiveness. From ballads and legends the protest grows into the novel and the drama. In the drama it becomes a force. In the theatre outraged love, the gloomy secrets of family injustice, find their tribune, their court of appeal. The hearing of their case has moved thousands of hearts, wringing tears and cries of indignation against the serfdom of marriage and the forcible bondage of the family. The jury of the stalls and the boxes have over and over again acquitted individuals and found institutions guilty.

Meanwhile, in the period of political reconstructions and secular tendencies in thought, one of the two strong props of marriage is beginning to break down. As it becomes less and less of a sacrament—that is, loses its ultimate foundation—it has leaned more and more on the police. Only by the mystic intervention of a higher power can Christian marriage be justified. There is a certain logic in that, senseless, but still logic. The police-officer, putting on his tricolor scarf and celebrating the wedding with the civil code in his hand, is a far more absurd figure than the priest in his vestments, surrounded by incense, holy images, and miracles. Even the First Consul, Napoleon, the most bourgeois politician in matters of love and the family, perceived that marriage at the police-station was a poor affair, and tried to persuade Cambacérès[1] to add some obligatory phrase, some moral sentence, particularly one that would impress upon the bride her duty to be faithful to her husband (not a word about his) and to obey him.

---

[1] Cambacérès, Jean-Jacques (1753-1824), one of the nearest advisers of Napoleon, and compiler of the *Code Civil*. He attempted to dissuade Napoleon from the invasion of Russia.—(*Translator's Note.*)

As soon as marriage emerges from the sphere of mysticism, it becomes *expédient,* an external arrangement. It was introduced by the panic-stricken 'Bluebeards' (shaven nowadays, and changed into 'blue-chins') in judges' wigs, and academic coats, popular representatives and liberals, the priests of the civil code. Civil marriage is simply a state measure of economy, freeing the state from responsibility for the children and binding men more closely to property. Marriage without the intervention of the Church became a contract for the bodily enslavement of each to the other for life. The legislator has nothing to do with faith, with mystic fantasies, so long as the contract is fulfilled, and if not he will find means of punishment and enforcement. And why not punish it? In England, the traditional country of juridical development, a boy of sixteen, made drunk with ale and gin and enrolled in a regiment by an old recruiting sergeant with red ribbons on his hat, is subjected to the most horrible tortures. Why not punish a girl? Why not punish with shame, ruin, and forcible restoration to her master the girl who, with no clear understanding of what she is about, has contracted to love for life, and has permitted something extra, forgetting that the season-ticket is not transferable. But these new Bluebeards too have been attacked by the troubadours and novelists. Against the marriage of legal contract, a pathological, physiological dogma has been set up, the dogma of *the absolute infallibility of the passions and the incapacity of man to struggle against them.*

Those who were yesterday the slaves of marriage are now becoming the slaves of love. There is no law for love, there is no strength that can resist it.

With that, all rational control, all responsibility, every form of self-restraint is effaced. That man is in subjection to irresistible and overwhelming forces is a theory

THE TYRANNY OF LOVE

utterly opposed to rational freedom and to reason, to that formation of the character of a free man which all social theories aim at attaining by different paths.

Imaginary forces, if men accept them as real, have as much power as real ones, and that is because man's power of response is the same whatever force acts on him. The man who is afraid of ghosts is afraid in exactly the same way as the man who is afraid of mad dogs, and may as easily die of fright. The difference is that in one case the man may be shown that his fears are groundless, and in the other he cannot.

I refuse to admit the sovereign position given to *love* in life, I deny its autocratic power and protest against the pusillanimous excuse of having been carried away by it.

Surely we have not freed ourselves from every restraint on earth, from God and the devil, from the Roman and the criminal law, and proclaimed reason as our sole guide and standard, in order to lie down humbly, like Hercules at the feet of Omphale, or to fall asleep in the lap of Delilah? Surely woman has not sought to be free from the yoke of the family, from perpetual tutelage and the tyranny of father, husband, or brother, has not striven for her rights to independent work, to learning and the position of a citizen, only to begin over again cooing like a dove all her life and pining for a dozen Leone Leonis[1] instead of one.

Yes, it is for woman that I am most of all sorry in this question; she is hopelessly torn and destroyed by the all-devouring Moloch of love. She puts more faith in it, she suffers more from it. She is more concentrated on the sexual relation, more driven to love. . . . She is both intellectually more unstable and intellectually less trained than we.

I am sorry for her.

[1] Leone Leoni is the hero, or rather villain, whose name supplies the title of one of George Sand's earlier novels.—(*Translator's Note*.)

III

Has any one made a serious and honest attempt to break down conventional prejudices in female education? They are only broken down by experience, and so it is life and not convention that suffers.

People go round the questions we are discussing, as old women and children go round a graveyard or a place where a crime has been committed. Some are afraid of impure spirits, others of the pure truth, and are left in fantastic disorder and inconsistent chaos. There is as little serious consistency in our view of sexual relations as in practical spheres. We are still haunted by the possibility of combining Christian morality, which starts from negation of the flesh and leads towards the other world, with the realistic earthly morality of this world. People are annoyed at the two moralities not harmonising, and, to avoid spending time in worrying over the solution of the problem, pick out according to their tastes and retain what they like of the Church teaching, and reject what they do not care for; just as those who do not keep the fasts will zealously eat pancakes, and avoid dull religious services, whilst still observing religious festivities. Yet I should have thought it was high time to bring more harmony and manliness into conduct. Let him who respects the law remain under the law and not break it, but let him who does not accept it show himself openly and consciously independent of it.

A sober view of human relations is far more difficult for women than for us—of that there can be no doubt; they are more deceived by education, and know less of life, and so they more often stumble and break their heads and hearts than free themselves. They are always in revolt, and remain in slavery, strive for revolution, while most frequently they are propping up the existing regime. From childhood the girl is frightened of the

FEMALE EDUCATION

sexual relation as of some *fearful unclean secret* from which she is guarded and scared off as though it were a sin that had some magical power; and afterwards this same monstrous thing, this same *magnum ignotum* which leaves an ineffaceable stain, the remotest hint at which is shameful and sets her blushing, is made the object of her life. As soon as a boy can walk, he is given a toy sword to train him to murder, he is promised an hussar's uniform and epaulettes; while the girl is lulled to sleep with the hope of a rich and handsome bridegroom, and she dreams of epaulettes not on her own shoulders but on the shoulders of her predestined husband.

> 'Dors, dors, mon enfant,
> Jusqu'à l'age de quinze ans,
> A quinze ans faut te réveiller,
> A quinze ans faut te marier.'

One must marvel at the fine human nature which is not ruined by such an education—we might have expected that all the little girls so lulled for fifteen years would set to work speedily to replace those slain by the boys who have been trained from childhood with weapons of slaughter.

The Christian teaching imposes the terror of the 'flesh' before the creature is conscious of its sex; it awakens the dreadful question in the child, instils terror into the adolescent soul, and when the time to answer it is come—another doctrine, as we have said, raises her sexual calling to the sought-for ideal for the girl: the schoolgirl becomes the bride, and the same mystery, the same sin but purified and sanctified, becomes the crown of her education, the hope of her relations, the goal of all her efforts, almost a social duty. Accomplishments, learning, education, intelligence, beauty, wealth, grace, all are devoted to her *sanctioned* fall . . . to the very same sin, the thought of which was looked on as a crime but which has now changed its essential nature by a miracle like that by which the Pope, when held up on a journey, changed a meat dish into a Lenten dish by his blessing.

In short, the whole training—negative and positive—of a woman remains a training for sexual relations; round them all her subsequent life turns. From them she runs, towards them she runs, by them is disgraced, by them is made proud. . . . To-day she preserves the negative holiness of sexlessness, to-day she can only whisper, blushing, of love to her bosom friend; to-morrow, in the face of the crowd, in glare and noise, in the light of chandeliers and strains of music, she is flung into the arms of a man.

Bride, wife, mother, only in old age as grandmother a woman is set free from sexual life, and then becomes an independent creature, especially if the grandfather is dead. Woman, struck down by love, does not soon escape. . . . Pregnancy, suckling, child-rearing are all the development of the same mystery, the same act of love; in woman it persists not in the memory only, but in blood and body, in her it ferments and matures and rends without breaking its tie.

Christianity breathed with its feverish monastic asceticism, with its romantic nonsense, upon this physiologically strong, deep relation, and blew it into the frenzied and destructive flames of jealousy, revenge, punishment, and insult.

For a woman to extricate herself from this chaos is an heroic feat—only rare and exceptional natures accomplish it; other women are tortured, and if they do not go out of their minds it is only thanks to the frivolity with which we all live without over-subtlety in the face of terrible catastrophes and misfortunes, senselessly passing from day to day, from one chance event to another and from one contradiction to another.

What breadth, what beauty and power of human nature and development there must be in a woman to get over all the fences, all the barriers, within which she is held captive!

I have seen one such struggle and one such victory. . . .

Chapter 42

The Coup d'État — The Procureur of the late Republic — The Voice of the Cow in the Wilderness — Banishment of the Procureur — Order and Civilisation Triumphant

'VIVE *la mort, friends! And a happy new year! Now we shall be consistent, now we shall not be false to our own ideas, shall not be terrified at the realisation of what we have foreseen, shall not abjure the knowledge we have reached by the path of tribulation. Now we shall be strong and stand up for our convictions.*

'*We saw death approaching long ago; we may grieve, we may feel sympathy, but we cannot be surprised, we cannot be despairing or downcast. Quite the contrary, we ought to lift up our heads, we are justified. We have been called birds of ill omen invoking disaster, we have been reproached for heresy, for ignorance of the people, for proud isolation, for childish resentment, while we have only been guilty of seeing the truth and speaking it openly. Our words, which are still the same, are now the consolation, the encouragement of those who are terrified by the events in Paris.*'—('Letters from France and Italy,' No. 14. Nice, December 31, 1851.)

One morning (I remember it was the 4th of December) our cook, Pasquale Rocca, came in to me, and with a look of pleasure announced that flysheets were being sold in the streets with the news that 'Buonaparte has dismissed the Assembly and appointed a red government.' Who were the zealous servants of Napoleon who spread such rumours among the people even outside France (Nice was at that time Italian), I do not know; but what numbers there must have been of agents of all sorts, political stokers, whipping the public up and raising the temperature, since there were enough of them even for Nice!

An hour later Vogt, Hoetsky, Mathieu, and others turned up: all were surprised . . . Mathieu, a typical specimen of a French revolutionary, was beside himself.

Bald, with a skull the shape of a walnut—that is, a typically Gallic skull, not spacious but obstinate—with a big, dark, unkempt beard, a rather good-natured expression, and little eyes, Mathieu was like a prophet, like a crazy saint, like an augur, and like his bird. He was a lawyer, and in the happy days of the February republic had been a *procureur* or a deputy *procureur* somewhere. He was a revolutionary to the tips of his finger-nails; he gave himself up to the revolution as people give themselves up to religion, with implicit faith, never dared either to understand or to doubt or to be over-subtle, but loved and believed, called Ledru-Rollin 'Ledru,' and Louis Blanc simply 'Blanc,' used the word *citoyen* whenever he could, and was perpetually conspiring.

On receiving the news of the 2nd of December he disappeared, and returned two days later completely convinced that France was rising, *que cela chauffe,* and especially in the south, in the department of Var near Draguignan. The great thing to be done was to enter into relations with the leaders of the insurrection. . . . He had seen some of them, and had settled with them overnight, passing through Var, to collect trustworthy and important persons together at a certain spot, for consultation. . . . But that the gendarmes might not get wind of it, it was settled on both sides to give as a signal the moo of a cow. If things went well, Orsini meant to bring all his friends, and, though not quite confident that Mathieu's view of the position was correct, he set off with him to cross the frontier. Orsini came back shaking his head, though, true to his revolutionary and somewhat *condottieri* temperament, he proceeded to prepare his comrades and collect arms. Mathieu vanished.

Twenty-four hours later, Rocca woke me at four o'clock in the morning: 'Two gentlemen just arrived from a journey; they urgently want to see you, they say. One of them gave me this note.' '*Citoyen*, for God's sake give bearer three or four hundred francs at once, if possible; urgently necessary.—MATHIEU.'

I snatched up the money and went downstairs: two remarkable individuals were sitting in the half-dark by the window; accustomed as I am to all the uniforms of revolution, I was yet struck by the appearance of my visitors. Both were covered with mud and clay to their knees; one was wearing a thick red woollen scarf; both had shabby overcoats, a sash round their waistcoats, and big pistols in the sash; and the rest was as usual— unkempt shocks of hair, big beards, and tiny pipes. One of them, beginning with the word *citoyen*, delivered a speech in which he touched upon my civic virtues and the money expected by Mathieu. I gave him the money. 'Is he in safety?' I asked. 'Yes,' answered his ambassador; 'we're going to join him at once on the other side of the Var. He is buying a boat.'

'A boat! what for?'

'Citoyen Mathieu has the whole plan for landing— the infamous coward of a boatman would not let us have the boat on credit. . . .'

'What, a landing in France . . . with one boat. . . . ?'

'It is a secret, *citoyen*, for the time.'

'*Comme de raison*.'

'Would you like a receipt?'

'Oh, no need of that!'

Next day Mathieu himself appeared, also muddy to the ears, and worn out with fatigue; he had been mooing like a cow all night, had several times fancied he heard an answer, went towards it, and found a real bull or a cow. Orsini, who had been waiting somewhere for him for ten hours at a stretch, also came back. The difference between them was that Orsini, washed, and as always, dressed neatly and tastefully, looked like a man who had just walked out of his bedroom; while Mathieu bore all the outward signs of destroying the peace of the state, and attempting to raise a rebellion. Then the boat question had to be considered. Trouble is never far off, and he might easily ruin half a dozen of his own countrymen and half a dozen of the Italians. To stop or dissuade him was impossible. The leaders who had come to me in the night appeared with him; one might be certain that he would compromise not only the French but all of us in Nice. Hoetsky undertook to manage him, and did so like an artist.

Hoetsky's window, with a little balcony, looked straight out on the sea-shore. In the morning he saw Mathieu wandering with a mysterious air along the beach . . . Hoetsky began making signs to him; Mathieu saw them and signed that he would come to him presently; but Hoetsky, assuming an air of the most terrible alarm, telegraphed to him with his fingers that danger was imminent, and insisted on his coming up to the balcony at once. Mathieu, looking round him, stole up on tiptoe. 'You don't know?' Hoetsky asked him. 'What?' 'A squadron of French gendarmes has come into Nice.' 'You don't say so!'

'Sh—sh—sh. . . . They are looking for you and your friends. They mean to make a house-to-house search among us—you will be caught at once; don't go out into the street.'

'*Violation du territoire* . . . I shall protest.'

'Of course; only, now you must escape.'

'I will go to Ste. Hélène, to Herzen's.'

'You must be mad! That's simply giving yourself up to them. His villa is on the frontier, with a huge garden, and no one will even know that you have been arrested—besides, Rocca saw two gendarmes at the gate, even yesterday.'

Mathieu sank into thought.

'Go by sea to Vogt's, hide there for the time, and he, by the way, will give you the best advice.'

Mathieu went by the sea-coast—that is, twice as far round—to Vogt's, and began telling him word for word his conversation with Hoetsky. Vogt instantly grasped the position and observed to him: 'The great thing, dear Mathieu, is not to lose one instant. Within two hours you must go to Turin: the diligence passes the other side of the hill; I will take a seat, and take you there by the path.'

'I'll run home for my things . . .' and the *procureur* of the republic was a little flustered.

'That's even worse than going to Herzen's. Why, you must be crazy—gendarmes, agents, spies, I don't know what, are after you . . . and you want to run home to kiss your fat Provençale! What a Celadon![1] Porter!' shouted Vogt (his house-porter was a minute German, a killing person, very much like a coffee-pot that had not been washed for months, and absolutely devoted to Vogt). 'Make haste and write that you want a shirt, handkerchiefs, clothes; he 'll fetch them, and if you like bring your Dulcinea too so that you may kiss and weep to your heart's content.'

Mathieu was so overcome with feeling that he embraced Vogt.

Hoetsky arrived. 'Make haste, make haste!' he said with an ominous air.

Meanwhile the porter came back, his Dulcinea came also—they had only to wait for the diligence to

---

[1] A character in the famous romance *Astrée* by Victor d'Urfé (1568-1626), adopted into the Russian language as the type of the faithful and devoted swain.—(*Translator's Note*.)

come into sight beyond the hill. The seat had been taken.

'I suppose you are cutting up rotten dogs or rabbits again?' Hoetsky asked Vogt; *'quel chien de métier . . . !'*

'No, I'm not.'

'Upon my soul, the stench in your room is like the catacombs at Naples.'

'I notice it myself, but I can't make it out; it comes from the corner. . . . There must be a dead rat under the floor—it's an awful stink,' and he picked up Mathieu's overcoat lying on a chair. It appeared that the smell came from the overcoat.

'What the devil have you got in your overcoat?' Vogt asked him.

'Nothing!'

'Oh, it must be my fault,' observed Dulcinea, blushing, 'I put a pound of Limburg cheese, *un peu trop fait*, in his pocket for the journey.'

'I congratulate your neighbours in the diligence,' shouted Vogt, laughing as no one else in the world can laugh.

'Well, it's time to start—march!'

And Hoetsky and Vogt saw the agitator off on his way to Turin.

In Turin Mathieu presented himself before the Minister of the Interior with a protest. The latter received him with irritation and laughter. 'How could you imagine that French gendarmes could arrest people in the kingdom of Sardinia? You must be unwell.'

Mathieu referred to the testimony of Vogt and Hoetsky.

'Your friends,' said the Minister, 'have been having a joke at your expense.'

Mathieu wrote to Vogt; he reeled off a string of nonsense, I do not know what, in answer. But Mathieu was offended, particularly with Hoetsky, and a few weeks later wrote a letter to me in which, among other things, he said: 'You, *citoyen*, alone among these gentlemen, took no part in this treacherous intrigue against me. . . .'

What adds to the characteristic oddity of the affair is that there was a very serious rising in Var, that masses of the population really did revolt, and that the rising was suppressed with the habitual French bloodthirstiness. How was it Mathieu and his bodyguard, for all their zeal and their mooing, did not know how to get in contact with the rebels? No one suspects him or his comrades of intentionally going to mess about in the mud and not wanting to go where there was danger—far from it. That is not in the spirit of the French, of whom Delphine Gay said that 'they are afraid of everything except bullets,' and still less in the spirit *de la démocratie militante* and the red republic. . . . Why did Mathieu go to the right when the revolting peasants were on the left?

A few days later—like yellow leaves driven before the wind—the luckless victims of the suppressed rising began streaming into Nice. There were so many of them that the Piedmont government allowed them to remain for a time in a sort of bivouac or gypsy camp near the town. How many ruined fortunes and privations have we seen in these camps!—that is the horrible side behind the scenes of civil wars; usually concealed behind the big framework and gay scene-painting of such events as the 2nd of December.

Here were simple peasants, gloomily pining for home, for their land, and naïvely saying: 'We are not rebels at all—and not *"partageux"*; we tried to defend public order as good citizens: *ce sont ces coquins* who called us out' (*i.e.* the officials, mayors, and gendarmes)—'they were false to their oath and their duty, and must we now die of hunger in a foreign land or face a court-martial? . . . Where s the justice in that?'

LUCKLESS VICTIMS

And indeed, a *coup d'état* like the 2nd of December destroys more than men: it destroys all morality, every conception of good and evil in a whole population; it is a lesson of corruption which cannot pass without effect. Among them were soldiers too, *troupiers,* in a permanent state of wonder at finding themselves, contrary to all discipline and their captains' orders, on a different side from their flag and their regiment. The number of these was not great, however. There were also simple bourgeois of humble means, who never make the same repulsive impression on me as the more pretentious —pitiful, narrow-minded people, they had somehow, in the midst of the petty cheating of trade, laboriously assimilated two or three notions or half-notions of their duties, and they had risen in defence of them when they saw their holy things trampled upon.

'It is the triumph of egoism,' they said; 'yes, yes, of egoism, and where there is egoism there is vice; every one ought to do his duty without egoism.'

There were, too, of course, town workmen, the real genuine element of revolution, striving to obtain *la sociale* by decree—and to pay out the bourgeois and the aristocrat as they paid them out.

Of course, among them there were wounded, terribly wounded, too. I remember two middle-aged peasants who had crawled, leaving a track of blood, from the frontier to a suburb where the inhabitants picked them up half dead. A gendarme had been chasing them, and, seeing the frontier was not far off, he fired at one and shattered his shoulder. . . . The wounded man still ran on. . . . The gendarme fired once more, the wounded man fell; then he galloped after the other and overtook him, first with a bullet and then himself. The second wounded man surrendered; the gendarme tied him in haste to his horse, and all at once missed the first man . . . he had crawled to a copse and started running. . . . To overtake him on horseback was difficult, especially with the other wounded man; to leave the horse behind impossible. . . . The gendarme shot his prisoner '*à bout portant*' from the top of his head downwards; the man fell unconscious: the bullet tore open the whole right side of his face, splintering the bones. When he came to himself there was no one there; he made his way along familiar paths trodden by the smugglers as far as Var, and crossed it and passed through it almost bleeding to death; there he found his comrade utterly exhausted, and with him succeeded in *surviving* as far as the first houses of Ste. Hélène. There, as I have said, the inhabitants took care of them. The first man said that after being shot he had hidden in some bushes, that afterwards he had heard voices, that the pursuing gendarmes had probably come upon others and so made off.

How zealous are the French police!

This example was followed by the zealous *maires* and their deputies, the *procureurs* of the *republic* and prefects; the zeal was displayed in the elections and counting of votes: all this was typically French, and familiar to everybody. I will only say that in remote parts the steps taken for attaining an immense majority at the polls were of a rustic simplicity. On the farther side of the Var, in the first village, the *maire* and brigadier of gendarmes sat beside the urns and looked at every ballot-paper any one put in, saying on the spot that they would make mince-meat of any rebel. The government voting-papers were printed on special paper—so it worked out that there were in the whole village only some five or six bold, unruly spirits who voted against the plebiscite; the rest, and with them the whole of France, voted for the Empire *in spe*.

SECTION TWO
RUSSIAN SHADOWS

I

N. I. SAZONOV

SAZONOV, Bakunin, Paris. Those names, those men, that city, take me back . . . back into the far-away past, to the days of youthful conspiracies, to the days of the cult of philosophy and the worship of revolution.

My youth with each is too precious for me not to pause over it. . . . With Sazonov, early in the 'thirties, I shared our boyish dreams of a plot *à la* Rienzi . . . with Bakunin, ten years later, in the sweat of my brains, I mastered Hegel.

Of Bakunin I have spoken already and shall have much more yet to say. His striking personality, his eccentric and vigorous appearance, everywhere—in the circle of Moscow youth, in the lecture-room of the Berlin University, among Weitling's communists, and Caussidière's Montagnards—his speeches in Prague, his leadership in Dresden, his trial, imprisonment, sentence to death, torture in Austria, deportation to Russia—where he vanished behind the terrible walls of the Alexeyevsky Ravelin-—make of him one of those individual figures which neither the contemporary world nor history can overlook.

That man had within him the latent power of a colossal activity for which there was no demand. Bakunin was capable of becoming an agitator, a tribune, a preacher, the head of a party or of a sect, an arch heretic or a fighter. Put him down anywhere you like, at any extreme point—an Anabaptist, a Jacobin, a comrade of Anacharsis Cloots or a friend of Gracchus

Babeuf—and he would have won over the masses and shaken the destinies of nations.

> 'But here under the yoke of Tsars,'

a Columbus without an America or a ship, after against his will serving two years in the artillery and two more in the ranks of Moscow Hegelianism, he made haste to leave the country in which an idea is persecuted as an evil intention, and an independent word as an offence against social morality.

After tearing himself from Russia in 1840, he did not return there until a picket of Austrian dragoons handed him over to a Russian officer of gendarmes in 1849.

The worshippers of teleology, the charming fatalists of rationalism, are still surprised at the provident appropriateness with which great talents and leaders appear as soon as there is a need for them; forgetting how many germs perish, are stifled without seeing the light, how many faculties and powers waste away because they are not wanted.

Sazonov's example is still more striking. Sazonov has passed without leaving a trace, and his death has been as unnoticed as the whole of his life. He died without carrying out one of the hopes that his friends built upon him.

It is easy to say he was to blame for his fate; but how can we weigh or appraise how much of the blame rests on the man and how much on his environment?

The age of Nicholas was a soul-destroying age; it murdered not only with labour in the mines and 'white straps,' but with its stifling, degrading atmosphere, with its, so to say, negative blows.

To deliver the funeral oration over the submerged beings of that period, worn out with striving to drag our ship off the sandbanks where it has foundered so deeply, is my speciality. For them I play the part of

Domazhirov, the old retired orderly of Prozorovsky's, now forgotten by everybody, but at one time a familiar figure in Moscow. With a powdered head, wearing a light green uniform of the days of Paul, he used to turn up at all the funerals in which a bishop officiated, and, taking the foremost place, led the procession, imagining that he was doing something important.

. . . In our second year at the university—that is, in the autumn of 1831—in the lecture-room of the faculty of physics and mathematics, Ogaryov and I met, among our new comrades, two with whom we became particularly intimate.

Our likings, our sympathies and antipathies, were all derived from the same source. We were fanatics and lads: learning, art, connections, home, and social position, everything was subordinated to one idea and one religion. Wherever there was an opening for appeal and propaganda, there we were on the spot with all our heart and understanding, persistently, indefatigably, devoting time, work, and even efforts to please.

We went into the lecture-room with the firm determination of founding in it the nucleus of a society in the image and semblance of the Decembrists, and so sought proselytes and followers. The first of our comrades to understand this clearly was Sazonov; we found him completely prepared, and at once made friends. He gave us his hand with full understanding, and next day brought us another student.

Sazonov had conspicuous gifts and conspicuous pride. He was eighteen or rather less, but in spite of that he had studied a great deal and had read everything in the world. He tried to dominate his comrades, and put no one on a level with himself. That was why he was more respected than loved by them. His friend, as handsome and soft as a girl, seemed asking sympathy and support; full of love and devotion, fresh from under his mother's wing, with noble impulses and half-childish dreams, he longed for warmth and tenderness, he clung to us and gave himself up entirely to us and our idea — his was the character of Vladimir Lensky, the character of Venevitinov.

. . . The day on which we sat side by side on one of the benches of the amphitheatre, glanced at each other with the full consciousness of our dedication to our league, our secret, our readiness to face death, our faith in the sacredness of our cause—and glanced with loving pride at the multitude of handsome young heads about us, as at a band of brothers—was a great day in our life. We gave each other our hands and *à la lettre* went out to preach freedom and struggle in all the four quarters of our youthful 'universe,' like the four deacons who go on Easter Day with the Four Gospels in their hands.

We preached in every place at every time . . . exactly what it was we preached it is hard to say. Our ideas were vague: we preached the Decembrists and the French Revolution, then advocated St. Simonism and the same revolution; we advocated a constitution and a republic, the reading of political works and the concentration of forces in one society. Most of all we preached hatred for every form of violence, for every sort of arbitrary tyranny practised by governments.

Our society in reality was never formed; but our propaganda sent down deep roots in all the faculties, and extended far beyond the university walls.

Since those days our propaganda has gone on uninterrupted, all our lives, from university lecture-room to London printing-press. Our whole life has been the carrying out of our boyish programme as far as lay in our power. It is not hard to follow the connecting thread through the questions we have touched upon, through the interests aroused by us, in journals, in lectures, in literary circles. . . . Though it took different forms and developed, our propaganda remained true to itself and retained its individual character in every surrounding.

Punishment lifted us up and gave us the prestige of prison and exile. We came back to Moscow, 'authorities' at five-and-twenty. We were joined by Byelinsky, Granovsky, and Bakunin, while through our articles in *Notes on the Fatherland* we ourselves joined the Petersburg movement of the Lyceum students and the young literary men. The Petrashev group were our younger brothers as the Decembrists were our elder ones. To be silent about the importance of our circle because I belonged to it would be hypocritical and stupid. Quite the contrary: whenever in my memoirs I come upon those days, on old friends of the 'thirties and the 'forties, I purposely pause and speak regardless of repetition if only I can make the younger generation better acquainted with them. It does not know them, it has forgotten them, it does not care for them, and denounces them as unpractical and unbusinesslike, as men who did not know so well where they were going; it is angry with them, and rejects them wholesale as out of date, as idle and superfluous men, as fantastic dreamers, forgetting that the value of men of the past, their significance and the hall-mark of them, depends less on the comparison of the sum of knowledge, and the manner of formulating problems of the old period and of the new, than on the energy and strength they brought to their solution. I have a desperate longing to save the younger generation from the ingratitude of history, and even from the mistakes of history. It is time for the fathers to cease devouring their children like Saturn, but it is time for the children, too, to cease following the example of the natives of Kamschatka, who kill off their old people.

Boldly, and with full conviction, I say once more of

our comrades of those days 'that they were a wonderful set of young men, that such a circle of talented, pure-hearted, cultured, intelligent, and devoted men I have never met,' and I have wandered pretty widely about the world among all classes, and especially the revolutionary ones. I am not only speaking of my own circle of intimate friends; I am bound to say the same thing as emphatically of Stankevitch's circle and the Slavophils. Young men, horror-stricken by the infamies of the life about them, surrounded by gloom and oppressive misery, gave up all and went in search of a way out. They sacrificed everything that others strive after—social position, wealth, everything which the traditional life offered them, to which environment and example drew them, to which their family urged them—for the sake of their convictions, and they remained true to them. Such men cannot be simply put on the archives and forgotten.

They are persecuted, arrested, put under police supervision, exiled, dragged from place to place, overwhelmed with insults and humiliations—they remain the same: ten years pass—they are still the same: twenty, thirty years pass—they are still the same. I demand that a recognition be accorded them and justice be done to them.

To this simple demand I have heard a strange objection, and more than once, too: 'You, and even more the Decembristi, were the dilettanti of revolutionary ideas; interest in the cause was for you a luxury, something romantic; you say yourselves that you all *sacrificed* social position; you had means, so for you the revolution was not a question of bread and butter and of human existence, the question of life and death . . . .'

'I imagine,' I answered once, 'that for those who were executed it was. . . .'

'Anyway, they were not momentous, inevitable

questions for you. You like to be revolutionaries, and that of course is better than if you like to be senators or governors; for us the struggle with the existing order is not a matter of choice, it is due to our social position. Between you and us there is the difference between the man who has fallen into the water and the man who is bathing; both have to swim, but one does it from necessity and the other for pleasure.'

To refuse recognition to men because they have done from inner impulse what others *are going* to do from necessity is remarkably like the monastic asceticism which only attaches value to duties the fulfilment of which is very disgusting.

Extreme views of this sort easily take root among us; and though the roots do not go deep, they are as hard to eradicate as horse-radish.

We are greatly given to theoretical pedantry and argumentativeness. This German propensity is in us associated with a special national element—which we might call the Araktcheyev element—a ruthlessness, a passionate rigidity, and an eagerness to despatch our victims. To satisfy his grenadier ideal, Araktcheyev flogged living peasants to death; we flog to death ideas, arts, humanity, past leaders, anything you like. In dauntless array we advance step by step to the limit and overshoot it, never sinning against logic but only against *truth*; unaware, we go on further and further, forgetting that real sense and real understanding of life are shown precisely in stopping short before the extreme . . . that is the *halte* of moderation, of truth, of beauty, that is the perfect balance of the organism.

The oligarchic pretension of the have-nots to be the exclusive sufferers from the social system and to possess a monopoly of the feeling of social injustice is as unjust as all forms of exclusiveness and monopoly. Neither through Christian mercy nor through democratic envy will you ever get beyond charity and violent spoliation, the division of property and universal poverty. In the Church it has remained a theme for rhetoric and a sentimental exercise in compassion; in the ultra-democrats, as Proudhon has observed, it is confined to the feeling of envy and hatred; and in neither case has it gone on to any constructive ideas, to any practical result.

In what way are men to blame who understood the pain of the sufferers before they themselves did, and showed it them, and, what was more, the way of escape too? It was not through starvation that St. Simon the descendant of Charlemagne, and Robert Owen the manufacturer, either of them became apostles of socialism.

This view will not persist; it lacks warmth, goodness, breadth. I should not have referred to it if these critics had not included on their black lists, not only our names, but those of the men who sowed the first seeds of all that has come up and will come up—the Decembrists whom we so deeply honour.

This digression is hardly in place here.

Sazonov was, in fact, an idle man, and wasted immense abilities; frittering his life away in all sorts of trivialities abroad, he was lost like a soldier taken prisoner in his first battle and never able to get home again.

When we were arrested in 1834 and clapped into prison, Sazonov and Ketscher were, by some miracle, untouched. They both lived almost uninterruptedly in Moscow, and talked a great deal but wrote little, and no letters of theirs were found in the possession of any of us. We were sent into exile; Sazonov's mother succeeded in getting a passport for him to go to Italy. His going abroad and being separated from us may have laid the foundation of all that followed in his life, which was that of a star with no fixed orbit, falling and leaving no trace.

A year later he returned to Moscow; it was just at

one of the most stifling and oppressive periods of the last reign. In Moscow he was met by a dead level calm, nowhere a shade of sympathy, nowhere a word of life. We, in the *reserves* of exile, were cherishing our past life, were living in hope and memory, were working and learning something of the coarse realities of provincial existence.

In Moscow everything reminded Sazonov of our absence. Of his old friends, the only one on the spot was Ketscher, with whom Sazonov, a man of stiff and aristocratic manners, was less able to be intimate than with any of the rest. Ketscher, as we have said, was an intellectual savage—a cultured one, a pioneer from Fenimore Cooper, returning intentionally to the primeval state of the human race, rude on principle, slovenly through theory, a student of five-and-thirty in the part of a Schilleresque youth. Sazonov struggled on and on in Moscow—he was consumed by boredom, he had no motive for work, for activity. He tried moving to Petersburg; that was even worse: *à la longue* he could not stand it, and went to Paris with no definite plan. Those were the days when France and Paris still had a spell of magic for us. Our tourists glided over the polished surface of French life, knowing nothing of its rough side, and were in raptures over everything—over the liberal speeches, over the songs of Béranger and the caricatures of Philipon. It was the same with Sazonov. But he found nothing to do there either. Noisy, lively idleness succeeded to his life of dumbness and oppression. In Russia he had been bound hand and foot, here he was a stranger to every one and everything. Another long series of years of aimless excitement and over-stimulated nerves began for him in Paris. He was incapable of concentrating, of devoting himself to intellectual work without waiting for some impelling force from outside; it was not in his character. The impersonal interest in science was not strong enough in him; he was looking for some activity, and would have been ready for any amount of work so long as it was conspicuous, so long as it could be rapidly applied and realised in practice — and it must have been, too, with noise and acclamation, amidst applause and the outcry of his enemies. Not finding such work, he flung himself into the dissipations of Paris.

. . . Yet his eyes, too, glowed and filled with tears at the memories of our dreams as students. In the recesses of his deeply wounded vanity there still was faith that the revolution in Russia was close at hand, and that he was called to play a great part in it. It seemed as though he were carousing only *meanwhile,* in the wearisome suspense of waiting for the great work before him, and were convinced that one fine evening he would be summoned from the table in the Café Anglais and borne off to govern Russia. . . . He kept intent watch on what was being done, and impatiently awaited the moment when he would have to take part in earnest and utter the last decisive word.

After my first noisy days in Paris, more serious conversation began, and at once it was evident that we were tuned to very different keys. Sazonov and Bakunin were (like Wysocki and the members of the Polish Central Committee later on) displeased that the news I brought was more concerning the literary and university world than political spheres. They were expecting to be told about parties, secret societies, ministerial crises (under Nicholas!), the opposition (in 1847!), while I talked about professorships, about Granovsky's public lectures, about Byelinsky's articles, about the state of mind of the students and even of the seminarists. They had been too long divorced from Russian life, and had entered too thoroughly into the interests of the 'all-world' revolution and French problems to remember that among us the appearance of *Dead Souls* was an event of far more consequence than the appointment of a couple of Paskevitches as field-marshals and a couple of Filarets as metropolitans. With no Russian books and papers and no regular means of communication, they judged of everything in Russia theoretically and from memory, which throws an artificial light on everything far away.

The difference of our views almost led to a breach between us. It happened like this. On the day before Byelinsky left Paris we saw him home in the evening, and went for a walk in the Champs-Élysées. I saw with terrible clearness that all was over for Byelinsky, that I was pressing his hand for the last time. The mighty, passionate fighter had burnt himself out, death had laid its unmistakable imprint on his face, wan with suffering; he was in acute consumption, but still full of holy energy and holy indignation, still full of his agonising, angry love for Russia. I had a lump in my throat and for a long time I walked in silence, when the unlucky argument which had been ten times already *sur le tapis* was renewed once more.

'It is a pity,' observed Sazonov, 'that Byelinsky has had no career but journalistic work, and under the censorship, too.'

'I think it is hard to reproach him, of all people, for doing little,' I answered.

'Well, with abilities like his he might in other circumstances and in another field have done rather more. . . .'

I felt vexed and wounded. 'But do tell me, please, you now, who are not under the censorship, who are so full of faith in yourselves, so full of strength and talent, what have you done? Or what are you doing? Surely you don't imagine that walking from one end of Paris to the other every day to discuss the boundaries of Poland and Russia with Sluzalski or Chotkewicz is doing something? Or that your talks in cafés and at home, where five fools listen and understand nothing, while another five understand nothing and talk, is doing something?'

'Wait a bit, wait a bit,' said Sazonov, by now considerably nettled: 'you forget our position.'

'What position? You have been living here for years in freedom, in no dire extremity: what more do you want? Positions are created. Strong men make themselves acknowledged and force themselves in. Come, come: one critical article of Byelinsky's is of far more value for the younger generation than playing at being conspirators and politicians. You are living in a sort of delirium and somnambulism, in a perpetual optical illusion with which you deceive your own eyes. . . .'

I was particularly irritated at the time by the two different standards which not only Sazonov but Russians in general applied in appreciating people. Their severe criticism of their own people was transformed into slavish worship before French celebrities. It was annoying to see our friends kow-tow before those champion babblers, who flung them a word, a phrase, a commonplace, uttered with *vitesse accélérée;* and the more meekly the Russians behaved, the more they blushed and tried to conceal their idols' ignorance (as tender parents and sensitive husbands do), the more the latter gave themselves airs and swaggered before their hyperborean Anarchases.[1]

Sazonov even as a student in Russia had been fond of surrounding himself with a retinue of all sorts of mediocrities, who listened to him and followed his lead; and here, too, he was surrounded by all sorts of *lazzarone* of the literary haunts, feeble in mind and body, penny-a-liners, journalistic scavengers such as the gaunt Jules

[1] The reference is to the *Voyage du jeune Anarchasis*, by Barthélemy (1779).—(*Translator's Note.*)

Vécourt, the half-crazy Tardif de Melot, the unknown but great poet Bouilhet;[1] in his chorus, too, were the most narrow-minded Poles, followers of Towjanski, and dull-witted German atheists. How it was they did not bore him is his secret. He almost always brought one or two attendants from his chorus even when he came to me, although I was always bored by them and did not conceal the fact. It seemed particularly odd, too, that he himself was in the position of a Jules Vécourt in his relation to the Marrasts, the Ribeyrolles,[2] and even lesser celebrities.

All this is not quite intelligible for contemporary visitors to Paris. It must not be forgotten that the present Paris is not the *real* Paris, but a new one.

Having become a sort of gathering-place for the whole world Paris has ceased to be a pre-eminently French city. In old days all France was in Paris, and nothing besides; now all Europe is there, and the two Americas besides, but there is less of itself: it has become merged in its function of a world-hotel, a caravanserai, and has lost its individual personality, which once inspired ardent love and burning hate, boundless respect and unlimited aversion.

I need hardly say that the attitude of foreigners to modern Paris has changed. The Allied troops who bivouacked in the Place de la Révolution knew that they had taken a foreign town. The tourist who puts up there now regards Paris as his own; he buys it, he plays with it, and knows very well that he is essential to Paris, and that the old Babylon has rigged herself out, rouged and powdered, not for her own sake but for his.

---

[1] Bouilhet, Louis, was a great friend of Flaubert, with whom he collaborated. His own works include *Hélène Peyron*, and a very successful drama, *La Conjuration d'Amboise*.

[2] Ribeyrolles, a talented writer on *La Réforme*, the organ of the Extreme Left, of which Flocon was editor.—(*Translator's Notes.*)

In 1847 I found still the old Paris—moreover, Paris with a quickened pulse, that had been singing Béranger's songs, with the chorus *'Vive la réforme!'* changed unawares into *'Vive la République!'*

Russians still in those days lived in Paris with an ever-present sense of thankfulness to Providence (and to the regular despatch of remittances) that they were living in it, that they were strolling in the Palais Royal and visiting French people. They frankly worshipped lions and lionesses of every description—celebrated doctors and dancing-girls, the dentist Désirabode and the mad Ma-Pa, and all the literary charlatans and political jugglers of the day.

I hate the systematic, *prémédité* insolence which is the fashion among us. I recognise in it the family traits of the old bullying and arrogance of our officers and landowners, adapted to the manners of Vassilyevsky Island and its streets. But it must not be forgotten that our cringing before West European authorities has come out of the same barracks, the same government offices, the same antechambers, though it has come out of the other door and is addressed to the grand gentleman, the office chief or the commanding officer. In our lack of anything whatever to which to do homage, except brute force and its symbols, stars and ranks in the service, the craving for some table of grades of merit is easy to understand; but, on the other hand, to what men have not the best of our contemporaries bowed down with tender devotion! Even before Werder and Ruge, those mighty dullards of Hegelianism. From this reverence for Germans it may easily be gathered how far they went in their attitude to Frenchmen, to men who are really remarkable—to Pierre Leroux, for instance, or George Sand herself. . . .

I am ashamed that I was at first carried away, and thought that to talk in a café with the historian of the

Ten Years,[1] or at Bakunin's with Proudhon, was something like a promotion, an honour; but in me all attempts at idolatry and fetish-worship do not last long, and very soon give way to complete scepticism.

Three months after I arrived in Paris I began strenuously attacking this form of snobbery, and it was just when my opposition to it was at its height that the argument about Byelinsky took place. Bakunin, with his usual good-heartedness, half assented and laughed; but Sazonov resented it, and continued to regard me as a profane outsider in questions of practical politics. Shortly afterwards I confirmed him in this conviction.

The revolution of February was a complete triumph for him; his journalistic friends received posts in the government, thrones were tottering and leaning for support on poets and doctors. German princelings were asking advice and help from professors and journalists, who only the day before had been persecuted. The Liberals taught them how to fit their narrow crowns on more firmly, that they might not be carried off by the rising hurricane. Sazonov wrote to me in Rome, letter after letter, urging me to come *home*, to Paris, to the one and indivisible republic.

On my return from Italy I found Sazonov preoccupied. Bakunin was not there; he had already gone off to stir up the Western Slavs.

'You don't mean to say,' Sazonov said to me at our first interview, 'that you don't see that our *time has come*?'

'How do you mean?'

'The Russian Government is in an *impasse*.'

'Why! what has happened? A republic has not been proclaimed in the Peter-Paul Fortress, has it?'

'*Entendons-nous*, I don't imagine that we shall have

[1] Louis Blanc, author of *L'Histoire de Dix Ans*, one of the most widely read books of the epoch.—(*Translator's Note*.)

a twenty-fourth of February to-morrow in Russia. No, but the state of public opinion, the torrent of liberal ideas, Austria broken to pieces, Prussia with a constitution, will force the men about the Winter Palace to think a little. They cannot do less than dole out some sort of constitution, *un simulacre de charte*: well, and with that,' he added with a certain impressiveness, 'they must have a liberal, cultured ministry who can speak the language of to-day. Have you thought of that?'

'No!'

'You queer fellow! Where are they going to get cultured ministers?'

'Oh, they'll find them right enough if they want them; but I fancy they won't look for them.'

'This scepticism is quite out of place now; *history is being made*, and very rapidly too. Think a minute—the government will have no choice but to appeal to *us*.'

I looked at him, trying to make out whether he was joking. His face was quite serious, it looked a little flushed and nervous with excitement.

'You mean literally to *us*?'

'Whether to us personally or to our circle does not matter. But just think again: to whom else can they turn?'

'Which portfolio will you undertake?'

'It's silly of you to laugh. It's our misfortune that we don't know how to take advantage of opportunities, *ni se faire valoir*. You keep thinking about your little articles: articles are all very well, but times are changed now; one day in power is worth more than a whole volume of them.'

Sazonov looked with compassion on my unpracticalness, and at last found less sceptical people who put faith in his approaching advent to power. At the end of 1848, two or three German refugees were very regular visitors at the little evening gatherings that were held at Sazonov's. Among them was an Austrian lieutenant who had distinguished himself as a staff-officer under Messenhauser.[1] Once as he was going out at two o'clock at night in a heavy downpour of rain, the officer complained of his hard lot, reflecting on the considerable distance between the Rue Blanche and the Quartier Latin.

'Why were you forced to trudge all that way in such weather?'

'Of course, I was not forced; but, you know, Herr von Sessanoff is vexed if one does not turn up, and I believe that we ought to maintain good relations with him. You know better than I do that with his talent and intellect . . . with the position he occupies in his party, what he may rise to be in the coming revolution in Russia. . . .'

'Well, Sazonov,' I said to him next day, 'you have found Archimedes' point; there is a man who believes in your future portfolio, and that man is Lieutenant So-and-So.'

Time passed, the revolution in Russia did not come off, and no one sent envoys to fetch us home. The sinister days of June had come; Sazonov undertook to write a leading article for the *Epoch*, He spent a long time working at it; read aloud a few fragments, made corrections and alterations, and only just finished it by the winter. He thought it essential 'to explain the last revolution to Russia.' 'Do not expect me,' he wrote at the beginning, 'to describe events; others will do that better than I could. I am giving you the significance, the idea of the revolution which has taken

[1] The real name of Messenhauser was Cæsar Wengel, a soldier and writer, who took an active part in the rising of 1848, first in Lemberg and then in Vienna. On the suppression of the rising he was sentenced to be shot, and asked that as an officer he might give the word of command to the soldiers who were to shoot him, and so conducted the business of his own execution with remarkable composure.—(*Translator's Note*.)

place.' Humble work was not enough for him; whenever he did take up the pen, he wanted to do something extraordinary, something momentous; his mind was always haunted by Tchaadayev's letter. The article reached Petersburg, was read in friendly circles, and made no impression.

In the summer of 1848, Sazonov founded an International Club. To it he brought all his Tardifs, Germans, and Messianists. With a beaming face he walked up and down the empty room in a dark blue dress-suit. He opened the International Club with a speech addressed to five or six listeners (of whom I was one[1]) by way of audience, the rest of the party being on the platform in the capacity of committee. Sazonov was followed by Tardif de Melot, a dishevelled figure looking half-asleep, who stood up and boomed off a poem in honour of the Club.

Sazonov frowned, but it was too late to stop the poet.

> 'Worcel, Sassonoff, Elinski, Del Balzo, Leonard . . .
> Et vous tous . . .'

Tardif de Melot bawled with a sort of ecstatic exasperation, unaware of the laughter.

Two or three days afterwards Sazonov sent me one thousand copies of the programme of the opening ceremony; with that the Club ended. Only later on we heard that one of the representatives of humanity, who at that congress represented Spain in particular, and delivered a speech in which he called the executive power *potence ehécoutive*, supposing that was French, narrowly escaped the gallows in England and was sentenced to penal servitude for forging some document.

The failure to become a minister and the collapse of

[1] I was in those days what the Poles call a 'passport man,' and had not yet cut off all possibility of return to Russia.—(*Author's Note.*)

the Club were followed by more modest but far more possible attempts as a journalist. When *La Tribune des Peuples* was established with Mickiewicz as chief editor, Sazonov took a leading position on the paper, wrote two or three very good articles . . . and then ceased, and before the failure of the *Tribune* —that is, before the 13 th of June 1849—he was on bad terms with all the staff. To him it all seemed petty and poor, *il se sentait dérogé,* was vexed at it, finished nothing, dropped what he had begun and flung aside what was half done.

In 1849 I suggested to Proudhon to give the post of foreign editor of the *Voix du Peuple* to Sazonov. With his knowledge of four languages, of literature, of politics, of the history of all the European nations, and his wide acquaintance with political parties, he might have done wonders for the French with this part of the paper. Proudhon had nothing to do with the internal arrangements of the foreign news department, it was in my hands, but I could do nothing from Geneva. A month later Sazonov handed the foreign editorship to Hoetsky and severed his connection with the paper. 'I have a great respect for Proudhon,' he wrote to me in Geneva, 'but there is not room on one journal for two such personalities as mine and his.'

A year later Sazonov joined *La Réforme*, then being revived by the followers of Mazzini. Lamennais was the chief editor. But on that paper also there was not room for two great men. Sazonov worked on it for three months, and then threw up *La Réforme*. With Proudhon he had fortunately parted peacefully, but he quarrelled with Lamennais. Sazonov charged the niggardly old man with using the funds of the paper for his personal ends. Lamennais, recalling the habits of his clerical youth, resorted to what is the *ultima ratio* in Western Europe, and spread concerning Sazonov the suggestion that he might be an agent of the Russian Government.

The last time I saw Sazonov was in Switzerland in 1851. He had been deported from France, and was living in Geneva. This was at the very greyest, most oppressive period; a brutal reaction was triumphant everywhere. Sazonov's faith in France and in the coming change in the ministry in Petersburg was shaken. He was bored and worried by his idle life, did not succeed with any work, caught at everything without perseverance, lost his temper, and drank. Moreover, the life of petty cares and the everlasting struggle with creditors, the effort to obtain money, together with the talent for flinging it away and the incapacity for ordering his life, brought a great deal of nervous irritability and dismal prose into Sazonov's daily existence; by then his life of reckless gaiety was no longer an enjoyment but a habit, while in old days he really had known how to enjoy himself.

A few words about his domestic life will not be out of place, especially as it was distinguished by the same note of gay recklessness, and was not without its striking contrasts in colour.

In the early years of his Parisian life Sazonov met a wealthy widow, and his connection with her drew him still further into a life of luxury. She went off to Russia, leaving him plenty of money and their daughter to bring up. The widow had scarcely had time to reach Petersburg when her place was filled by a buxom Italian with a voice at which the walls of Jericho would have fallen once more.

Two or three years later the widow took it into her head to pay her friend and her daughter a quite unexpected visit. She was struck by the Italian woman.

'What person is this?' she asked, scanning her from head to foot.

'Lili's nurse, and a very good one.'

'But how can she teach her to speak French with such an accent? That's a pity. I had better find a Parisian and you get rid of this one.'

'*Mais, ma chère* . . .'

'*Mais, mon cher* . . .' and the widow took her daughter away.

This was not only an emotional but a financial crisis. Sazonov was far from being poor; his sisters sent him twenty thousand francs a year from the revenue of his estate. But, being accustomed to spend it recklessly, he did not think of diminishing his establishment, but resorted to borrowing. He borrowed right and left, got what he could from Russia out of his sisters, borrowed from friends and enemies, borrowed from money-lenders, from fools, from Russians and non-Russians. For a long time he managed and kept afloat in this way, but at last got into trouble, and was thrown into Clichy, as I have mentioned already.

It was during this period that his elder sister's husband died. Hearing that their brother was in prison, the two sisters came to get him out. As is always the case, they knew nothing of the manner of life of their Nikolinka. The two sisters adored him, regarded him as a genius, and were impatiently awaiting the moment when he would appear to the world in all his power and glory.

They were met by various disillusionments which surprised them the more as they were so unexpected. On the morning after their arrival, taking with them Count Chotkewicz, a friend of Sazonov's, with them, they went to buy him out as a surprise. Chotkewicz left them in the carriage and went away promising to return in a minute with their brother. Hour after hour passed, Nikolinka did not appear . . . no doubt the formalities take a long time, thought the ladies waiting wearily in the cab. . . . At last Chotkewicz ran up alone, flushed in the face, and smelling strongly of spirituous liquor. He announced that Sazonov would be with them directly; that he was just giving a farewell lunch to his companions and treating them to wine; that this was the usual thing. This was rather a stab to the tender hearts of the fair travellers . . . but . . . but here at last their Nikolinka, solid, stout, and perspiring, flung himself into their arms, and they set off homewards satisfied and happy.

They had heard something . . . about some Italian woman . . . an ardent daughter of Italy, unable to resist the genius from the hyperborean north, who had been enchanted by her southern voice and the fire of her eyes. . . . Blushing and abashed, they indicated the timid desire to make her acquaintance. He agreed to everything, and went home. Two days later the sisters planned a second surprise for their brother, which was even less successful than the first.

At eleven o'clock one hot morning the sisters set off to have a look at this Francesca da Rimini and her *ménage* with Nikolinka. The younger sister opened the door, and stopped short. . . . In the small drawing-room Sazonov was sitting on the carpeted floor in extreme deshabille, and beside him the stout Signora P., scantily veiled in a light dressing-gown. The signora was laughing with the full force of her lusty Italian lungs at something Nikolinka was telling her. Beside them stood a pail of ice, and in it, tilted on one side, was a bottle of champagne.

What happened next I do not know, but the effect produced was strong and lasting. The younger sister came to consult me about this incident, of which she spoke with tears and sobs. I tried to comfort her by assurances that the first days after Clichy were different from the average.

All this was followed by a prosaic move into smaller

lodgings. . . . The valet, who was a master at putting on a cravat of impenetrably solid silk and adroitly sticking a pearl pin into it, was dismissed, and after him the pin itself appeared in a shop window.

So passed another five years. Sazonov went to Paris from Switzerland, and then went back again from Paris to Switzerland. To get rid of the buxom Italian, he devised the most original plan—he married her and then left her.

Something had come between us; he did not treat me openly in a matter that was very dear to my heart. I could not get over it.

Meantime a new epoch was beginning for Russia, Sazonov was eager to take part in it: wrote articles[1] that were unsuccessful, tried to return to Russia and did not succeed, and finally left Paris. For a long while nothing was heard of him.

One day a Russian who had just come from Switzerland to London said to me: 'An old friend of yours was buried the day before I left Geneva.'

'Who was that?'

'Sazonov; and only fancy, there was not one Russian at his funeral.'

And it sent a stab to my heart to think with remorse that I had abandoned him for so long . . . .

(*Written in* 1863.)

II

THE ENGELSONS

They are both dead. He was not more than thirty-five; she was younger.

He died ten years ago in Jersey: his coffin was followed to the grave by his widow, his child, and a sturdily built,

[1] His article on 'The Position of Russia in the All-World Exhibition' was published in vol. ii. of the *Polar Star*.—(*Author's Note*.)

dishevelled-looking old man with large, marked, rough features; in his face were mingled genius and frenzy, fanaticism and irony, the intensity of an Old Testament prophet and a Jacobin of the year 1793. That old man was Pierre Leroux.

She died at the beginning of 1865 in Spain. I heard of her death a few months later.

I have not heard where the child is.

The man of whom I am speaking was once near and dear to me; he first tended deep wounds when they were fresh; he was a brother, a sister to me. She, scarcely knowing what she was doing, estranged him from me. He became my enemy. . . .

The news of her death brought them back to my memory again. . . .

I took up the manuscript I had written about them in 1859, and read it through by way of psalter over the dead.

For a long time I hesitated whether to print it or not, and only lately decided to do so. My intention is good, and my story is true. I do not want to cast reproaches on their grave, but together with the reader to trace once again, in fresh instances, the intricate, morbid warping of character in the last generation under Nicholas.

CHÂTEAU BOISSIÈRE, *December* 31, 1865.

I

At the beginning of 1850 a Russian arrived in Nice with his wife. They were pointed out to me on the parade. They both belonged to the class who were waiting for the turn of the tide: he was thin, pale, consumptive, with reddish fair hair; she was a beauty who had faded early, worn-out, half-shattered, exhausted.

A doctor living in the household of a Russian lady

told me that the fair gentleman had been a Lyceum student, that he was reading *Vom andern Ufer*, that he had been mixed up in the Petrashev case, and consequently wished to make my acquaintance. I answered that I was always glad to meet a good Russian, especially a Lyceum student, and one who had had a hand in a case of which I knew little, but which had been for me like the olive branch brought by the dove to Noah's ark.

Some days passed without my seeing either the doctor or the new Russian. Suddenly between nine and ten one evening a card was brought me; it was he. Karl Vogt and I were sitting in the dining-room. I told the servant to ask the visitor upstairs into the drawing-room, and went upstairs before the rest. There I found him, pale, trembling, apparently in a feverish condition. He could scarcely tell me his name; when he was a little calmer, he jumped up from his chair, rushed at me, kissed me effusively, and before I could quite recover myself, with the words, 'So at last I am really seeing you,' he kissed my hand. 'What are you about? Upon my soul!' I said, but by then he was in tears.

I looked at him in perplexity; was this nervous instability or simply madness?

Apologising and showering compliments on me, he told me with extraordinary rapidity and much gesticulation that I had saved his life, and this was how. Desperate with acute depression in Petersburg, expelled from the Lyceum for some nonsense or other, disgusted with a job in the service which he had been obliged to accept, and seeing no solution for himself personally, nor for things in general, he had made up his mind to poison himself, and a few hours before carrying out his design went wandering aimlessly about the streets: came to Izler's and picked up a volume of the *Notes of the Fatherland*. My article, 'A propos of a Drama,' was in it. Reading it gradually absorbed his attention; he felt better, he felt ashamed of having so weakly given in to sorrow and despair when public interests were springing up on all sides and calling for all who were young, for all who had strength, and instead of taking poison Engelson asked for half a bottle of madeira, read the article over again, and from that time became my ardent admirer.

He sat on till late at night, and went away asking leave to come again soon. Through his tangled talk, continually interspersed with anecdotes and digressions, one could see a richly endowed brain, unmistakable dialectic ability, and, still more clearly, something warped and distorted that flung him from one extreme to the other, from an indignation intensified by sorrow, and made poignant by misfortune, to ironical clowning, from tears to affectation.

He left me with a strange impression. At first I did not quite believe in him, then I was tired by him—he seemed to affect one's nerves too much; but by degrees I grew used to his oddities, and was glad of an original person to break the monotonous boredom induced by the vast majority of Western Europeans.

Engelson had read a great deal and studied a great deal, he was a linguist and a philologist, and brought into everything the scepticism with which we are so familiar, and which exacts so high a price for the pain it leaves. In old days they would have said of him that he had read himself silly. His over-stimulated intellectual activity was too much for the strength of his frail organism. Wine, with which he conquered fatigue and stimulated himself, fanned his thoughts and imagination into long, bright tongues of fire, that were rapidly consuming his sick body.

His disorderly living and drinking, his perpetual, irritable mental activity, his conspicuous many-sidedness and his conspicuous futility, his utter idleness, his extreme violence of feeling and extreme apathy, vividly recalled the past to me, in spite of the immense difference between all this and our old ways in Moscow. Again I heard the sounds not only of my own language but of my own thought. He had been a witness of the reign of terror in Petersburg after 1848, and he knew the literary circles. Entirely cut off from Russia as I was at that time, I listened greedily to his accounts.

We took to seeing each other often, nearly every evening.

His wife, too, was a strange creature. Her face, by nature handsome, was racked by neuralgic pains and a sort of restless anxiety. She was a Russified-Norwegian, and spoke Russian with a slight accent which suited her. As a rule she was more silent and reserved than he. Their home life was not cheerful: there was something nervous, *unheimlich*, strained, about them; there was something lacking in their life, and something superfluous in it, and one felt this continually like electricity, unseen and menacing, in the air.

I often found them in the large room which served them as bedroom and sitting-room in the hotel, in a state of utter prostration. She, with tear-stained eyes, helpless in one corner; he pale as death, with white lips, distraught, and silent in the other. . . . So they would sit at times for whole hours, whole days together, and that a few yards from the dark blue Mediterranean, from groves of orange-trees, to which everything—the sapphire sky and the bright noisy gaiety of southern life—invited one. They did not actually quarrel; it was not a case of jealousy nor estrangement, nor any tangible cause, indeed. . . . He would suddenly get up, go to her, fall on his knees and sometimes with sobs repeat: 'I have been your ruin, my child, your ruin!' and she would weep and believe that he had been her ruin. 'When shall I die and leave him in freedom?' she used to say to me.

All this was new to me, and I felt so sorry for them that I wanted to cry with them, and even more to say to them: 'Oh, come, come, you are not so miserable and not so bad, you are both splendid people; let us take a boat and drown sorrow in the dark blue sea.' I did do this sometimes, and succeeded in drawing them out of themselves. But by next morning the paroxysm would return. . . . They were somehow so on each other's nerves, and had reached such an hysterical *impasse*, that the slightest word destroyed the harmony and, as it were, called up furies again from the bottom of their hearts.

I sometimes fancied that, continually tearing open their wounds, they found a sort of stinging enjoyment in the pain; that this gnawing at each other had become necessary to them, like vodka or pickle. But unfortunately the physique of both was unmistakably beginning to be exhausted; they were on the high road to the lunatic asylum or the grave.

Her mind, by no means without talents, was undisciplined and at the same time depraved; her character was far more complex, and in a certain sense she had far more fortitude and strength than he had. Moreover, she had not a shade of the unity, the consistency, that unhappy consistency which he retained even in the most violent extremes and the sharpest contradictions. In her, side by side with her despair, her desire to die, her habit of moaning and groaning, there was a thirst for worldly pleasures and a concealed coquetry, a love for dress and luxury, denied as it were intentionally, to spite herself. She was always dressed becomingly and with taste. She longed to be an emancipated woman according to the ideas of the period, and the victim of an immense, original, psychic unhappiness, like George Sand's heroines . . . but her old accustomed, traditional life dragged her like a heavy weight towards quite a different sphere.

What gave poetic charm to Engelson, and did much to make up for his defects, and what served as a safety-valve for himself, she could not understand. She could not follow his racing thought, his rapid transitions from despair to wit and laughter, from candid mirth to candid tears. She lagged behind, losing the thread, distracted. . . . His caricatures of his own gloomy thoughts were beyond her comprehension. When Engelson, after a perfect feast of puns and jokes, mockery and teasing, getting more and more into the spirit of the thing, began acting regular scenes at which one could only laugh helplessly, she would go out of the room, exasperated; she was offended at 'his unseemly behaviour before outsiders.' He usually noticed this, and as nothing could stop him when once he was set going, he would play the fool more extravagantly than ever, and then waltz round with her and ask her with glowing cheeks and perspiring brows: *'Ach ,mein lieber Gott, Alexandra Christianovna, war es denn nicht respectabel?'* She would weep more than ever, till he suddenly changed, grew gloomy and morose, drank glass after glass of brandy, and went home, or simply fell asleep upon the sofa.

Next day I had to reconcile them and make the peace, and he so earnestly kissed her hands and so funnily asked to be forgiven his sins, that even she could not restrain herself sometimes and laughed with us.

I must explain in what these performances, which were such a source of woe to poor Alexandra Christianovna, consisted. Engelson's comic talent was unmistakable and immense; such biting satire was never equalled by Levassor, hardly by Grasso at his best, and Gorbunov in some of his stories. Moreover, half of it was improvised; he would bring in additions and variations while preserving the same framework. If he had cared to train and develop this gift, he would certainly have been in the foremost ranks of *satirical* comedians, but Engelson never trained nor developed anything in himself. Talents shot up like vigorous wild plants and were choked in his unstable soul, both by domestic cares which took up half his time, and by his habit of catching at everything in the world from philology and chemistry to political economy and philosophy. In this respect Engelson was a typical Russian, although his father was of Finnish extraction.

He acted everything in the world—officials and Russian gentlemen, priests and police-constables; but the best of his performances were concerned with Nicholas, for whom he had a profound, sincere, and active hatred. He would take a chair *à la* Napoleon, sit astride it, and sternly ride up to a corps on parade . . . epaulettes, hats, casques shaking all round him . . . it is Nicholas at a review; he is moved to wrath, and, turning his horse, says to the commanding officer, 'Bad'; the commanding officer listens with reverent awe, looks after Nicholas, and then, dropping his voice and gasping with fury, whispers to the general of the division: 'You appear, your Excellency, to be busy about something else and not your duties. What a wretched division! what regimental commanders! I'll teach them.'

The general of the division turns redder and redder, and pounces on the first colonel he comes across, and so from one grade to the next, with incredibly true, almost imperceptible nuances, the Imperial 'bad' passes down to the sergeant, at whom the squadron commanding officer swears like a trooper, and who, without answering, pokes the scabbard of his sword with all his might into the ribs of the nearest soldier, who has done nothing.

Engelson would portray with amazing fidelity, not

only the characteristics of each rank, but also each man's movement as he tugged at his horse in his fury and then raged at it for not standing still.

Another performance was of a more peaceful kind. The Emperor Nicholas is dancing the French quadrille. *Vis-à-vis* is a foreign diplomat, on one side a general, stiff as on parade, on the other a civilian grandee. This was a perfect *chef-d'œuvre*. Engelson would take one of us for his partner. The flower of it all was Nicholas —playing the autocratic Tsar over the quadrille, the conscious firmness of every step, the brilliant perfection of each movement, together with the indulgent and gracious glance at his partner, which is transformed at once into a command to the general, and warning not to forget himself to the civilian gentleman. To describe this in words is impossible. The general, who, rigidly erect, with his elbows a little rounded, with strained attention walks in time through the figures under the stern observation of his gracious monarch, and the distracted civilian with his legs shaking under him from terror, with a smile on his face and almost a tear in his eye—all this was performed so that a man who had never seen Nicholas could thoroughly grasp the agonising ordeal of an imperial quadrille, and the danger of having the Most High as a *vis-à-vis*. I forgot to say that the foreign diplomat was the only one who danced with studied negligence and great finish, concealing the uncomfortable feeling of uneasiness of which the most valiant is conscious when he has a lighted cigar close to a barrel of gunpowder.

But although Engelson's grimacing and foolery roused his wife's indignation, it does not follow that there was any more unison or harmony about her; quite the contrary, there was an absolute chaos in her head, that was destructive of all order, of all consistency, and made her impossible to cope with. In her case I learnt for the first time how little you can do with logic in discussion with a woman, especially when the discussion relates to practical affairs. In Engelson the lack of harmony was like the mental confusion after a fire, after a funeral, after a crime perhaps; but in her case it was like an untidy room in which everything is flung about higgledy-piggledy—children's toys, a wedding dress, a prayer-book, a novel of George Sand's, slippers, flowers, plates. In her half-conscious ideas and half-undermined beliefs, in her claims to an impossible freedom and to independence of all customary external bonds, there was something suggestive of a child of eight, a girl of eighteen, and an old woman of eighty. Many times I told her that. And, strange to say, even her face was prematurely faded; it looked old from the absence of some of her teeth, and at the same time it retained a childish expression.

Engelson was entirely to blame for the chaos in her mind.

His wife was the spoilt child of a mother who had adored her. An elderly, phlegmatic official of Swedish origin sought her in marriage when she was eighteen. In a moment of childish caprice and vexation with her mother, she agreed to marry him. She wanted to be her own mistress and sit at the head of the table.

When the honeymoon of freedom, visits, and fine clothes was over, the bride was insufferably bored; although her husband behaved with strict propriety, took her to the theatre and arranged evening tea-parties for her, she had an aversion for him; she struggled with him for three or four years, grew tired of it, and went back to her mother. They were divorced. Her mother died, and she was left alone, suffering and melancholy, with her health prematurely broken in the struggle with her absurd marriage, with emptiness and hunger in her heart and an idle brain.

It was just at this time that Engelson was expelled from the Lyceum. He was nervous, irritable, and, with a passionate yearning for love and a morbid lack of confidence in himself, was consumed by *amour-propre*. . . . He had made her acquaintance while her mother was living, and they became great friends after her death. It would have been strange if he had not fallen in love with her. Whether the feeling were likely to be lasting or not, he was bound to love her passionately; everything helped to bring this about . . . the fact that she was a woman without a husband, a widow and not a widow, a bride and not a bride, and that she was pining for something, was in love with another man, and made miserable by her love. This other was an 'energetic young fellow,' an officer and a literary man, but a desperate gambler. They quarrelled over this invincible passion for play; later on, he shot himself.

Engelson never left her side; he comforted her, amused her, occupied her. It was his first and last love. She wanted to study, or rather to learn without studying; he undertook to be her Mentor—she asked for books.

The first book Engelson gave her was Feuerbach's *Das Wesen des Christenthums*. He took the place of commentator, and day by day he pulled from under the feet of his Héloïse, who could not step on firm ground for the Chinese shoes of her early Christian training, the prop by means of which she might somehow have kept her balance.

Emancipation from the traditional morality, said Goethe, never leads to good unless the mind has grown strong; indeed, only reason is worthy to replace the religion of duty. Here was a woman sleeping the deep slumber of moral security, lulled by traditions and full of the dreams natural to a patriarchal soul, tinged with Christianity, tinged with romantic and moral notions; and Engelson tried to educate her at one blow on the method of English nurses, who, when the baby screams from stomach-ache, pour a glass of gin into its mouth. He flung into her immature, childish conceptions a rankling ferment with which men are rarely equal to coping, which he himself could not cope with but only understand.

Overwhelmed by the overthrow of all her moral conceptions and all her religious convictions, and finding in Engelson himself nothing but doubt, nothing but irony and denial of the old, she lost the only compass, the only guide she had left, and was like a boat adrift at sea, twisting and turning without a rudder. The equilibrium arrived at by life itself, resting—like the opposite weights of a pendulum—on absurdities which exclude each other and are maintained by so doing, was broken.

She flung herself into reading with avidity, understanding and not understanding, and mixing up the philosophy of her nurses with the philosophy of Hegel, sentimental socialism with the economic conceptions of conventional housekeeping. With all that, her health grew worse, boredom and misery continued; she pined and grew thin, had a desperate longing to go abroad, and was afraid of persecutions and enemies of some sort.

After a prolonged struggle, Engelson, rallying all his forces, said to her: 'You want to travel; how can you go alone? . . . You will meet with all sorts of unpleasantness, you will be lost without a friend, without a protector with the right to protect you. You know that I would lay down my life for you . . . give me your hand—I will care for you, soothe you, watch over you. . . . I will be your father, your mother, your nurse, and your husband, but it must be legally. I will be with you, near you. . . .'

This was said by a man under thirty, and passionately in love. She was touched, and accepted him as her husband unconditionally. A short, time afterwards they went abroad.

Such was the past of my new acquaintances. When Engelson told me all this, when he bitterly complained that this marriage had been the ruin of them both, and I saw for myself how they were fretting away in a sort of moral furnace which they intentionally fanned, I came to the conviction that this unhappiness was due to their having known too little of each other beforehand, their being too closely bound together now, their having built their life too much on personal feeling, and their putting too much faith in being husband and wife. If they could have parted, each might have sighed in freedom, have grown calm, and perhaps begun to blossom afresh. Time would have shown whether they were really so necessary to each other; in any case, the delirium would have been broken for a time without catastrophe. I did not conceal my opinion from Engelson; he agreed with me. But all this was a *mirage*; in reality he had not the strength to leave her, nor she to take the plunge. . . . They secretly *wanted* to hover on the brink of these resolutions without carrying them into execution.

My view was too sane and simple to be correct in regard to such intricately pathological characters and such sick nerves.

II

The type to which Engelson belonged was at that time rather new to me. At the beginning of the 'forties I had seen such a type only in embryo. It developed in Petersburg towards the end of Byelinsky's career, and was formed after I left and before Tchernyshevsky appeared. It was the type of the Petrashev group and their friends. That group was made up of young and gifted men, extremely intelligent and extremely cultured, but nervous, morbid, and warped by their surroundings.

Among them there was no example of striking stupidity, no one who wrote ungrammatically—those types belong to quite a different period; but in them there was something degenerate, abnormal.

The followers of Petrashev made a bold and ardent dash into activity, and astonished all Russia by the *Dictionary of Foreign Words*. The intense mental activity of the 'forties was their heritage, and they passed straight from German philosophy into Fourier's phalanstery, into becoming followers of Kant.

Surrounded by petty and worthless people, proud of the attentions of the police, and conscious of their own superiority, from the very time they left school they prized too highly their negative achievement, or rather their possible achievement. This led to immoderate vanity—not that youthful healthy vanity becoming in a lad who dreams of a great future, becoming in a man in the fulness of his powers and in the fulness of activity, not that which in old days has led men to perform miracles of daring and to endure chains and death for the sake of glory, but, on the contrary, a morbid vanity, hindering all work through its vast pretensions, irritable, ready to take offence, conceited to the point of rudeness, and at the same time diffident.

Between their pretensions and their appreciation by their neighbours the distance was immeasurable. Society will not accept blank cheques for the future, but insists on work being completed before giving personal recognition. They had little power of hard work and perseverance; they only had enough of each for understanding and assimilating what had been worked out by others. They wanted to have harvests for the intention of sowing, and to be rewarded for having their granaries full. 'The insulting way in which they were overlooked by society' worried them, made them unjust to others, and reduced them to despair and *Fratzenhaftigkeit*.

In the person of Engelson J studied the difference between that generation and our own. Later on I met many men not so talented, not so cultured, but with the same obviously morbid warp in all their composition.

A terrible sin lies at the door of the government of Nicholas in this moral destruction of a generation, in this spiritual depraving of its children. The wonder is that the strong and healthy, though warped, still survived. Every one knows the celebrated list of instructions to teachers in the Cadet Corps. In the Lyceum things were better, but of late years it, too, had incurred the hatred of Nicholas. The whole system of government education lay in instilling the religion of obedience, leading up to power as its reward. The feelings of the young, naturally radiant, were coarsely driven inwards, and replaced by ambition and jealous, envious rivalry. What did not perish came out sick, deranged. . . . Together with burning pride, they were inoculated with a sort of spiritlessness, a sense of impotence, of fatigue before beginning work. Young men became hypochondriacal, suspicious, tired before they were twenty. They were all tainted with the passion for introspection, self-analysis, self-accusation; they scrupulously believed their psychic experiences, and loved making endless confessions and giving descriptions of neurotic incidents of their lives. In later years it happened to me several times to receive the confessions not only of men but of women belonging to this category. After watching with sympathy their remorse, their pathological self-castigation, which approached gross calumny upon themselves, I at last came to the conviction that this was only one of the forms of the same vanity. One had but to cease protesting and sympathising and to agree with the repentant sinners, to see how readily malignant and how mercilessly vindictive these Magdalens —of both sexes—became. With them, like the Christian priest before the mighty of this world, you are only privileged solemnly to absolve their sins and to keep silent.

These nervous people, though excessively ready to take offence, shuddering like a sensitive plant at the faintest rough handling, are incredibly harsh in their own language. As a rule, when it came to revenging themselves, there was no moderation in their language—a terrible defect of taste, which betrays a profound contempt for the person addressed and an insulting indulgence for self. This lack of restraint among Russians comes from the homes of landowners, from government offices and army barracks; but how is it that it has survived and developed in the younger generation whilst skipping ours? That is a psychological problem.

In our old student circles we scolded each other roundly, argued roughly and emphatically, but in the most violent fray something remained outside the pale. . . . For our nervous friends of Engelson's generation this limit did not exist, they did not think it necessary to restrain themselves; for the sake of a vain and momentary vindictiveness, for the sake of getting the upper hand in an argument, they spared nothing, and I have often, with horror and amazement, seen them— including Engelson himself—without a trace of pity, fling the most precious pearls into the corrosive fluid of their bitterness, 'and weep afterwards.' With the change of the nervous current, remorse would follow, and entreaties for forgiveness from the outraged idol. They are not fastidious, and pour filth into the very cup from which they drink.

Their repentances are sincere, but do not prevent repetitions of the offence. Some spring regulating and controlling the action of the wheels within them is broken; the wheels turn with tenfold swiftness, doing no work, but injuring the machine; harmonious combination is broken, the aesthetic mean is lost; there is no living with them, and there is no living for them themselves.

Happiness does not exist for them, they are not able to take care of it. The slightest cause provokes them to ruthless antagonism and makes them behave rudely with every one near them. By irony they have ruined and spoilt as much in life as the Germans have by mawkish sentimentality. Strange to say, these people are greedily anxious to be loved, they seek enjoyment, and when they lift the cup to their lips some evil spirit jogs their arm, the wine is spilt upon the floor, and the cup, passionately flung down, rolls in the mud.

III

The Engelsons soon went away to Rome and Naples; they meant to be away for six months, and returned in six weeks. Seeing nothing, they trailed their boredom about Italy, sorrowed in Rome and grieved in Naples, and at last made up their minds to come back to Nice— 'to you for healing,' he wrote to me from Genoa.

Their gloomy depression had increased while they were away. In addition to their nervous hysteria, there were now quarrels which assumed a more and more exasperated and envenomed character. Engelson was to blame for his unrestrained language and cruel words, but she always provoked them, provoked them intentionally, with secret spite and peculiar success in his most good-natured moments; he was never allowed to forget himself for an instant.

Engelson was incapable of holding his tongue; talking to me was a comfort to him, and so he used to tell me everything, even more than he ought, which was awkward for me. I felt that I could not be so open with them as they were with me. Talking came easy to him, complaining comforted him for a time—it did not me.

One day, sitting in a little tavern with me, Engelson said that he was being worn out in the daily struggle, that there was no way of escape from it, that again the thought of cutting short his life seemed to him the only salvation. . . . With his nervous impulsiveness it might well be expected that if a pistol or a glass of poison did come in his way he would sooner or later make an attempt with one or the other.

I was sorry for him. And both of them were to be pitied. She might have been a happy woman if her husband had been a man of serene temper who would have known how to develop her slowly, to be light-hearted in his merriment, and in case of need to influence her, not merely by persuasion but also by authority— grave authority, without irony. There are immature natures which cannot guide themselves, just as there are persons of lymphatic constitution who need a corset to escape curvature of the spine.

While I was thinking of that, Engelson, going on with his talk, came to the same conclusion himself. 'That woman does not love me,' he said, 'and cannot love me; what she does understand and looks for in me is bad, and what is good in me is so much Chinese to her. She is corrupted by bourgeois ideas, by her external *Respektabilität*, her petty domesticity. We torment each other, we are tormenting each other to death; I see that clearly.'

It seemed to me that if a man could talk in that way of the woman nearest to him, the chief tie between them was broken. And so I admitted to him that, having watched their life together for a long time past with deep sympathy, I had often asked myself why they went on living together. 'Your wife is pining for Petersburg, for her brothers and her old nurse; why don't you arrange for her to go home, and you to remain here?'

'I've thought of it a thousand times; it's the one

thing I wish for. But in the first place, she has no one to go with; and in the second, she would be bored to death in Petersburg.'

'Well, but she's bored to death here. As for having no one to send her with, that's a relic of our old Russian notions. You can take your wife to the steamer at Stettin, and the steamer will find its way by itself. If you haven't the money, I'll lend it you.'

'You're right, and that's what I shall certainly do. I am sorry for her, my heart aches for her, all the love I have in me I have concentrated on her. I sought in her not only a wife, but a creature whom I could develop and educate after my own fancy. I thought that she would be my child—the task was beyond my strength. But who could have guessed that I should find such contradictions, such stubbornness?'—he paused, and then added: 'To tell you all I think—she needs a different husband . . . if a man turned up worthy of her whom she could love, I would give her up to him, and we should both recover—that would be better than Petersburg.'

I took all this *au pied de la lettre*. That he was sincere, there is no doubt. That is just the difficulty with these impulsive, uncontrolled creatures; they can, like good actors, enter so thoroughly into different parts, and so identify themselves with them, that a cardboard dagger seems to them the real thing, and they shed genuine tears over 'Hecuba.'

We were then living together at Ste. Hélène. Two days after my conversation with Engelson, Madame Engelson, with a tear-stained face, came into the drawing-room late in the evening, a candle in her hand; she set the candle on the table, and said she wanted to have a little talk with me. We sat down . . . after a brief and obscure prelude touching upon the fate which pursued her, on Engelson's unfortunate character and her own, she announced that she had made up her mind to return to Petersburg, and did not know how to do it. 'You alone have influence over him; persuade him to let me go really. I know that in moments of vexation he is ready in words to put me in the posting-chaise at once, but all that is only words. Persuade him, save us both, and give me your word to look after him just at first, comfort him . . . it will be hard for him, he is ill and nervous.' And again sobbing, she hid her face in her handkerchief.

I did not believe in the depth of her woe, but I saw very clearly what a false move I had made by speaking openly to Engelson; it was evident to me that he had repeated our conversation to her.

I had no choice left; I repeated my own words to her, softening them in form. She got up, thanked me, and added that if she did not go she would throw herself into the sea; that she had that evening been burning a great many papers, and wished to put some others in a sealed packet in my keeping. It was clear to me that she was by no means so passionately anxious to go away, but through some self-indulgent caprice wanted to drag on and pine away in melancholy. Moreover, I saw that, if she were wavering without any settled plan, he was not wavering but distinctly did not want her to go. She had great power over him; she knew this, and, building upon it, allowed him to rage, to rear, to foam at the bit, knowing that, however he might jib, things would go not as he willed but as she willed.

She never forgave me for my advice; she feared my influence, though she had unmistakable proof of my powerlessness.

For ten days there was no talk about going away. Then followed periodical skirmishes. Once or twice a week she would come to me with tear-stained eyes and announce that now all was over, and that next day she would get ready to go to Petersburg or to the bottom of the sea. Engelson would come out of his room, twitching convulsively, with a green face and trembling hands; he would vanish for some ten hours, and would come back covered with dust, exhausted and rather drunk, would take a passport to be viséd, or obtain a permit for Genoa;. then it would all subside again and fall back into the every-day routine.

Externally, Madame Engelson was completely reconciled with me, but from that time she began to conceive something like a hatred for me. Before that she had disputed with me and been angry without concealing it . . . now she became extraordinarily amiable. She was annoyed that I had seen through something; that I had not been touched by her tragic destiny or taken her for an unhappy victim, but had looked on her as a capricious invalid; that, far from shedding tears of platonic sympathy with her, I doubted whether she did not find enjoyment rather than distress in tears, heart-rending scenes, explanations lasting several hours, and so on and so on.

Time passed, and by degrees much was changed. With the rapidity which only occurs in nervous invalids she regained her health, became more lively, and even more careful of her dress. And although the most nonsensical things would lead again to the old scenes between her and Engelson, to a farewell à la Socrates before the hemlock, and to a readiness to follow in Sappho's footsteps to the bottom of the sea, yet on the whole things went better. The woman who had been for ever lying down from weakness, for ever exhausted, drew herself up as erect as Sixtus v., and began to grow so stout that one day poor Kolya, sitting at dinner and looking at her full bosom, said, shaking his head: '*Sehr viel Milch.*'

It was evident that some new interest was occupying

her, that something had awakened her from her morbid lethargy. From the time of my open explanation with her, she had begun a persistent game, thinking over every move, like the gamblers *du Café Régent*, and patiently correcting her mistakes. Sometimes she betrayed herself and made a blunder, carried too far in one direction or the other, but she steadily returned to her original plan. This plan went now beyond the tightening of her grip over Engelson, and beyond revenging herself on me; she aimed at nothing less than getting us all, the whole household, in her power, and taking advantage of Natalie's being more and more seriously ill to control the education of the children and our whole life—or, if she failed, breaking off my relations with Engelson at all costs.

But before she could obtain complete success, there were many very difficult moves to be taken, painful concessions, cat-like tactics, and much patient waiting: she accomplished a great deal, but not everything. Engelson's incessant chatter hindered her as much as my open eyes.

She might have made a better use of the energy, the force and the persistence which she wasted on her craftily interwoven schemes . . . but personal feeling and vanity intoxicate people, and, once entering upon the dark game of intrigue, it is hard to stop and hard to see anything clearly. As a rule, light is only brought into the room after the crime has been committed; that is how it is that both the catastrophe and the sting of conscience are irremediable.

IV

. . . Of the misfortunes that fell upon me in 1851 and 1852 I speak in another place. Engelson brought me much comfort in my sorrow. I should have stayed a long time with him near the graveyard, but the restless vanity of his wife had no pity even on mourning.

Some weeks after the funeral, Engelson, agitated and melancholy, with evident reluctance and evidently not of his own initiative, asked me whether I were not thinking of entrusting the education of my children to his wife.

I answered that the children, except the eldest, Sasha, were going to Paris with Marya Kasparovna Reihel, and I openly admitted that I could not accept his suggestion.

My answer wounded him, and it hurt me to wound him. 'Tell me,' I said, 'speaking honestly, do you think your wife competent to educate children?'

'No,' Engelson answered, 'but . . . but perhaps it's a *planche de salut* for her; she is just as wretched as ever, and it would mean your trusting her, and a new duty.'

'Yes, but if the experiment didn't answer?'

'You are right; let us say no more about it; it is sad.'

Engelson really agreed with me, and said no more. But she had not expected so simple an answer; on this question I would not give in, and she would not, and, beside herself with vexation, she immediately made up her mind to take Engelson away from Nice. Three days later he told me he was going to Genoa.

'What is the matter?' I asked; 'and why are you going so soon?'

'Well, you see for yourself my wife does not get on with you, nor with your friends, so I've made up my mind . . . and perhaps it is for the best.'

And next day they went away.

Afterwards I left Nice. On my way through Genoa we met peaceably. Surrounded by our friends, among whom were Medici, Pisacane, Cosenz, and Mordini, she seemed calmer and better in health. Nevertheless, she could not let slip any chance for having a spiteful dig at me. I moved away, said nothing; that was no use. Even when I had gone to Lugano she kept up her poisoned *petits points*, and this in the rare postscripts to her husband's letters, as though with his *visa*.

At last these pin-pricks, at a time when I was utterly crushed by grief and distress, drove me out of all patience. I had done nothing to deserve them, nothing to provoke them. On getting one of her spiteful postscripts saying that Engelson would still have to pay dearly for his wholehearted devotion to friends who would do nothing for him, I wrote to Engelson that it was time to put a stop to this.

'I do not understand,' I wrote, 'why your wife has got a grudge against me. If it is because I did not give my children into her keeping, surely that is no justification for it?' I reminded him of our last conversation, and added: 'We know that Saturn devoured his own children, but for any one to show his gratitude to his friends for their sympathy by bestowing his children's education on them is something unheard of.'

She never forgave me that sally, but, what is far more remarkable, he never forgave me for it either, though at first he showed no sign of resenting it . . . but he reproached me with those words a year later. . . .

I went to London; Engelson settled for the winter in Genoa, and afterwards moved to Paris.[1]

V

The proverb, 'He who has not been in the sea has not prayed to God,' may be varied in this way: the woman who has not had children does not know what disinterested devotion is, and this is particularly true of married women; in them childlessness almost always

[1] A series of very remarkable letters of his, of which I propose to publish a considerable number some day, date from this period.— (*Author's Note*.)

develops a coarse egoism—if; that is, some impersonal interest does not incidentally save them. The old maid has some belated yearnings that soften her, she is still seeking and still hoping: the childless woman with a husband has reached her haven successfully; at first she instinctively grieves at having no children, then she takes comfort and lives for her own pleasure, and, if she is not successful in that, for *her own sorrow*, or for somebody else's displeasure, somebody else's sorrow, if it is only her maid's. The birth of a child may save her. A child trains its mother in sacrifice, in giving way, in eagerly spending her time not on herself, and trains her to indifference to all external reward, recognition, gratitude. A mother does not keep an account with a baby; she requires nothing from it but to be well, to be hungry, to sleep—and to smile. Without drawing the woman out of the home, the baby transforms her into a citizen.

It is quite a different thing when another woman's child comes for any reason whatever, and especially unavoidably, into the house of a childless woman. She will perhaps dress it up and play with it, but only when she cares to; she will spoil it when she is pleased to; at all other times the child will knock in vain at the doors of the heart that has grown hard or slothful from self-indulgence. In short, the child can reckon upon all the spoiling and pampering which would be given to a dog or a canary, but nothing more.

One of our friends had a daughter whose mother was a young widow. With a view to the mother's marrying again, an attempt was made to get the child away, and she was kidnapped in the father's absence. After a prolonged search the little girl was found; but the father, having been turned out of France, could not come to Paris to fetch her, and besides he had not the money. Not knowing what to do with her, he asked

Engelson to take her for a little while. Engelson consented, but very quickly regretted it. The child was naughty—indeed, considering the irregular way in which she had been brought up, it is quite likely she was very naughty; but, all the same, her naughtiness was that of a child of five years old, and Engelson was too humane and understanding to be capable of turning against a child for naughtiness. And indeed the trouble was not that she was naughty; the child hindered, not him so much as his wife, though she never did anything. Engelson, with a sort of exasperation, complained to me in his letters of the child!

In regard to her father, Engelson wrote to me: 'Is it not strange that H., who once agreed with you that my wife was *not a suitable person to bring up your children,* has entrusted his *own daughter to her?'*

He knew perfectly well that the father had not chosen Madame Engelson to bring up his little girl, but had been forced by actual necessity to have recourse to her assistance. There was something so cruel, so ungenerous in this remark that it sent a pang to my heart. I could not get used to this lack of mercy, this brutality of language which did not hesitate at anything! Intensely malignant insinuations which may in a moment of irritation occur to any one's mind, but which we could not bring our lips to utter, are spoken by people like Engelson with readiness and enjoyment at the slightest tiff.

Giving full vent to his irritation, Engelson in his letter incidentally attacked Tessier too, and other friends, and even Proudhon, for whom he had a great respect. Together with Engelson's letter came one from Tessier, who was also in Paris; he made some friendly jests about Engelson's 'tempers and tantrums,' without suspecting that the latter had been writing about him. I disliked the position of a sort of negative treachery, and I wrote to Engelson that it was a shame to talk in that abusive way of men with whom life itself has brought us into intimate relations; that they were, any way, good people, as he knew himself. In conclusion, I told him that it was a shame to exaggerate everything so, and to be sighing and groaning and reduced to despair over the naughtiness of a child of five.

This was enough. My ardent admirer, the friend who had kissed my hand in his enthusiasm, who came to me to share every grief and offered to shed his blood and lay down his life for me, not in word but in deed . . . this man, bound to me by his own confession and by my misfortunes, of which he was the witness, by the coffin which we had followed together, forgot everything. His vanity was wounded . . . he wanted to revenge himself, and he did revenge himself.

Four days later I received from him the following reply:—

'February 2nd, 1853.

'There are rumours that you have decided to come here;—Marya Kasparovna is, I believe, recovering (last week, any way, she seemed in better spirits, got up for five minutes, and has an appetite). Concerning the commission you gave me in regard to T., all I have to tell you is that the things the General asks him to get ready are not at T.'s, but were left by them at Vogt's in Geneva, and that Madame T. thinks your silence *peu gracieux*, and adds that a correspondence with you could not cause them any inconvenience.

'In short, I need not have written before you come if it had not occurred to me that silence may often be taken as a sign of assent. I do not wish to mislead you or keep you in error in regard to me: I do not agree with what you said in your last letter to me of January 28th.

'These were your words: "Come, now, is it worth while to get into such a state—'and oh, the baby—and oh dear, oh dear—and good God, what am I to do?' Just think: isn't it beneath you? surely, it's nothing new to you! You have seen life and know what people are. Every day I grow more indulgent and more aloof from others."

'To this I answer, without for the present going off into a dissertation on respectability in general, and without even congratulating you on your satisfaction with yourself, that of course a man is absurd who falls into a rage and a frenzy when he is bitten by gnats or bugs, but the man is even more absurd who under the same circumstances forces himself to assume an air of stoical indifference.

'You perhaps do not agree with this, for you put playing a part above everything. Don't be angry! Wait a minute! Let me finish. In the first chapter of your *Vom andern Ufer* in the Russian and German versions these are your words: "Man likes to produce an effect, to play a part, especially a tragic one; to suffer is good and noble, it presupposes unhappiness; suffering is a distraction, a comfort . . . yes, yes, it is a comfort." As I have said to you already in Nice, I was at first inclined to take this *dictum* of yours as a careless oversight, and not a happy one. At the time you answered that you did not remember the words.

'Though by no means applying those words exclusively to you—that is, not assuming that you judged in this case of men in general by yourself—I had hitherto imagined that this *dictum* of yours, like most of the *Reflexions de' La Rochefoucauld*, which it greatly resembles, like the description of the talented men of our period, once drawn in a masterly fashion by Byelinsky, was an "hyperbole, a jest." And so when I learnt that H. in Switzerland was indignant with the General for the way he behaved in your affair, I took his indignation, not for playing a part, but for real feeling, and wrote to you: "Yes, I see H. is a brother to me." When T., in the presence of a witness, declared that he had been sentenced for life—plus two years, I believed him too, and even repeated this to several people. Yesterday Madame T. told me her husband had never been sentenced at all. *Ergo,* in the eyes of the persons to whom I repeated his lie I am just such a *blagueur* as he. I do not like it. Who is to blame? I am, of course, because I was "young and credulous"; but they are to blame too, because they told a lie. I have never in Russia, nor anywhere, met such *blagueurs* as in Nice. In my letter to you of the 19th of January I told you that I want without *esclandre* to get away from these people; they are antipathetic to me. I wrote this to you because I wanted to be open with you. But *absorbed in yourself* you could not grasp this very simple idea. Or you would hardly, I suppose, have given me a most trivial commission to T. You, too, say that you are holding yourself aloof from people, but at the same time you ask them to write to you. I do not understand that sort of aloofness.

'Assuming that in serious matters to be frank is an essential condition of honesty, I have to tell you this, too, without loss of time. You write to me that when you have despatched the General to Australia, and dismissed every one else, you will be left with me and with your enemies—and that if, moreover, I were a little more stable, and less dependent upon my own and other people's nervous caprices and agitations, you would be disposed to make *un bout de chemin* with me. To this I am obliged to reply that, feeling in myself neither a taste nor a talent for playing parts, and especially tragic ones, I am ready to serve you with my advice, but not with my company.'

Of course, I had not supposed that a man who with tears and sobs had led me on to confidences difficult to utter, a man who had come so near to me and on whom I had leaned as on a brother in moments of weakness and helplessness, when my pain was beyond human endurance, that the eyewitness of all that had happened could regard my misery as stage trappings and scenery, of which I should take advantage to play a tragic part. In his ecstasies over my book he had been picking out stones in it and laying them up in his bosom to fling them at me when the chance might come. It was not enough for him to tear the present to pieces—he defiled and vulgarised the past: breaking with me, he could not show it the respect of dejected silence, but covered it with merciless abuse and ironical jeering.

This letter wounded me, wounded me very much.

I answered him sadly, with suppressed tears; I said good-bye to him, and asked him to break off our correspondence.

That was followed by complete silence between us. . . .

With Engelson once more something seemed to have snapped within me. I was even poorer, more isolated; there was coldness all about me, nothing near me. . . . At times a hand seemed held out to me more warmly; some fanatic of no understanding, not even seeing that we were not of the same religion, would approach hurriedly, and as hurriedly turn away. Though indeed I did not seek closer intimacy with any, I had grown accustomed to men coming and going, to all sorts of nonentities of whom one expected nothing, and to whom one gave nothing except a cigar, wine, and sometimes money. My one salvation lay in work; I was writing *My Past and Thoughts*, and was setting up a Russian printing-press in London.

VI

A year passed: the printing-press was in full swing, it was being noticed in London and feared in Russia. In the spring of 1854 I received a short manuscript from Marya Kasparovna. It was not difficult to guess it had been written by Engelson. I published it at once.

Then came a letter from him asking me to put an end to our unhappy misunderstanding and to let us meet again in common work. Of course, I held out both hands to him.

Instead of an answer he arrived in London himself for a few days, and stayed with me. Sobbing and laughing, he begged me to forget the past, was lavish in words of affection, and again seized my hand and pressed it to his lips. I embraced him, deeply touched, in the firm conviction that the quarrel would not be renewed.

But only a few days later clouds foreboding little good appeared on the horizon. The shade of fatalism, of Buonapartism, which had peeped out in his letters from Geneva had developed. From hatred for Nicholas and the rank and file of the French Revolution of 1848, he had passed over *armes et bagages* into the enemy's camp. We argued; he was obstinate. Knowing that he always rushed to extremes and came back as quickly, I waited for the turn of the tide, but it did not come.

Unhappily, Engelson was busy at that time with an amazing project with which he was passionately in love.

He had made a plan for an air battery—that is, a battery of balloons loaded with explosives and at the same time with printed proclamations. This was at the beginning of the Crimean War. Engelson proposed letting off such balloons from ships on the coast of the Baltic. I greatly disliked this scheme; what could one make of propaganda with projectiles? Where was the sense in it for us Russians to burn Finnish villages and help

Napoleon and England? Moreover, Engelson had discovered no new means of steering balloons. I made little opposition to his plan, supposing he would drop this nonsense of himself.

But not at all. He went off with his plan to Mazzini and Worcell. Mazzini said that things of that sort were not in his line, but that he was ready through his friends to send his plans to the Minister of War. The War Office gave an evasive reply, and put the project aside without a definite refusal. He asked me to gather together two or three of the military men among the refugees and put the balloon question to them. All were against it, and I told him over and over again that I, too, was against it; that our work, our strength, lay in propaganda, nothing but propaganda; that we should lose in moral prestige by siding with Napoleon, and should ruin ourselves in the eyes of Russia *faisant cause commune* with her enemies. Engelson lost his temper and was beside himself. He had come to London confident of a triumph, and, meeting with opposition even from me, imperceptibly returned to his hostile attitude. Soon afterwards he went to fetch his wife, and brought her in May to London. A complete transformation had taken place in their relations; she was expecting to be a mother, and he was rapturously delighted at the prospect of a child. Misunderstandings, quarrels, and explanations were all a thing of the past. She with a sort of insane, half-mad mysticism was turning tables and absorbed in spiritualism. The spirits told her many things, and among others predicted my speedy demise. He was reading Schopenhauer, and told me with a smile that he was doing all he could to encourage her mystic tendencies, that this faith and exaltation was bringing peace and calm into her soul.

With me she behaved affectionately, perhaps in expectation of my approaching death; would come to me with her work, and make me read aloud articles and chapters from *My Past and Thoughts*. When a month later differences arose again over Engelson's Buonapartism and air-balloons, she took the part of the reconciler—came to me begging me to spare a poor invalid, and assuring me that every spring Engelson was attacked by a hypochondriacal condition in which he did not know himself what he was doing.

Her serene gentleness was the gentleness of the conqueror, the mercy of complete triumph. Engelson, imagining that he held her under control by turning tables, lost sight of one thing—that she was not only twisting tables with her fingers, but him round her finger, and that he always gave the answers she wanted better than the tables did.

One evening Engelson began discussing his balloons again with a Frenchman, and said all sorts of biting things to him; the latter replied with irony, and of course that infuriated Engelson more than ever. He snatched up his hat and ran away. In the morning I went round to have it out with him on the subject.

I found him at his writing-table, his face still completely distorted with fury, and a frenzied expression in his eyes. He told me that the Frenchman (a refugee whom I had known for years and know still) was a spy, that he would unmask him, would kill him; and he gave me a letter he had only just written to a doctor of medicine in Paris; in the letter he implicated persons living in Paris, and slandered the refugees in London. I was dumbfounded.

'And do you mean to send that letter?'

'At once.'

'And by post?'

'Yes, by post.'

'That's treachery,' I said; and flung his scrawl on the table. 'If you send that letter . . .'

'Well, what?' he shouted, interrupting me in a wild, hoarse voice—'what are you trying to threaten me with? I'm not afraid of you nor of your nasty friends.' With this he leapt up, opened a big knife, and brandishing it about, shouted gasping: 'Come, come, show your mettle . . . I'll teach you . . . wouldn't you like to try . . . come on!'

I turned to his wife, and saying, 'Has he gone quite out of his mind? You had better get him away somewhere . . . ,' went out of the house.

On this occasion, too, Madame Engelson played the part of peacemaker. She came to me in the morning entreating me to forget what had passed the day before. He had torn up the letter—was ill and gloomy. She took it all as a calamity, as physical derangement, was afraid that he was seriously ill, and shed tears. I yielded to her entreaties.

After that we moved to Richmond, and Engelson did the same. The birth of a son and the first months of looking after him gave Engelson new life; he was off his head with joy. When the baby was born he embraced and kissed effusively first the maid and then his old landlady. Anxiety over the baby's health, the novelty of paternal feeling, the novelty of the baby himself, occupied Engelson for some months, and all went well again.

All at once I got a big envelope from him, accompanied by a note asking me to read the enclosed document and tell him my opinion candidly. It was a letter to the French Minister of War. In it he again proposed air-balloons, bombs, and manifestoes. I thought it all bad, from the quarter to which he was appealing down to the language, which was lacking in dignity, and I told him so.

Engelson answered by a rude note and began to sulk. After that he gave me another manuscript to publish.

I did not conceal from him that it would produce a very bad effect on Russian readers, and that I did not advise publishing it. Engelson reproached me with wanting to set up a censorship, and said that he supposed I had founded the printing-press exclusively to publish my own immortal works. I did publish the manuscript, but my instinct had been right. It aroused general indignation in Russia.

All this indicated that a new rupture was not far off. I must own that this time I felt no great regret. I was weary of this fever varied by paroxysms of friendship and hatred, of having my hands kissed and then getting a moral box on the ears. Engelson had overpassed the limit beyond which not even memories nor gratitude could save the situation. I liked him less and less, and waited coolly for what was to come. At that point an event occurred so important that for a time all quarrels and dissensions were eclipsed by a single feeling of joy and expectation.

On the morning of the fourth of March I went as usual at eight o'clock into my study, opened the *Times*, read a dozen times and did not understand, did not dare to understand, the grammatical sense of the words at the head of the news column: *The death of the Emperor of Russia*.

Hardly knowing what I was doing, I rushed with the *Times* in my hands into the dining-room; I looked for the children and the servants to tell them the great news, and with tears of joy in my eyes gave them the newspaper. . . . I felt as though several years had rolled off my shoulders. It was impossible to stay indoors. Engelson was at that time living in Richmond. I hurriedly put on my coat and hat and was about to go to him, but he anticipated me, and was already in the hall; we fell on each other's necks and could say nothing but: 'Well, at last he is dead!' Engelson, as his way was, capered about, kissed every one in the house, sang and danced; and we had hardly recovered ourselves when a carriage suddenly stopped at the front door and some one gave a violent tug at the bell: three Poles had driven full speed from London to Twickenham, without waiting for a train, to congratulate me.

I ordered champagne; no one reflected that it was only eleven o'clock in the morning, or earlier. Then, quite aimlessly, we all went off to London. In the streets, on the Exchange, in the restaurants, people were talking of nothing but the death of Nicholas; I did not see one man who did not breathe more easily from knowing that that sore was taken out of the eye of humanity, and did not rejoice that that oppressive tyrant in the big boots had at last returned to clay.

On Sunday my house was full all day; French and Polish refugees, Germans, Italians, even English acquaintances kept coming and going with beaming faces. It was a bright, warm day; after dinner we went out into the garden.

Some lads were playing on the bank of the Thames. I called them up to the railing and told them we were celebrating the death of their enemy, and flung them a handful of small silver for beer and sweets. 'Hurrah! hurrah!' shouted the lads. 'Impernikel is dead! Impernikel is dead!'

My visitors too began flinging them sixpences and threepenny-bits; the lads bought ale and tarts and cakes, got hold of a concertina, and began dancing. After that, as long as I lived at Twickenham, the lads used to take off their caps when they met me in the street, and shout: 'Impernikel is dead! hurrah!'

The death of Nicholas multiplied our hopes and energies tenfold. I at once wrote the letter to the Emperor Alexander, afterwards published, and made up my mind to bring out the *Polar Star* at once.

'May reason prevail!' broke involuntarily from my tongue at the head of my programme. 'The *Polar Star*[1] has been hidden behind the storm-clouds of the reign of Nicholas; Nicholas has gone, and the *Polar Star* appears again on the day which is our Good Friday, the day on which five gibbets became for us five crucifixes.'

It was a powerful, stimulating impetus; we set to work with redoubled energy. I announced that I was bringing out the *Polar Star*; Engelson at last took up his article on socialism about which he had been talking in Italy. It might have been expected that we should go on working for a couple of years or.. more . . . but his irritable vanity made any work with him insufferable. His wife encouraged his infatuation. 'My husband's article,' she used to say, 'will be taken as a new epoch in the history of Russian thought. If he writes nothing else, his place in history will be assured.'

The article, 'What is the State?' was good, but its success did not justify his wife's anticipations. Moreover, it appeared at the wrong moment. Awakening Russia demanded, just at that time, practical advice, and not philosophical treatises *à la* Proudhon and Schopenhauer.

The whole of the article had not yet been published, when a new quarrel of a different character from all the preceding ones almost completely severed all relations between us.

One day when I was with them I spoke jestingly of their having sent for the third time for a doctor for their baby, who had a cold in its head and a slight chill.

'So because we are poor,' said Madame Engelson, and all her old spiteful hatred a hundred times intensified flamed in her face, 'our little one is to die without medical

---

[1] The *Polar Star* is the name of the paper edited by Ryleyev, one of the five Decembrists hanged by Nicholas in 1825. On the anniversary of their execution Herzen brought out the first number of his paper of the same name.—(*Translator's Note*.)

assistance? And you say that? You, a socialist and the friend of my husband, who refuse him fifty pounds, and are exploiting him over his lessons.'

I listened in amazement, and asked Engelson whether he shared this view or not. He was embarrassed, his face flushed in patches, he besought her to be silent. . . . She went on. I got up and, interrupting her, said: 'You are ill and are nursing your baby, I am not going to answer you, but I am not going to listen either. . . . You will hardly think it strange that I shall not set foot in your house again.'

Engelson, distraught and melancholy, caught up his hat and came out into the street with me: 'Don't take *au pied de la lettre* the unbridled language of an hysterical woman. . . .' He went off into a muddle of explanations. 'I will come and give my lesson to-morrow,' he said. I shook hands with him and went home without a word.

All this calls for explanations, and the most painful ones, too, relating not to opinions and public affairs but to the kitchen and account books. Nevertheless, I will make an effort to clear up this side of our relations too Squeamishness, that sentimentalism of purity, is out of place in pathological investigation.

The Engelsons were scarcely entitled to reckon themselves poor people. They received ten thousand francs a year from Russia, and he could easily earn another five thousand by translations, reviews, and school-books; Engelson was a proficient linguist. Trübner's, the booksellers, had ordered a lexicon of Russian roots and a grammar from him; he could, like Pierre Leroux, like Kinkel, like Esquiros, give lessons. But, like a regular Russian, he took up everything—the dictionary, the translations, and the lessons—never finished anything, never put himself out, and never earned a farthing.

Neither husband nor wife was prudent or capable

of managing their affairs. The continual fever in which they lived prevented them from thinking about household management. He had come from Russia with no definite plan, and remained in Europe with no definite object. He had taken no steps whatever to secure his property, and *un beau jour*, panic-stricken, made a hasty arrangement of some sort by which he limited his income to ten thousand francs, a sum which he did not receive quite punctually, but always received sooner or later.

That Engelson would not make both ends meet with his ten thousand francs was evident; that he would not know how to economise was equally clear; all that was left for him was to work or to borrow. At first, after coming to London, he borrowed about forty pounds from me . . . a little time afterwards he asked for money again. . . . I had a serious and friendly talk with him about this, and told him I was ready to help him, but that I absolutely refused to lend him more than ten pounds a month. Engelson frowned. However, he did twice take a ten-pound note; then suddenly he wrote to me that he needed fifty pounds, and, if I did not care to lend it him or did not trust him, he begged me to get it for him by pawning some diamonds. All this could hardly be taken seriously; if he had really wanted to pawn the diamonds, he ought to have taken them to some pawnbroker and not to me. . . . Knowing him and being sorry for him, I wrote that I would pawn the diamonds for fifty pounds, if they would give that, and would send him the money. Next day I sent a cheque, but the diamonds, which he would certainly have sold or pawned, I put away to keep for him. He took n0notice of the fact that no interest was asked for the fift0pounds, and believed that I had pawned the diamonds.

The second point relating to the lessons is even simpler. While I was in London, S. gave Russian lessons to my children, charging four shillings an hour.

In Richmond, Engelson offered to take S.'s place. I asked him about terms; he answered that it was difficult for him to talk of terms with me, but that, as he had no money, he would take what I had paid S.

On reaching home I wrote a letter to Engelson: I reminded him that he had himself fixed the terms for the lessons, but that I begged him to take double the amount for all the lessons in the past. Then I wrote what had led me to keep his diamonds, and sent them back to him.

He sent a confused answer, thanked me, expressed vexation, and came in the evening himself, and went on coming as before. His wife I did not see again.

VII

A month later, Zeno Swentoslawski, and with him Linton,[1] the English republican, were dining with me. Engelson came in towards the end of dinner. Swentoslawski, the purest-hearted and best of men, a fanatic who at over fifty retained the reckless fire of a Pole and the impulsive impetuosity of a boy of fifteen, was urging the necessity of our returning to Russia and beginning a keen propaganda in print there. He undertook to convey the type, and so on.

After listening to him, I said half in jest to Engelson: 'I say, you know, *on nous accusera de lâcheté* if he goes alone.'

Engelson made a grimace and went away.

Next day I went up to London and did not come back till the evening; my son, who was lying down with

[1] W. J. Linton, a friend of Mazzini, and author of a series of sketches of Italian, French, and Polish exiles, and of Herzen, called *European Republicans*. His wife, Mrs. Lynn Linton, a prominent figure some forty years ago, wrote several novels, and created a journalistic sensation by an onslaught on 'The Girl of the Period.'— (*Translator's Note*.)

a feverish attack, told me, in great excitement, that Engelson had come in my absence, that he had abused me terribly, had said that he would pay me out, that he was not going to put up with my authority any longer, and that he did not need me now *since his article had been published*. I did not know what to think, whether Sasha was delirious from fever or Engelson had come in dead drunk.

From Malwida von Meysenbug[1] I learnt more. She told me with horror of his violence. 'Herzen,' he had shouted in a nervous, gasping voice, 'called me *lâche* yesterday in the presence of two strangers.' Malwida interrupted him, saying that I had not been talking about him at all, that I had said '*on nous taxera de lâcheté*,' speaking of all of us generally. 'If Herzen feels that he is doing something mean, let him speak for himself, but I will not allow him to speak like that of me, and in the presence of two blackguards too.'

My elder girl, then ten years old, had run in at the sound of his shouts. Engelson had gone on: 'No, this is the end of it, it is enough. I am not accustomed to it, I will not allow myself to be trifled with, I will show him whom he has to deal with . . . ,' pulled a revolver out of his pocket and went on shouting, 'It is loaded, it is loaded, I will wait for him. . . .'

Malwida got up and told him that she insisted on his leaving her, that she was not obliged to listen to his wild ravings, that she could only put down his behaviour to illness. 'I am going,' he said; 'don't trouble; but first I want to ask you to give Herzen this letter.' He opened

[1] Baroness Malwida von Meysenbug, authoress of *Memoirs of an Idealist*, was a great friend of Wagner, and also of Nietzsche, whom she cared for at times with motherly kindness. At this date she was living in Herzen's house as the governess of his children, the youngest of whom, Olga, remained in her charge for many years.—(*Translator's Note.*)

it and began reading it aloud; the letter was a string of abuse.

Malwida von Meysenbug refused the commission, asking him why he expected her to act as an intermediary in forwarding such a letter.

'I will find means without your help,' observed Engelson, and went away.

He did not send the letter, but a day later he sent me a note; in it, without saying one word about what had passed, he wrote that he had an attack of hæmorrhage, that he could not come to me, and begged me to send the children to him.

I said that there was no answer, and again all diplomatic relations were broken off; hostile relations remained. Engelson did not let slip a chance of turning them to account.

From Richmond I moved in the autumn of 1855 to St. John's Wood. Engelson was forgotten for some months. Suddenly, in the spring of 1856, I received a note, suggestive of a duel, from Orsini, whom I had seen two days previously.

Coldly and courteously, he asked me to let him know whether it was the truth that Saffi and I were spreading a rumour that he was an Austrian spy. He asked me either to give an unqualified *démenti*, or to indicate from whom I had heard this abominable calumny.

Orsini was justified; I should have done the same in his place. Perhaps he ought to have had more confidence in Saffi and in me—but the insult was terrific.

Any one who knew anything of Orsini's character would understand that such a man, attacked in the most holy of holies of his honour, could not stop short at half measures. The affair could only be settled by our *absolute* innocence or by the death of some one.

From the first minute it was clear to me that the blow came from Engelson. He no doubt reckoned on one side of Orsini's character, but fortunately there was another which he had overlooked. Orsini combined with violent passions an intense power of self-control; he was cautious among dangers, thought over every step he took, and never reached a decision on the spur of the moment, because when once he had reached a decision he wasted no time in criticism, in doubt, in reconsideration, but carried it out. We saw this later in the Rue Lepelletier. He acted in the same way now. He tried without haste to investigate the matter, to find out who was guilty, and then, if he succeeded, to kill him.

Engelson's second mistake lay in quite unnecessarily bringing in Saffi.

The facts were these. Six months before my rupture with Engelson I happened to be one morning at the house of Mrs. Milner-Gibson (the wife of the minister): there I found Saffi and Pianciani; they were saying something to her about Orsini. As I went away I asked Saffi what they had been talking about. 'Only fancy,' he answered: 'Mrs. Milner-Gibson had been told in Geneva that Orsini had been bribed in Austria. . . .' On reaching home at Richmond I had repeated this to Engelson. We were both then dissatisfied with Orsini. 'The devil take him entirely!' observed Engelson, and nothing more was said on the subject. When Orsini made his marvellous escape from Mantua we thought in our own circle of the accusation heard by Mrs. Milner-Gibson. The arrival of Orsini himself, his story, his wounded foot, entirely effaced this absurd suspicion.

I asked Orsini to give me an interview. He asked me to go the following evening. In the morning I went to Saffi and showed him Orsini's note. He at once offered to go with me, as indeed I expected he would. Ogaryov, who had only just arrived in London, was a witness of this interview.

Saffi described the conversation at Mrs. Milner-

Gibson's with the simplicity and straightforwardness which are his distinguishing characteristics. I filled in the rest of the story. Orsini thought a minute, and then said: 'Well, may I ask Mrs. Milner-Gibson about this?'

'Of course,' answered Saffi.

'Yes, I believe I have been too hasty; but,' he asked me, 'tell me, why did you speak of it to an outsider instead of warning me?'

'You forget, Orsini, the time when it happened, and that the *outsider* to whom I spoke was at that time not an outsider; you know better than most people what he was then to me.'

'I have mentioned no one . . .'

'Let me finish. Why, do you suppose it is easy for a man to repeat such things? If these rumours had spread, perhaps I ought to have warned you—but who is speaking about it now? As for your having mentioned no one's name, you are making a great mistake there. Bring me face to face with my accuser, then it will be still more evident what part each has played in these slanders.'

Orsini smiled, got up, came to me, embraced me, embraced Saffi, and said: '*Amici*, we will end the matter; forgive me, let us forget all about it and talk of something else.'

'That's all very well, and you were perfectly right to ask me for an explanation, but why do you not name my accuser? In the first place, it is useless to conceal it . . . it was Engelson told you this.'

'Give me your word that you will drop the matter?'

'I will give you my word before two witnesses.'

'Well, you have guessed right.'

I anticipated this confirmation, yet it sent a pang to my heart as though I had still doubted it.

'Remember what you have promised,' Orsini added, after a brief silence.

'You need not worry about that. But to make up to me and to Saffi you might tell us how it happened; you see, we know all that matters.'

Orsini laughed. 'What curiosity!' he said. 'You know Engelson. He came to me the other day: I was in the dining-room'—(Orsini lived in a boarding-house)—'and having dinner alone. He had already dined. I asked for a bottle of sherry for him; he drank it, and at once began complaining of you—that you had ill-treated him, that you had broken off all relations with him—and after gossiping about all sorts of things asked how you had received me on my return. I answered that you had given me a very friendly welcome, that I had dined with you, and that I had been to you in the evening. . . . Engelson all at once began shouting: "That's just like them . . . I know those gentry; it's not long since he and his friend and admirer Saffi were saying that you were an Austrian spy, but now you 're famous again and in the fashion, and he is your friend!" "Engelson," I observed, "do you fully understand the gravity of what you 've just said?" "Fully, fully," he repeated. "Will you be ready under all circumstances to repeat your words?" "Under all circumstances!"

'When he had gone I took a sheet of paper and wrote you a letter. That's the whole story.'

We all went out into the street. Orsini, as though guessing what was passing within me, said by way of consolation, 'He's crazy.'

Soon afterwards Orsini went to Paris, and his beautiful classical head rolled bleeding on to the platform of the guillotine.

The first news of Engelson was the news of his death in Jersey.

No word of reconciliation, no word of remorse reached me. . . .

(1858.)

P.S.—In 1864 I received a strange letter from Naples. It spoke of the apparition of my wife's soul, and of her having appealed to me to turn to religion and purify my soul with it, and to abandon worldly vanities. . . .

The writer said that it was all written at the dictation of the spirit; the tone of the letter was warm, friendly, and ecstatic.

The letter was unsigned; I recognised the handwriting; it was from Madame Engelson.[1]

---

[1] With this ends that part of *My Past and Thoughts* which was corrected by the author in its final form and published in four volumes. The chapter which follows (in the next volume) is now published for the first time, and is that for which, as Herzen himself more than once says, he wrote all the rest.—(*Note to the Russian edition*, 1921.)